A HISTORY OF
JEWISH ART

A HISTORY OF
JEWISH ART

BY FRANZ LANDSBERGER, PH.D.

Hebrew Union College, Cincinnati

THE UNION OF AMERICAN HEBREW

CONGREGATIONS · *CINCINNATI*

1946

Editor's Introduction

ONE of the unknown fields in Jewish lore is that of Jewish art. There is a general and wide-spread impression that the Biblical prohibition which forbids the making of a likeness of anything that is in the heavens above, on the earth beneath, or in the water under the earth, cut off Jewish art at its very beginning. On the other hand, one need not be a student of the arts to recognize such distinguished Jewish names as Joseph Israels, Camille Pissarro, and Max Liebermann. We know that in our own day Jewish artists continue to be creative and are recognized not only in Jewish circles, but in the world of art as a whole.

What, then, are the facts?

The Union of American Hebrew Congregations sought an answer to this question and was eager now for some time to publish a book on the history of Jewish art and to open this fascinating field to English readers. The coming of Professor Franz Landsberger, an exile from Nazi Germany, to this country and to the Hebrew Union College, gave us the desired opportunity. Dr. Landsberger served as professor of history of art at the University of Breslau and as Director of the Jewish Museum in Berlin. He thus combines a knowledge of art in general with that of Jewish art in particular. The present work is the result of his many years of research in this field.

It consists of two parts. The first gives a description of Jewish art in life. It begins with a discussion of the problem of Jewish art and proceeds to describe art objects used in the synagogue and in the home, in the course of the Jewish year and throughout the life of the individual, from the cradle to the grave. The second part presents an historical treatment of Jewish art from its beginnings, through the ages, to our own day.

The book is accompanied by more than two hundred illustrations of art objects carefully selected to convey to the reader with concreteness and vividness, a sense of the achievement of the Jewish people in this significant area of world culture.

In thus presenting *A History of Jewish Art* to our readers, the Union of American Hebrew Congregations has once again pioneered in the field of Jewish education and scholarship. We have reason to feel that this unique work will arouse the interest of all cultured readers both Jewish and Christian.

While authentic in treatment, the book is written in a popular style so that it will be of interest to adults and to our older youth groups throughout the country. We trust that it will stimulate the organization of reading circles of men and women who will want to acquaint themselves with the important contribution which Jewish art has made in the history of civilization.

EMANUEL GAMORAN

Acknowledgments

THIS BOOK could not have come into being were it not for a combination of favorable circumstances. The Hebrew Union College not only saved me from the clutches of Nazism by calling me to its renowned halls, but also gave me ample opportunity to study in its marvelous library. Reposing confidence in me, the Union of American Hebrew Congregations invited me to write a book on Jewish art, its characteristics, and its history. The readers of the Commission on Jewish Education, Rabbi Leon Fram, Dr. Solomon B. Freehof, and Dr. Abba Hillel Silver, read my manuscript and offered valuable suggestions. Dr. Emanuel Gamoran, Educational Director of the Commission on Jewish Education, gave untiringly of his time, effort, and guidance to bring the book to completion. Mr. M. Myer Singer contributed his expert talents to the physical make-up and production of the book. Mrs. Adolph Marcus and Mrs. Sheldon H. Blank assisted in the translation of the manuscript.

It is with profound sincerity and appreciation that I extend my thanks to them and to all others, too numerous to mention, who, in one manner or another, have contributed to this book.

FRANZ LANDSBERGER

Cincinnati, Ohio
Hebrew Union College

vii

Contents

PART ONE

JEWISH LIFE AND ART

I.

The Problem of Jewish Art

Is THERE such a thing as Jewish Art? This question is often asked when the subject is mentioned. Generally the Second Commandment is then quoted. It expressly forbids making "any manner of likeness, of anything that is in heaven above, or that is in the earth beneath, or that is in the water under the earth." This commandment, it is said, completely eliminates the possibility of any Jewish art.

There is no doubt that, for thousands of years, Jewish art was severely hampered by the Second Commandment, but we must be careful not to exaggerate its influence. To begin with, we must bear in mind that the commandment was not always taken literally. The Bible does not imply in the words "any likeness" the imitation of nature as such, but the representation of particular objects, such as stars, calves, snakes, and fish, which were worshipped by other oriental peoples. "Thou shalt not bow down unto them, nor serve them." In the book of Deuteronomy (4:19) it is even forbidden to lift one's eyes to the stars, so as not to "be drawn away and worship them, and serve them."

Not long ago a synagogue, dating from the third century C.E., was discovered in Dura Europos in Syria. Its walls were covered from floor to ceiling with Biblical scenes. This certainly is not the only synagogue to have been thus ornamented, proving that at this time the Second Commandment was interpreted very freely. Even in the Middle Ages when Jewish law was scrupulously observed, Hebrew manuscripts

3

were decorated with Biblical figures because it was considered improbable that Jews would turn to them as objects of worship. In the centuries following the Middle Ages even portrait painting was tolerated in some countries. Since the Emancipation the Second Commandment has been adhered to only in respect to synagogue decoration.

It is to be noted also that the Second Commandment, regardless of its origin, obtained a firm hold in Israel only after centuries of struggle. Again and again we hear that statues of deities were erected in the Holy Land. The Bible always refers to them with disgust, as idols, and because of this we are inclined to forget that they were at the same time works of art.

Finally, the Second Commandment refers only to representational art—painting and sculpture—but not to architecture or artistic craftsmanship, neither of which attempts to imitate nature. The description of the Temple of Solomon evidences the interest which Jews had in such a house of worship. As for the applied arts, we know how lavishly all ritual objects in the Temple were decorated and we know also that synagogues in later times were similarly adorned.

In this connection a passage should be quoted which is today less familiar than the Second Commandment but was, in former times, taken much to heart. In the Talmud the Biblical words: "This is my God and I will adorn Him" are explained thus: "Make a beautiful suko in His honor, a beautiful lulov, a beautiful shofor, beautiful tsitsis and a beautiful Scroll of the Law, and write it with fine ink, a fine reed, and a skilled penman, and wrap it about with beautiful silks" (b. Sabbath 133 b). How vividly this expresses the desire to worship God with beautiful objects made for His service.

It thus appears that the Jews had many more art objects than is generally believed; it is to an acquaintanceship with these that this book is dedicated.

Doubts concerning the existence of Jewish art arise from still other quarters. Were the artists who created these works of art, Jews? Joseph Pijoan, the Spanish art historian, recently said of the Biblical Jews in his *History of Art*: "The Jewish nation, which through its literature, occupied so prominent a position in the Orient, possessed no aptitude for plastic art" (Vol. I, p. 153).

There is no doubt that literature held a greater appeal for the Jews of old than the plastic arts; but is it necessary to go so far as to deny the Jews of the Biblical period *all* aptitude for art? This point of view is usually based on the tradition that the Temple of Solomon, the greatest architectural achievement of Biblical times, was constructed by a Phoenician—Hiram by name. But the First Book of Kings (7:14) states only that he knew "to work all works in brass." In Second Chronicles (2:13) which was written later, many other artistic gifts are attributed to him, but this versatility is certainly only an imitation of the versatility attributed to the artist Bezalel as described in Exodus in connection with the erection of the Tent of Meeting.

The two columns to which people refer when speaking of Hiram's architectural work are not columns in the architectural sense, but sacred monuments. They were not placed *in* the Temple, but *in front* of it, and were not of stone, but of brass. A foreigner, who was, by the way, the son of a Jewish mother, was employed for the difficult task of brass-founding in much the same way as, in the Italy of the Renaissance, artists from other towns were sent for, to complete such difficult tasks as the founding of an equestrian statue, when the native artist's skill was inadequate.

Even if we grant that a few Jewish works of art in ancient times were executed by non-Jews, there is no reason to doubt that most of them were made by Jewish artists. There is enough evidence to justify this assumption.

Concerning the post-Biblical period up to modern times the argument has sometimes been advanced that the Jews—at least the Jews living in Christian countries—could not have functioned as artists because they were excluded from the Christian art guilds, in which apprentices were trained. But these guilds did not make their appearance until the centuries following the first millennium of our era. Consequently they could have had no effect on Jewish art prior to that period.

Later on, when the Jews were forbidden to enter Christian guilds, they sought to acquire the necessary knowledge from masters among their own people. Here and there Jewish craftsmen became so numerous that they were able to found their own guilds. We hear of some in Spain and in Sicily during the Middle Ages, and in Eastern Europe in recent times.

Furthermore the Christian guilds did not embrace all branches of art and craftsmanship. They included neither the scribes who illuminated their manuscripts, nor the bookbinders who used costly materials for their work, nor the seal engravers, nor the embroiderers.

These facts then substantiate the belief that the Jews had manifold opportunities for creating works of art, and we shall see how well they used these opportunities.

It is not to be denied that Jews often employed gentile artists when Jewish artists were not available. Endless persecutions and wanderings, restrictions on building, and the small size of many communities sometimes made it impossible for Jews to find among their own numbers artists who could accomplish the tasks set them. But, on the other hand, we hear that at times Jews were employed by Gentiles on account of their artistic ability. In Spain, for instance, Jewish goldsmiths were so popular that in the year 1415, Pope Benedict XIII forbade Christians to use Jewish craftsmen for their goblets and crucifixes.[1] In Spain, too, the Jews even made altar paintings, until Queen Isabella, in the year 1480, appointed a special artist whose duty it became to prevent this.[2]

In the face of these facts, it is surely no longer possible to doubt the aptitude of the Jew in all branches of art. Had the gift of artistry not always been inherent in the Jews how would it have been possible for them to produce such a surprising number of fine Jewish artists in the nineteenth and twentieth centuries?

A final doubt is sometimes expressed as follows: Can these works of art, created by Jews, in a deeper sense, be called Jewish art? Is it an art noticeably different from every other art? Our first impulse is to answer "no," and to insist that the Jews never developed an artistic style of their own. As long as they lived in the Holy Land, the larger and culturally more developed oriental nations, and later on the Greeks, had a decided influence upon Jewish art. In the Middle Ages, the Jews lived as minorities among other peoples and adopted their art patterns. Since the Emancipation, Jews have so intermingled with non-Jews that their artistic activities have been colored by their environment. Such being the case, say the skeptics, it would be more nearly correct to consider Jewish art not as something apart, but as submerged in the art of the people among whom they lived.

These arguments will have to be considered more seriously than the previous ones. It is true that Jewish art has been permeated with all these foreign influences. The

Temple of Solomon was in all probability similar to other oriental temples. The synagogues, at least those from Hellenistic times on, reflect Greek influence, modified only by slight oriental characteristics. The synagogues of the Middle Ages appear to be Spanish when constructed in Spain, and German when constructed in Germany. In China, in the city of K'ai-fêng Fu, there was a synagogue which bore a great resemblance to the pagodas.

Joseph Israels is, by tradition, a Dutch artist; Lieberman was imbued with the German realism of the nineteenth century; Pissarro trod the path of the French Impressionists.

Nevertheless it may be correct to consider Jewish art as a separate entity. We know that non-Jews were not always willing to accept Jewish art as a part of their national art, although generally speaking, Jewish artists of the nineteenth and twentieth centuries were accorded the same recognition as other artists, at least until Hitler's rise to power. Also the ancient Jewish past was diligently studied by archaeologists of every creed. The publications resulting from the discovery of the synagogue in Dura Europos were very numerous! Yet the long period of Jewish art between the early centuries and the nineteenth century of our era has received practically no attention. Where does any history of Spanish art mention the magnificent Spanish-Jewish illuminated manuscripts, and where in any history of German art does one find a word concerning the splendor of the Darmstadt Haggadah? This neglect may derive from difficulties arising from the Hebrew text of these manuscripts. They are certainly worth careful attention.

Still another point should be observed when Jewish art is considered as a separate entity. Roman art is, as we know, an echo of Greek art. Japanese art is derived from Chinese art; American art is a branch of European art. And yet the art of each of these—the Romans, the Japanese, and the Americans—has always been dealt with as a special field. Why should this not apply to Jewish art? Let us suppose that Jewish art closely resembles the art of its surroundings; how many questions still remain which can only be answered in dealing with Jewish art as such? To what social level does Jewish art belong? Is this art the creation of a few outstanding personalities, or does it emerge from the masses so that it can be considered as folk-art? To what heights did the best examples of Jewish art attain? The value of a work of art does not depend upon the originality of the single forms, but upon the way in which these forms are combined to create a whole. Consequently, even though the Temple of Solomon showed the influence of other oriental art, it may have been a structure of particular and individual beauty. King Solomon with the abundant means at his disposal wished to create an outstanding edifice, and would hardly have been satisfied with a feeble copy of other temples. This we can only surmise. But we do know, for instance, of the existence of wooden synagogues built by Jewish architects in Poland in the seventeenth and eighteenth centuries. These architects made ample use of the motifs of East-European wood constructions, but they combined them in a style of their own, thereby creating attractive works of art.

There are still other questions which we can ask concerning the art of the Jews. What kind of technique did they favor? This leads to some interesting observations. To mention one: the Jews were excellent seal engravers as far back as Biblical times, when this art flourished throughout the Orient. They retained this skill when scattered throughout the world, and when they came in contact with peoples not so familiar with this art the Jews were employed as crafts-

men. As late as the nineteenth and twentieth centuries, the
Jews still excelled in this and in the related arts of coin
minting and medal casting. In a similar way they were able
to benefit themselves and the peoples among whom they
lived, by bringing to the Western world various other oriental crafts. Jewish art must be understood as a whole in order
to grasp the full import of this fact.

In the freedom achieved by the Emancipation of the
nineteenth century, the Jews fully embraced the plastic arts.
Thereby they certainly contributed far more to art in general than they had previously contributed by the creation
of seals, coins and medals. The question now arises as to
which new fields of activity they added to the original skills.
How great was their contribution to the art of portrait and
landscape painting, the designing of posters and cartoons,
and to theatrical art? Furthermore are the Jews to be considered as the progressive or the conservative element in the
continuous change of artistic styles characteristic of this
epoch?

Just one more point must be mentioned in favor of con-
sidering Jewish art as a separate entity amongst other arts.
If one wishes fully to understand a work of art, one must
look at it not only with one's eyes but also with an historical
understanding for the mental processes which brought them
into being. In order to illustrate this point, let us take a
synagogue of the Middle Ages—the famous Altneuschul in
Prague. Inwardly and outwardly, it resembles a Gothic
church. Looking at it, therefore, from the point of view of
form, one can say it shows nothing specifically Jewish, and
that as an architectural form it is simply derived from Christian church construction. Yet if one traces the origin of the
synagogue to its source, one must come to the conclusion
that the mediaeval churches are rather patterned after the

synagogues. Among the ancient pagan temples, which were designed as dwelling places for deities, the Jews began to erect synagogues, not as an abode for God but rather as a house of meeting for worshippers who came to pray to an invisible Lord. The churches followed the synagogues in this conception. Consequently, the gentile architects began to construct their churches after the manner of synagogues. It was not until later that the churches developed a richer and more differentiated style and passed on their changing forms to the synagogues. This act accounts for the similarity between the Altneuschul in Prague and the Gothic church.

This similarity of synagogue and church is more striking when the synagogue is empty, that is to say, when it is not being used for services. But now let us take a look at an old synagogue during a Sabbath service. Only men are visible because the women are seated in an adjoining room or in a latticed gallery, hidden from the eyes of the men. The men are wrapped in prayer-shawls, which formerly covered the whole body. The Torah curtain is drawn aside, the Holy Ark is opened and the richly decorated Torah Scroll is solemnly carried to the reading platform. This platform usually stands in the center of the synagogue. Around this we see the worshippers, not seated in straight rows, but carelessly grouped at individual desks. These ceremonies and these objects were foreign to the churches of the Middle Ages, or to be more accurate, they had been gradually omitted from the Christian ritual.

Out of the needs of the Jewish ritual, there gradually came into being many cult objects which were intended for use in the synagogue and in the home. Among these objects were such things as Chanuko candelabra and richly decorated Haggadahs. These things were unknown to the Gentiles, but were essential to Jewish life, and were therefore lovingly adorned. Even if such an object was made by a non-Jew, the Christian artist creating an object needed for Jewish ritual had to reproduce Jewish symbols. It is noticeable that Jews have always clung with great tenacity to these symbols, most of them derived from the Tent of Meeting and the Temple. We find them on ancient mosaics, on lamps and glasses, on miniatures of the Middle Ages, on Torah curtains of the baroque period, and on nineteenth century tablets which were hung on the eastern wall of a dwelling to indicate to one who prays which direction he should face.

Though the object represented by the Jewish artist is an expression of the Jewish faith, and belongs to the ritual of Judaism, it would be incorrect to say that the Jewish element in art is *only* to be found in its content and not in its form. The seven-branched candelabrum is decorated with oriental designs, but the fact that it has seven branches and in this respect is unique in the Orient, gives it a special Jewish form. The same applies to the eight-armed Chanuko candelabrum, derived from the former. The elaboration of the Torah Scroll, with mantle, rimonim, shield and pointer, gives to the Torah its particular exterior, even though the design of the single objects follows the pattern of the lands of their origin. A decorated Haggadah may easily be distinguished by its style as French, German, or Italian, but the Hebrew characters and particularly the Hebrew initials, give it the characteristic Jewish touch.

But what about the period following the Emancipation, when the synagogue and the ritual accessories receded into the background of Jewish artistic activities? It was possible even then to create an art marked by Jewish traits. Just at this time the Jewish artist felt the desire to depict the Jew in his own atmosphere. Certainly such a work need not necessarily show particular traits of Jewish art; gentile artists have also painted Jewish themes. But some prominent Jewish artists, particularly in the twentieth century, were able to realize the meaning of Judaism in its deeper sense; they depicted the characteristic mingling of worldly gaiety and religious fervor. The detailed explanation of these paintings will be given later on, when we deal with Jewish art in our own times.

The Jewish artist since the Emancipation has not only adopted the forms of European art, but also its content, and painted portraits, landscapes, still-life and domestic scenes. He can, however, give a Jewish touch to these works also in proportion to the intensity of his Jewish feelings. Plastic art, as all art, is a mirror for the human soul and all that the soul contains. The individual character of the artist, as well as his national and social background, are expressed in his art. That is why we turn to works of art in order to understand the character of a race or a people. The essential traits and characteristics of a civilization are permanently stamped upon its works of art.

I am fully aware that the question has been frequently discussed as to what extent Jews were able to preserve their original characteristics, those which they possessed when they were still a nation. But it is especially Jewish art, since the Emancipation, which seems to prove that such traits have persisted, and we shall have occasion to refer to them later on, when we deal with this period.

All these arguments are not intended to minimize what we have termed the "Problem of Jewish Art." It is still conceded that the Second Commandment had a crippling effect upon Jewish art. The restrictions placed upon the Jews and consequently on their art, by external influences, must be clearly understood. Furthermore, there is no doubt that the Jews, owing to their perpetual wanderings, were, and still are, constantly influenced by their new surroundings. In spite of all these deterrents, Jewish art, Jewish artists and some Jewish characteristics have always existed. To discuss these works of art, these artists, and these characteristics, is the object of this book.

II

Synagogue and Home

"MAKE a beautiful suko in His honor, a beautiful lu-lov, a beautiful shofor, beautiful tsitsis, and a beautiful Scroll of the Law, and write it with fine ink, a fine reed, and a skilled penman, and wrap it about with beautiful silks." Once again we quote these words from the Talmud, which show the intensity of the Jews' craving for beauty in the service of the Lord.

But what is a suko, a lulov, a shofor, and what are tsitsis? A Jew educated in the Jewish ritual will know, but we would like this book to awaken an interest in Jewish art in general, and for this purpose a lack of familiarity with Jewish life and customs makes the task more difficult. Furthermore, even the modern Orthodox Jew is only acquainted with the legally prescribed rites of his faith. Around these rites have arisen a number of ceremonies and customs which have accumulated in the course of centuries. These ceremonies and customs have gathered to themselves objects which serve as symbols, and these ritual objects are at the same time objects of art. It is our purpose to describe, not the ritual, but the art object, and to appraise its aesthetic value.

In this review we shall not touch upon the accessories of the Tent of Meeting and the Temple. These we shall discuss when we deal with the history of Jewish art. At present we will take up this survey at the point where Jewish life centers around the synagogue, or more specifically, when the rites and customs, which had increased in number during the centuries, had attained their maximum development. This happened just before the Emancipation. Since then, much has become lost which, until that period, had been faithfully preserved.

The illustrations in this book will eliminate the necessity of detailed descriptions and at the same time they will train the eye towards a better understanding of the forms of those works of art. The pious Jew is often too closely bound to the religious significance of his ritual, to see these works from an aesthetic point of view.

Whether one or another work of art, which serves us as an example, is the product of a non-Jew, need not concern us here. We have already mentioned that all works which are of Jewish content also belong to Jewish art.

Furthermore the word "art" must be correctly understood. Frequently these works were carried out by non-professional artists—by simple, art-loving men and women. They all participated in beautifying their ritual implements. Today we term all such art "folk-art." This is not meant in a derogatory sense; on the contrary, we admire the freshness and ingenuousness of the designs and the genuine love of color which are characteristic of folk-art.

It is often very difficult to state when these works came into existence, because folk-art clings tenaciously to old forms, elsewhere extinct. Sometimes one even finds a mixture of forms or of different styles or periods. The term "jargon" has not only been applied to language but to Jewish art works of this description as well. We would like to avoid this expression because such a mixture is pertinent to *all* folk-art.

Let us begin with such an object of folk-art, a wooden hammer (Fig. 1). It comes from Poland, and is said to date from the nineteenth century; to judge by its style, it could

1. WOODEN HAMMER OF THE "SCHULKLOPFER"
Poland, 19th century

well have been made earlier. This hammer was used to summon the worshippers to the synagogue by knocking on their doors or windows. Chimes, as in churches, muezzin, announcing the different times of prayer, as in the mosques, have never been adopted by the Jews. They preferred the more personal way of employing a special man, called a *Schulklopfer,* who went knocking from door to door. This hammer, therefore, is a practical object, but its maker was conscious of the fact that it would be used exclusively for summoning people to the synagogue. Therefore it deserved to have a beautiful shape. Hence, the hammer is curved and its two ends are shaped like lions, holding pieces of meat between their teeth. The lion is the symbol of Judaism. On both sides of the shaft verses from the Psalms are engraved, relating to the use of the hammer. "In the house of God we walked with the throng" is written on one side; "Let my prayer be unto Thee, O Lord, in an acceptable time," on the other (Psalms 55:15 and 69:14). This combination of pictorial and verbal decoration is frequently found in folk-art. The Jew with his highly trained reasoning powers favored this method. He liked to read and to visualize at the same time, and so he combined the graceful and the didactic.

2. TORAH SCROLL

Summoned by the hammer, we enter the synagogue, and the first object of interest is the Torah Scroll, containing the Pentateuch (Fig. 2). Around it the Jewish service is centered, and its reading continues through the entire Jewish year. For thousands of years the Jews have refrained from changing its exterior. The Scroll has most likely been left exactly as it was at the time of the first synagogues, written on parchment in the beautiful lettering which was developed in ancient Judaism, though we do not know the exact date of its origin. The square characters, the variety of horizontal and vertical, of thin lines and heavy bars, give it an aesthetic charm of its own.

The Scroll itself is nothing specifically Jewish, it was generally used in Antiquity. During the first centuries of our era it was replaced by books, first written by hand, but from the fifteenth century on, printed, at least in Christian countries.

For their Torah the Jews clung to the traditional scroll form. However a special type of scroll arose, worthy of mention. While one single roll was generally used in Antiquity, a double roll with two handles was adopted for the reading of the Torah.[3] The Jews were well aware of this characteristic, for we read in the Talmud, "All other scrolls are rolled from beginning to end, but the Scroll of the Law is rolled towards its center, and a pillar (shaft) is made for it at both ends" (b. Baba Batra 14 a). A sage who lived before the destruction of the Second Temple, adds, "Thus used the scribes of Jerusalem to make their scrolls." In the Holy City the custom originated while the Temple was still standing, and it spread over the Jewish world.

Two reasons can be found for the use of the double roll with its handles. When opened, the rolls immediately marked the place where the reader should start, and the touching of the Scroll itself, which was forbidden (b. Sabbath 14 a), was avoided by holding the handles.

We may assume, however, that there were also aesthetic reasons for the double roll, which, with its symmetry and balance of height and width, appealed strongly to the eye. Finally there may have been a pleasing similarity to the two stone tablets containing the Ten Commandments.

No embellishment of the script itself was permitted with the exception of some crownlike designs at the top of certain letters. Now and then in Antiquity and during the Middle Ages, attempts were made to write the whole text of the Pentateuch or special words, in gold.[4] But this did not meet with general approval, and so the custom disappeared.

Nevertheless the desire to adorn the beloved Torah existed and cried for satisfaction. A way out was found by decorating the exterior. The handles were beautifully turned and often richly inlaid with ivory or mother-of-pearl.

3. ITALIAN TORAH BINDER
Embroidered in 1736 by Magdalena Bassan.
New York, Jewish Museum.

Another manner of decorating the closed Scroll was devised. The rolls had to be tied with straps to prevent them from sliding and to protect them from dust. The Talmud, as we have mentioned before, suggests that the Torah be wrapped in "beautiful silks." These silk straps were painted or embroidered. The illustration (Fig. 3) shows an Italian Torah binder of the eighteenth century with colorful embroidery of tendrils and pomegranates. Proudly the Jewish artist has stitched her name on it.

In some European countries, especially in Germany, a charming custom arose. When the male infant was taken to the synagogue for the first time, a richly decorated binder, made from several of the baby's swaddling clothes, was wrapped around the Torah. This custom will be dealt with later.

Another opportunity for decorating the Torah was found in the cover which gave further protection to the Scroll. Similar covers were used by the heathen world for secular rolls. The Jews wanted their covers to be specially durable as the scrolls were used for centuries. In addition, the veneration felt for the precious contents of the Torah were an incentive to beautiful ornamentation.

Two forms of covering exist. In the Orient, metal, cylindrical containers came into use. They could be opened and the Torah was then read without being lifted from its case. The beauty of the Palestinian cover, dated 1754, lies in the gracefully hammered silver metal-work and in its crown-like top (Fig. 4).

In Europe the cover is made of cloth. Beautiful materials, like silk, velvet, and brocade, are chosen and finely embroidered. One of the most precious examples dating from the same period as the Palestinian container, is the English Torah cover in Figure 5. Long fringes are attached to the

4. (Left) TORAH CASE. Palestine, 1754. Cincinnati, Hebrew Union College.
5. (Right) TORAH COVER. England, 18th century. London, Jewish Museum.

mantle and also to the short top cover. An embroidered strip stretches over both and pictures a minute Ark with its Torah Scroll.

Both the metal and the cloth cover show yet another decoration; two metal ornaments are pulled over the upper ends of the rollers. They are called rimonim, pomegranates. The Palestinian container on Figure 4 clearly indicates why they were given this name. Originally, they seem to have been shaped like pomegranates, an old Jewish

6. TORAH CROWN
*Germany, 1821. Last at Kassel,
Jewish Community.*

symbol mentioned in the description of the garment of the high priest and in that of the two pillars before Solomon's Temple. These *metal* rimonim, matching the *metal* Torah cases may have originated in the Orient. In Europe, this round shape was gradually developed into a longer and elaborate top piece, as we can see from Figure 5. S'fardic Jews also made rimonim in the shape of towers.

Both kinds of rimonim have small bells which tinkle as the Torah is carried around. This again reminds us of the garment of the high priest, as we read: "A golden bell and a pomegranate, upon the skirts of the robe around about. And it shall be upon Aaron to minister; and the sound thereof shall be heard when he goeth in unto the holy place before the Lord, and when he cometh out, that he die not" (Exodus 28:34–35).

The ringing of the bells is said to protect the high priest from death, as sounds are generally thought to guard us against evil powers. No doubt this was the reason why the little bells were fastened to the Torah which had to be carried to and from its Holy Ark.

Sometimes, in place of the rimonim, crowns were used; the term "crown of the Torah" from the Sayings of the Fathers (1:17) may have been taken literally in creating these ornaments. Two separate crowns are placed on each roller, or one single crown covers both. The beautiful example in Figure 6 shows this latter form. Its raised parts are

intentionally like a king's crown, not like the simpler crown
of a prince, or a duke.

Another way of fastening the crowns is sometimes found,
especially in Italy. Instead of being a substitute for the
rimonim, the crown is an additional ornament covering the
mantle. This creates almost too much tinsel and glitter.

With all this the desire for decorating the Torah did not
seem to be appeased, and in later times two more opportunities were found for adding splendor to the beloved Scroll.
A metal shield was hung on a chain over the Torah cover,
stressing the front of the cover. This shield could be justified on practical grounds. On some holidays several Torah
Scrolls were needed, each one for reading a different por-

7. TORAH SHIELD
*Holland, 1607. Amsterdam,
Portuguese Community.*

tion of the Scripture. For distinguishing the scrolls the
shields had small interchangeable plates with the name of
the holiday on which they were to be read. But centuries
had elapsed without the use of these shields, and some of
them do not even have the helpful name-plates. It seems

to us that the main reason for creating the breastplates was
an aesthetic urge rather than a practical need. The breast-
plate, shown in Figure 7, which was donated to the synagogue of Amsterdam in 1607, is the earliest Torah shield
known to us. Its style is still simple and yet very tasteful
with the frame of tendrils and the crown set upon the top
of the shield. Later on the size of the breastplates was increased, and we often find ornaments in the form of objects
and persons relating to the Temple and the Tent of Meeting: the two tablets with the Ten Commandments, the two
pillars in front of the Temple, the figures of Moses and
Aaron.

The allusion to Aaron is emphasized if the breast-plate
is decorated with precious stones, as it sometimes is. It then
reminds us strongly of the precious stones on the breast-
plate of the high priest. The little bells, which sometimes
hang from the shields, recall once more the garment of the
high priest.

The pointer, the last object which was added to the
Torah in later times, may be justified on practical grounds.
The reader wished to follow the lines of the text more easily,
yet he dared not touch the Holy Scriptures with his finger.
A simple wooden marker would have been suitable for this
purpose, but when the pointer is made of wood, we find
it carefully and artistically carved. Frequently it is made of
precious materials like silver, ivory, or sometimes even in
part of coral. Our example (Fig. 8) which is of silver, shows
how the artist tried to produce an interesting effect by using
a spiral design. At the same time it shows an ornament characteristic of all pointers, a hand with a pointed index finger.
This is the substitute for the real hand. Similar hands may
be seen on scepters, and it is possible that the association
was intentional. One can see that many possible interpreta-

8. TORAH POINTER
Cincinnati, Hebrew Union College

tions inspired the imagination of the pious Jew as he looked
on these ritual objects.

Naturally, the beautiful Torah rolls required an equally
beautiful shrine. Heathen rolls were likewise often kept in
special, embellished bookcases. This desire for ornamentation was greatly intensified when the bookcase was meant
to hold the rolls of the Pentateuch. For one thing, the location designated for it could not be left to mere chance. A
place of great holiness in the synagogue was selected—the
wall which faced in the direction of the Holy City, Jerusalem. Furthermore several steps lead up to it, the elevation
being symbolic of spiritual loftiness. Finally the area immediately surrounding the Ark is often separated from the
congregation by a fence. These fences, made of stone in
Antiquity, but later of wood or iron, were artistically designed (Fig. 150).

The embellishment of the Ark itself depended upon one
of two circumstances; the shrine either stood apart in front
of the wall, or receded into it. Some old shrines from Italy
have been preserved which show both types. How attractive,
for instance, is the wooden Ark from the synagogue of
Modena, carved more than four hundred years ago in
Gothic style (Fig. 113). With its base, its delicately carved

9. TORAH SHRINE
Italy, 18th century. Padua, Scuola Italiana.

squares in place of windows and its cornice, it resembles an Italian Gothic palazzo.

Our second example, shown in Figure 9, also comes from Italy and represents the second type of the Ark of the Law. It is placed in a niche. Three steps lead up to it and finely ornamented metal doors close it. Since the eye sees only the front, this front is splendidly decorated. The Ark is flanked by mighty columns carrying a rich entablature and a still more richly decorated gable. This Torah shrine was made roughly two hundred years later than the wooden Ark shown in Figure 113. During this period Italian art had developed an ever-increasing richness and abundance which is a characteristic of the baroque style.

The Torah curtain, the poroches, offered further opportunity for decoration. There were two places where it could be hung, both places utilized since early times. One method was to hang the curtain behind the doors of the Ark. No doubt, this was done for a practical reason—it afforded further protection for the Scrolls. This became the custom in Italy and in S'fardic synagogues. The other method was to hang the curtains on the outside, fastened to the Ark or to the niche in which the Ark stood.[5] This was surely reminiscent of the curtain in the Tent of Meeting and the Temple. There, too, the curtain hung before a chamber in which, according to the Bible, stood the Ark containing the Tablets of the Law.

When this method was observed it became necessary to conceal the unsightly cords by means of which the curtains were drawn. A top-piece or kapores, named after the ark-cover in the Tent of Meeting was provided to serve this purpose. This type of curtain was used in the Ashk'nazic

synagogues and became more and more elaborate and beautiful through the employment of fine materials such as silk,
damask, velvet, and brocade, and rich embroideries of gold
and silver thread. The curtain of a German synagogue of
the eighteenth century is a good example of this style (Fig.
10). The two spiral columns are copies of the columns in
the Church of St. Peter's in Rome; which columns are there
displayed, though erroneously, as from the Temple of Solomon. The grape-vines entwined about them are familiar
symbols in Jewish literature. They betoken the Jewish
people (Hosea 10:1), the world, Jerusalem, and the Torah
(b. Hullin 92 a). The fact that the top-piece was known
as kapores frequently caused it to be associated with the
Tent of Meeting and its furnishings. On the curtain here
illustrated, reading from right to left, we see depicted the
two Tablets of the Law rising over the Ark of the Covenant,
the laver of brass, the seven-branched candelabrum, the
altar of burnt offerings, and the table of showbread.

Many synagogues have several curtains, simpler for week-
days, more ornamental for the festivals. In consonance with
the mood of the New Year and the Day of Atonement the
colored curtains are replaced by white ones. Occasionally
a black curtain was used on the Ninth of Ov, when the destruction of the Second Temple was commemorated, or else
no curtain at all, to symbolize the emptiness of Jerusalem
robbed of its treasures. Here and there, also, we find special
curtains for circumcisions and weddings.

To conclude our description, we mention a special lamp
placed near the Ark. It is called the perpetual light because
it is never allowed to go out. Like the Torah curtain, the
lamp reminds us of Biblical times, for a similar light is already mentioned in the Tent of Meeting (Lev. 24:1–4). The
type of lamp which is now in general use was not in exist-

10. TORAH CURTAIN

Embroidered by Jacob Koppel Gans, 1727. Last at Krumbach, Germany.

ence before the Hellenistic period. At that time lamps consisting of glass bowls which were hung from chains became popular and, as so often happens, they were then adapted to religious purposes. Lifted high above the congregation, their transparent substance and open flame seemed to inspire religious feeling, the uplifting of the soul towards God. The beautifully curved oriental lamp in Figure 11 dates back to the seventeenth century. Hebrew letters and ornaments painted in gold form a contrast to the dark green

11. Perpetual Light
Damascus, 1694. London,
Jewish Museum.

color of the bowl. The links of the chains have the form of the letter "S" and terminate in a holder in the shape of a bell.

Let us now turn our attention to the elevated platform, the bimo, from which the Torah was read. While the place for the Holy Ark was prescribed by ritual law, no such regulation existed concerning the position of the bimo. In Spain, in Germany, and in Eastern Europe it was usually placed in the center of the synagogue; this arrangement had the advantage that the reading could be heard equally well in every part of the synagogue.[6] At the same time it clearly demonstrated that the reading of the Torah was the nucleus of the service. The physical center was symbolic of the spiritual center.

In other countries, especially in Italy, the bimo was placed against the wall opposite the Ark, allowing more space for the congregation. In the *Scuola Italiana* in Padua, whose Ark was shown in Figure 9, we find that the latter arrangement prevailed (Fig. 12). It does not seem to be a mere coincidence that the Italian architects preferred this

12. BIMO
Italy, 18th century. Padua, Scuola Italiana.

method. The beauty of a wide space which would have been spoiled by a center platform appealed to them. Because of their keen sense of balance they liked to give the Torah shrine and bimo equal importance in position and size.

There is a third possible position for the bimo. Examples are to be found in synagogues of southern France. In Carpentras and Cavaillon, Provence, it also faces the Ark, but on a special balcony above the heads of the congregation.

In spite of all this variety, one basic principle is adhered to: a definite distance is kept between the Ark and the bimo and its meaning is both ritual and aesthetic. After lifting the Torah Scroll from the shrine, it was solemnly carried to and from the bimo, and this procession formed a striking contrast to the motionless congregation. This contrast disappeared when the Liberal and Reform synagogues began to give up the separate bimo, and instead, combined it with the desks from which the prayers were read and the sermon was delivered. Furthermore, these desks thus placed, obstructed the view of the Torah shrine. In former days it was possible better to appreciate the moment when the beautiful curtain was drawn aside, when the carved doors were opened and the Torah Scrolls appeared, not just one roll, but several and each one in its costly array. On some holidays several Torah Scrolls were used. Apart from this necessity, the pious always wished to increase the number of Torah Scrolls. It was considered a deed of devotion to write or to order a Torah Scroll, and to have it richly decorated.

There were steps leading to the bimo just as there were steps leading to the Ark (Fig. 12). Two staircases were generally used, one for carrying up the Torah, the other for returning it to its shrine. In our illustration the staircase is elegantly curved and provided with carved railings. Thin pillars rise high above the platform, carrying a lofty ceiling like a canopy. Because of all these ornamental details, the bimo has become a work of art beyond its mere practical use.

There is a desk on the bimo on which the Torah is unrolled. The desk as well was often richly carved, and the cloth that covered it was beautifully embroidered. Again ritual and aesthetic considerations were combined. The Scroll of the Law must not be placed on the bare wood; the cover on which it rested must be beautiful.

The synagogue had a second desk, the amud, designed for the cantor. Its place was close to the Ark so that the cantor was facing east, yet not directly in front of it, so as not to obstruct the view of the Ark (Fig. 150).

The illustration also shows a sign over the cantor's desk with an inscription reminding him of his sacred office. It is called the shivisi tablet, according to the first verse of Psalm 16: "I have set the Lord always before me." The tablet, too, was artistically decorated. When it was made of

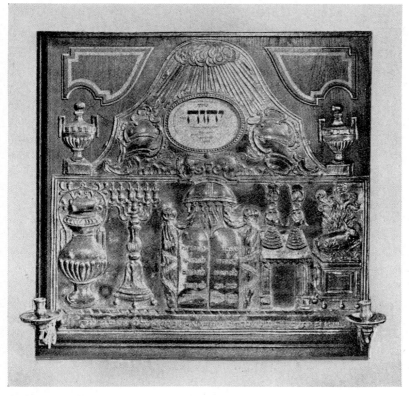

13. SHIVISI TABLET
Germany, about 1800. New York, Jewish Museum.

cardboard or wood, it consisted of silhouettes depicting ornaments and Jewish symbols. Our example (Fig. 13) is made of gilded silver. The verse is written in the oval space, and the enlarged name of the Lord is stressed by rays emanating from a cloud. In the center of the lower half, the two Tablets of the Law are shown in the open Tent of Meeting. To the right and left there are the seven-branched candelabrum, the basin, the table with the showbread, and the altar for burnt offerings. Again and again the thoughts of the Jews are centered around the lost sanctuaries, not only in retrospect, but in the hope of their eventual reconstruction.

A candle holder is attached to each side of the tablet. The candles throw the light on the desk and give a flickering shimmer to the golden tablet. Now and then special amud candelabra are placed on the desk.

There were still other lamps in the synagogue. The Chanuko candelabrum stood beside the cantor's desk. It will be described in connection with the festivals. Close to the Ark there is also a long row of Yahrzeit lights, in memory of the deceased members of the congregation. These are lighted year after year on the anniversary of their death. The candle holders are mostly made of iron and without decorations, as befits the Jewish conception of death. Attached to the walls or hanging from the ceiling are numerous lamps which have no

14. ALMS BOX
Poland, 1557. Cracow, Rema Synagogue.

ritual significance, but are much loved by the pious Jew. They are shaped like other lamps, but they were often made with special care and expressly for use in the synagogue (Fig. 112). Since the Jewish festivals begin in the evening, these lamps play an important part in the synagogue and give it a picturesque air. To the Jew, light is a symbol of the Law, of life, and a protection against evil. In the Elijah synagogue in Jerusalem there is a perpetual lamp with a metal hand at the top.[7] In the Orient an open hand is a well-known defense against evil powers.

An object which today no longer has the deep significance it possessed in the past is the seat of the leader of the synagogue. In ancient times it was known as the "seat of Moses." The term indicates the great importance attached to the leader of the congregation, who was regarded as a successor of Moses. His place was opposite the congregation so that he could keep his eye on the worshippers during the service.

In olden times this chair was made of stone (Fig. 88), while in later centuries wooden seats were used. For large congregations, chairs for other dignitaries were added. The main synagogue of Alexandria is said to have had seventy-one seats "corresponding to the seventy-one members of the great Sanhedrin, not one of them containing less than twenty-one talents of gold," as the Talmud reports (b. Sukkah 51 b). Figure 9 shows one of the syna-

15. ALMS BOX
From the synagogue in Witzenhausen, Germany

gogues of Padua where we see two chairs on either side of the Torah shrine. They are of wood and carefully carved.

In the lobby of a synagogue certain other ritual objects worth mentioning may be found. One often sees wall basins with a faucet, because the ritual of washing before entering the synagogue is not done by dipping the hands into the water, but by holding them under the faucet. There are also costly silver bowls and pitchers used for pouring water over the hands of the Kohanim, the descendants of the old family of priests. This act was essential before the priest could proceed to give the blessing to the congregation.

Alms boxes attached to the wall of the lobby were made

16. CARRYING THE LAW
By William Rothenstein. Johannesburg, South Africa, Art Gallery.

in a variety of materials and shapes. Some Polish containers in Renaissance and baroque style are outstanding. A very fine specimen belongs to the Rema Synagogue in Cracow (Fig. 14). This box is framed by pilasters carrying an entablature and a richly decorated gable. The inscription reads, "gold, silver, copper," meaning that even the smallest contribution is welcome.

17. PRAYER-SHAWL AND CAP
Last at Berlin, Jewish Museum

Another example is the wooden alms box from which an arm protrudes. The coins are placed in a slot in the palm of the hand, and then they fall into the box. This box, in its naive and lifelike execution, is such a striking example of genuine folk-art, that we include it among the illustrations (Fig. 15).

The picture would not be complete without the figures of the worshippers wrapped in their prayer-shawls. Originally, this shawl, or talis, was the secular dress of the Jew, and its use has continued in the synagogue just as the secular book roll has been preserved in the form of the Torah Scroll. This is probably due to the fact that, from Biblical times on, a few threads, the so-called tsitsis, which had a ritual significance, were attached to the four corners of the Jew's garment. The principal ornaments of the prayer-shawls

18. T'FILIN CASES
New York, Jewish Museum

were some dark blue or black stripes running parallel to the edges which, in their functional simplicity, appeal to contemporary taste. Since no reference to them is made in ritual literature, we may assume that these stripes originated in secular garments. They may be an elaboration of the "clavi" which were to be found on the dress of the Roman citizen. This theory is supported by the synagogue murals from the third century of our era which were excavated in Dura Europos. Several of the pictured Jews (Fig. 92) not only have the tsitsis on their Roman dress, but also the abovementioned clavi. The noted Jewish-English painter, William Rothenstein, tells us, in his autobiography, how fascinated he was when he saw these prayer-shawls as he witnessed an Orthodox service.[8] In the Orthodox synagogue they reach to the ground, while in more liberal synagogues they are often shortened. This picturesque sight inspired Rothenstein to paint several canvases, of which we reproduce one here (Fig. 16).

Sometimes a still more elaborate ornamentation of the prayer-shawls was employed, for instance, embroidering Biblical verses referring to the ritual of the tsitsis.[9] In Holland and Italy, probably not before the seventeenth century, shawls were found which were rich in colorful decorations, and they were used on festive occasions instead of the severe black and white ones. The Jewish Museum in Berlin had in its possession a shawl of silver damask, the back and borders of which were finely embroidered in shades of many colors. Gold and silver threads added to the costly and harmonious effect of this shawl (Fig. 17). Note the richly embroidered collar and cap. Similar collars, usually of gold or silver material, are sometimes added to the regular prayer-shawl. They are called "atoro" (crown), perhaps because the edge of the prayer-shawl was pulled over the forehead, and, when it was made of gold or silver, it greatly resembled a diadem or a crown.

At home, too, when saying the morning prayer, a pious Jew wraps himself in the shawl. At the same time he obeys another ritual law by winding phylacteries (t'filin) around his head and left arm. These are leather straps and boxes, the latter containing paragraphs from the Torah. Both lack decoration, but we mention them because they were sometimes kept in metal cases which were richly ornamented. Our examples, from the Jewish Museum in New York (Fig. 18), are of exquisite silver filigree work, a technique in which the Jews delighted, and acquired a high degree of artistic skill. The narrow confines of the ghetto tended to direct the mind and eye to small and limited objects.

19. SILVER M'ZUZO
Poland, about 1800

The prayer-shawl and the phylacteries have led us to
speak of the Jewish home, to which we will now turn our
attention. At the entrance and at the door of each room we
notice a narrow capsule, the m'zuzo. It contains a small roll
with Bible verses written on one side and the word *Shadai*
(Almighty) on the other. This word can be seen through
the little opening in the m'zuzo. The Bible requires this
writing to be placed on every door-post that we may be
constantly reminded of God. However, the Bible does not
actually mention the m'zuzo. We do not know when the
capsules originated. But we do know that they formerly had
an artistic design, whereas today, probably intentionally,
they are quite inconspicuous. When they were made of
wood the surface was carved with designs and Jewish symbols. Our illustration (Fig. 19) shows that precious metals
were also in use. The sides are bordered by a sawlike edge,
while coils in the classic style are placed at the top and bottom. In a playful mood the artist has added shutters to the
opening, and flowered designs extend all over the m'zuzo.

In the living-room a tablet hangs on one wall, indicating
the direction of Jerusalem, the direction one should face
when praying. This was the east wall for European Jews,
so the tablet was labeled mizrach, meaning "east." Since
it frequently has the same verses from the Psalms as the
shivisi tablet over the cantor's desk which we have already
mentioned, it is not always easy to distinguish the one from
the other. For the mizrach, as well as for the shivisi tablet,
silhouettes are often used for decoration. Our example
(Fig. 20) from Eastern Europe shows two circles, each containing one syllable of the word "mizrach." The crown with
the double eagle indicates that the tablet was made in Russia or Austria, and the hands raised in blessing show the
owner to be a Kohen. All other ornaments relate to the lost

20. MIZRACH TABLET
Leningrad, Jewish Museum

sanctuaries, such as the cherubim and the seven-branched candelabrum in the center which almost fades into the pattern of the tendrils. Snakes winding around the pillars of the temple stand for the adversaries of the Jews. Between them we see storks, the enemies of the snakes, suggesting that the foes of the Jews will eventually be destroyed.[10]

The story behind the tablet is very involved, and the artistic interpretation is no less complicated. There is no bare place left in the stencil. *Horror vacui,* fear of emptiness, as the art student calls this tendency, is characteristic of primitive art, as well as of folk-art. The Jews loved this richness of form and content. It was as much appreciated as the intricacies of a Talmudic discussion, with the difference that it was a feast for the eyes as well as for the brain.

III.

The Jewish Year

IN OUR discussion of the ritual objects in the synagogue and in the Jewish home, we have only taken into consideration those which are in regular use. We will now turn our attention to those objects which were reserved for the different holidays of the Jewish year.

Let us begin with the Sabbath. It is a day of rest and peace to be contrasted to the Jew's week-long struggle in an often hostile world. In the Jewish home we find a copper or brass lamp hanging from the ceiling, though in Italy it was usually attached to a metal arm projecting from the wall. The lamp was part of the regular equipment of the Jewish home, yet, it was only lit once every week, on Friday evening when the Sabbath began. Outgrowing its secular use, the lamp became a ritual object, and this fact influenced its shape. It was constructed in the shape of a star, with lights burning from its points. The number of points varied. Seven points are rarely to be found, probably because the Talmudic law forbade any revival of the seven-branched candelabrum after it had been lost (b. Rosh ha-Shanah 24 a). The top of the lamp, which is shaped like a saw, enabled the user to raise and lower it (Fig. 21). Small rounded metal pieces connect each corner of the star with a little pan underneath. The excess oil flows into this receptacle.

Besides the hanging lamp, there is also a type of standing candlestick used on Friday evenings. Nowadays it usually has one socket, but formerly it often had several. In Central

and Eastern Europe the kind shown in Figure 22 was much
in use. It is called the Cracow lamp, for it was made by the
Jewish coppersmiths of Cracow, in Poland. A shaft rises
from the well-rounded foot, spreading out into an elaborate
web of tendrils. The figures of deer can be discerned in the
pattern, corresponding to the verse from Psalm 42: "As the
hart panteth after the water brooks, so panteth my soul after
Thee, O God."

When the table is set for the Sabbath meal, the chalo, the

22. SABBATH CANDLESTICK
Cincinnati, Hebrew Union College

21. HANGING SABBATH LAMP. *Cincinnati, private possession.*

special loaf of bread, is placed before the head of the household. A cloth is spread over it. Here again we come across the ceremony of covering and uncovering objects, which is so prominent in the Jewish ritual. The chalo covers are

23. CHALO COVER
Germany, 19th century. Cincinnati, Hebrew Union College.

often skilfully embroidered. Figure 23 shows such a cover with two raised chalos in their characteristic braided form. They are framed by the Hebrew blessing and the name of the owner. A border of colorful flowers and branches completes the design. This handiwork, from the first half of the nineteenth century, has all the charm of the period which the Germans call "Biedermeier."

A wine cup is placed on the table beside the chalo, and is blessed by the master of the household. The cup was often made especially for this ceremony. Similar goblets were used for the Seder service, and will be described later.

The end of the Sabbath day is marked by a special ritual, the Havdolo, literally "separation," of the holiday from the week-days. A blessing is said over some spices, and they are

25. SPICE-BOX
Cincinnati,
24. SPICE-BOX
Germany, 16th century
Hebrew Union College

passed around. These spices are kept in a special spice-box, the b'somim box, and these boxes have been a source of considerable inspiration to Jewish art. The form of a tower is very popular. Similar boxes of such shape probably appeared first in Christian art. They are found in mediaeval pictures of the Adoration of the Magi, who, among other gifts, offer spices to the child Jesus.[11] When the Jews adopted this form they may have thought of the tower of spices men-

26. HAVDOLO CANDLE AND
SPICE-BOX

Germany, 18th century

tioned in the Song of Songs (5:13). Whatever the origin of the tower-shaped spice-boxes may have been, they vary widely in size and form. Sometimes they are round, sometimes square, and their sides may be plain or of exquisite filigree. Our example (Fig. 24) from the sixteenth century is one of the earliest of its kind. The resemblance to a church tower is avoided by the addition of gay little weather vanes characteristic of secular towers. This one has a small door for the insertion of the spices, and the scent comes through the screen above. The clock indicates that the spice-box is the model of a town hall tower, which also explains the presence of the figures of four watchmen on the gallery, guarding the city.

In Eastern Europe spice-boxes in the shape of flowers or fruit are preferred. Like the spices, they are natural carriers of scent. Our illustration (Fig. 25) shows a sunflower in a small vase. The artist did not trouble about correct botanic forms, for he added cones to the flower.

Sometimes gold and silver fish are used for spice-boxes, and the scent comes through small holes between the finely worked scales. In the nineteenth century, even models of railway engines have been made, a strange combination of an old custom and a modern invention! All these variations show again the Jew's love for things fanciful and subtle.

Another custom of the Havdolo service is the lighting of

a candle of unusual shape. It is made of several strands of
colored wax which are braided together. At times this
candle was put in a candle holder which could be joined to
the spice-box, as we can see from Figure 26. A drawer for
the spices is fastened over the spirally turned base in rococo
style. The candle is protected from breaking by slender
metal bars, lending further grace to the whole.

There was a prescribed manner of extinguishing the candle at the end of the ceremony. Some wine was poured on a
plate and the candle was then dipped in it. Havdolo plates
were made either of pewter or of porcelain, and their ritual
nature was emphasized by Hebrew words or symbols engraved or painted on them.

Let us now turn to those festivals which occur only once
every year. On the Jewish New Year, which comes in the
fall, the shofor is blown in the synagogue. It is the horn of
an animal, heated and then stretched, a primitive instrument, simple to manufacture, and limited in the range of its
tones. As so frequently happens, the Jews have faithfully
preserved an instrument of secular origin by using it for
their religious services. They feel strangely moved by its
penetrating sound.

The shofor is also blown on the Day of Atonement, and
in olden times it was sounded on other occasions as well.
Formerly these horns varied in appearance. For the New
Year, the horn of an ibex with a golden mouthpiece was
employed, for the Day of
Atonement, a ram's horn
with a silver mouthpiece,
and for the great ban, pronounced against transgres-
sors of the Law, the ram's
horn had to be black

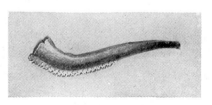

27. SHOFOR

28. BUCKLE

From a girdle worn on the Day of Atonement. New York, Jewish Museum.

(Mishnah, Rosh ha-Shanah III, 3–4). The modern synagogue uses only one horn, but still follows the previously mentioned Talmudic suggestion, "make a beautiful shofor." Our example (Fig. 27) shows a finely curved horn with an attractive saw-edge on one side. Sometimes it is engraved with designs and Hebrew words.

The Day of Atonement is spent in ascetic severity. In addition to the prayer-shawls, white garments are put on and tied around the waist. Even here the Jew could not refrain from adding an artistic buckle. The illustration in Figure 28 shows a vase with flowers in an oval center flanked by two lions. The drawing is naive, but the intuition of the artist in filling a blank space is worthy of note.

The Feast of Tabernacles is a harvest festival as well as a reminder of the time when the Jews were desert wanderers and lived in tents. The Law demands, therefore, that for seven days the Jews should exchange their homes for temporary booths. This imaginative custom led to a fanciful decoration of the booth. "Make a beautiful suko," says the

29. Sukos Meal
Engraving by Bernard Picart. Amsterdam, 1723.

Talmud, as we have quoted before. We find an enlightening
illustration in a French book of the eighteenth century dealing with the religious customs of different peoples (Fig. 29).
The wooden framework forms a dome above the walls. In
the center hangs a Sabbath lamp, surrounded by a crown of
garlands similar to the harvest crowns which the farmers
gave to their lords. Japanese lanterns hang from the roof,
and wall brackets holding candles are placed around the
room. This is again characteristic of the Jew's love of light.
Sometimes special mizrach tablets and other tablets, in
scribed and decorated, are added, so as to give the suko a
homelike appearance.

The esrog, the citron which the Jew holds in his hands
on this day, is kept in a special container. Such containers
were usually made of silver, and their form varied. Figure

30 shows a type which has been popular since the nineteenth century. The box is a naturalistic reproduction of the fruit itself.

Simchas Torah, the Feast of Rejoicing over the Law, is the day on which the last portion from the Torah is read. In thanksgiving for the Torah, all the scrolls are lifted from the Ark and carried in solemn procession through the synagogue. The children, too, are allowed to participate, and they hold paper flags in their hands as they follow the procession. In Western Europe the flags are quite simple, while in Eastern Europe they are frequently ornamented with woodcuts of lions, deer, and illustrations of men and children exultantly dancing and drinking (Fig. 31). These woodcuts are also examples of folk-art, and their charm is heightened rather than lessened by the naive draftsmanship.

30. ESROG BOX
Germany, 19th century

The Chanuko festival is dedicated to the successful revolt of Judas Maccabeus against the Syrian conqueror. At the restoration of the Temple, only one small bottle of oil was found which had not been desecrated by the invader. But. according to the well-known legend, the small flask lasted for eight days. In commemoration of this miracle, lights are burned for eight days, one on the first night, and one more on each succeeding night until on the last evening all eight candles are aglow. A ninth light, the shamos, or servant, was added for lighting the other candles. Obviously it was

31. SIMCHAS TORAH FLAG
Polish woodcut, 19th century

more practical to combine these candles on one stand. The Talmud already mentions such lamps and tells us that they should be placed at the gate or on the window-sill (b. Sabbath 21 b). Apparently the Jews wished to illuminate the Jewish quarter, and to proclaim publicly the joyous significance of the "Feast of Lights."

In order to fit the window-sill the lamp had to be small and narrow. Eight candles were mounted in a row in front of an upright handle, which later on developed into a kind of back. When made of metal it reflected the glow of the candles. In our illustration (Fig. 32) we show a Polish Chanuko lamp of this type from the eighteenth or early nineteenth century. The legs, sides, and back resemble a bench; so we feel justified in speaking of a "bench-type" lamp. The eight little oil phials are to remind us of the flask of oil found in the Temple. For symmetrical reasons, there are two sockets for the shamos instead of one. The wall is made of pierced work, a form of art very popular among Jews, as, for example, the paper sil-

32. CHANUKO LAMP
*Poland. Rabbi Philip Bernstein,
Rochester, N. Y.*

houettes of the mizrach tablets. In the center one sees the seven-branched candelabrum, its squareness contrasting with the curved lines of the lions and birds. Over the word "Chanuko" a loop is fastened, indicating that when not in

33. CHANUKO CANDLESTICK
Germany, 18th century. New York, Jewish Museum.

use, the lamp could be hung up, thus adding to the beauty of the room.

Besides the bench-type lamp, the "candelabrum-type" came into existence. It was no doubt derived from the seven-branched candelabrum of the Temple (Fig. 64) but the latter was of greater beauty because its odd number of arms gave it a natural center, and the arrangement of three arms on either side created an impression of amplitude without being confusing. To keep a similar balance, the Chanuko candelabrum was furnished with a ninth arm placed in the center. This was often extended above the other arms and crowned with a figure. In Eastern Europe the eagle was popularly used as a coat of arms, while Western artists ventured to place a human figure at the top. Judas Maccabeus served as a suitable figure, or Judith, who, according to Jewish tradition, killed Holofernes on the day of the Chanuko festival. She can be seen standing on the Chanuko candelabrum made in Frankfort-on-the-Main about 1700 (Fig. 33). The silver foot has been elaborately ornamented by colorful pictures painted in enamel. Above it a rampant lion is holding the coat of arms of the family which commissioned the lamp. The ninth light is attached to the central arm in the form of a small bowl.

The candelabrum-type, with its majestic shape, was well suited for the service in the synagogue, but was also used in a smaller size in the home. It became part of the regular equipment of the synagogue, though probably not before the fifteenth century.

For the festival of Chamisho Osor Bi-Sh'vot, the New Year of the Trees, special fruit bowls have recently been created.

In the Jewish month of Ador the Purim festival is celebrated in memory of the rescue of the Jews by Esther and

34. ESTHER SCROLL
Written by Arje Loeb ben Daniel in 1748. Cincinnati, Hebrew Union College.

Mordecai. "The beginning of Ador ushers in the joyous season," says the Talmud (b. Ta'anit 29 a). In many homes this joy was expressed by putting up wall tablets with Hebrew writing and designs of fish which are the constellation for the month of Ador. To give these days even more splendor, feasts were held and some wealthy families possessed special porcelain dishes for the occasion. The Hebrew Union College in Cincinnati owns a set of twelve plates made in Holland in 1785. A long Hebrew inscription runs from plate to plate.

There were special cake molds of wood for shaping the Purim cakes, and these molds were decorated with Jewish symbols and Hebrew words.

Jewish plays were performed referring to the story of Esther. The masks which were used by the actors have a singular power of expression.

The Book of Esther was read in the synagogue, and every time the name Haman was pronounced, the worshippers liked to show their disgust at the enemy of the Jews by shaking rattles. Even these noise makers were beautified with drawings of flowers or a picture of Haman on the gallows.[12]

Like the Torah, the story of Esther was read from a hand-written scroll. But while the Torah consists of a double roll, the brief story of Esther is written on a single roll. The scroll which was used at the service was without decoration, whereas for use at home it was permissible to have ornamented scrolls. The decoration varied; sometimes it consisted simply of geometric, floral, or architectural designs; in other instances the artist ventured to use human figures.[13] In this case it was customary to separate the columns of script by pictures of the main characters of the Esther story, while horizontal strips illustrating scenes from the same

story bordered the edges. The example shown in Figure 34 is in Renaissance style, though the copy itself dates from the eighteenth century. The figures also wear the dress of the sixteenth century. We must realize that in former times people attached less importance to the historical correctness of costumes. The story of Esther was looked upon as a symbol of persecution and salvation, which could recur at any period.

As with the Torah Scroll, the Jews wished also to protect the Esther scroll from damage. We saw that in the Orient the Torah Scroll was given a solid case. From this

Fellmann Photo Service

35. SILVER CASE FOR ESTHER SCROLL
New York, Jewish Museum

may have sprung the idea of making a similar container for the Esther scroll. For the simpler scrolls, wood was used, while the more valuable ones were given cases of ivory or silver. Unlike the containers for the Torah, these cases remained closed except for a slit through which the parchment was pulled for the reading. After reading, the roll was wound up by a handle which is to be seen at the bottom of the example, a work of the baroque period (Fig. 35).

36. PURIM PLATE
18th century. Paris, Musée Cluny.

This sums up the technical details. The artist's aim was to decorate the container to the best of his ability. If the script itself was illustrated, mere geometric or floral ornaments were sufficient for the cover. We frequently find the filigree technique employed for this purpose. Figure 35 shows a script without decoration; therefore a scene illustrating the Esther story has been embossed on the case. Notice the delicate metal edge of the roll and the beautiful little pointer, which is not found on every roll. The top is a crown often found on the Torah Scroll, but the crown of the Esther scroll cannot be removed.

Near the end of the Esther story we find the comment that the Jews should celebrate this day by giving presents to one another and sending gifts to the poor. For this purpose special gift plates were designed. When made of pewter, a star enclosing one or more fish was often engraved on the plate. It has already been mentioned that fish mark the month of Ador in the Zodiac. More elaborate decorations were possible on faience plates which were also in common use. Our example (Fig. 36) comes from Alsace and dates from the eighteenth century. The illustration shows the virtuous Mordecai riding on the king's horse as a reward for having detected a plot to assassinate the king. The malicious Haman leads the horse. Here again the dress of the characters is anachronistic. Haman wears the three-cornered hat of the rococo period, while Mordecai has a feathered hat of gigantic size. The bordering script, carefully spaced, is a reminder of the gifts, which according to the Book of Esther, should be given on this day.

Similar plates, larger in size, appear on the Seder evening, but before we discuss them, we must deal with the Passover (Pesach) festival in general. Like Purim, it celebrates the rescue from persecution, but the scene is set in the heroic times when God freed the Israelites from the slavery of Egypt. The significance of these events explains the splendor with which this festival is celebrated. The importance of the ritual is here shifted to the home, perhaps in order to impress the children with the ever-recurring Jewish fate of oppression and deliverance. The eve of the festival is remarkable for its multitude of ceremonies. In his novel, *The Rabbi of Bacharach*, Heinrich Heine has given us a description of the Seder which is so vivid that we would like to quote it in part here:

As soon as it is dark the mother of the family lights the lamps, spreads the table-cloth, places in the middle of the table three plates of unleavened bread, covers them with a napkin, and places on the pile six little dishes containing symbolic food, that is, an egg, lettuce, horse-radish, the bone of a lamb, and a brown mixture of raisins, cinnamon, and nuts. At this table the father of the family takes his seat among relations and friends, and reads to them from a very curious book, called the Haggadah, the contents of which are a strange mixture of legends of their forefathers, wondrous tales of

37. SEDER GOBLET

Germany, 18th century.
Last at Breslau, Germany,
Jewish Museum.

Egypt, questions of theology, prayers, and festival songs. During this feast there is a grand supper, and even during the reading symbolical food is eaten and the Passover bread tasted, while four cups of red wine are drunk.

Heine does not mention that the father of the family is clothed in the same white garment which he wears on the Day of Atonement. He is leaning on cushions which at times were appropriately embroidered and decorated. In addition, a silver basin for washing and a finely embroidered towel were placed close at hand.

The four cups of wine which Heine mentions are drunk from a silver goblet. It resembles the goblet used on Friday nights, but its special function is revealed in the words and pictures which adorn it. It has the shape either of a goblet or of a chalice, Figure 37 showing the latter type. The full grace of the rococo period is demonstrated in the elegantly shaped foot; and the finely curved cup which rests upon it is neither too heavy nor too light. Branches and grapes are delicately woven over the surface.

On this evening a second goblet is used. It is reserved for the prophet Elijah, whose visit is expected.

With regard to the symbolic food of the Seder, let us begin with the unleavened bread, called matso. It is a reminder of the bread which the Israelites ate on their desert wanderings. Today, it is machine made and matter-of-fact in form. Formerly the dough was worked into an attractive shape with iron combs and wheels. This procedure is clearly shown in a miniature found in a German Haggadah of the fifteenth century (Fig. 38). The whole family was busy with preparations for the holiday in much the same way as Christian families delighted in the coloring of Easter eggs for the Easter holidays.

We must add to Heine's description of the Seder, that the three matsos are placed on a special plate, usually made of pewter. When the plate is engraved, it frequently has a star pattern like the star on the Purim gift plate. But instead of the fish, the Passover lamb is placed in the center (Fig. 39). Around the edge, different scenes are engraved relating to the song, "An Only Kid," which is sung on the Seder night. With great pride the German-Jewish artist has added his name, Joel ben Jehuda, and the date, 1779.

The matso, like the chalo, in the Friday evening cere-

38. ORNAMENTATION OF MATSO
From a German Haggadah of the 15th century.
Nuremberg, Germanisches Museum.

39. SEDER PLATE
Germany, 1779. Cincinnati, Hebrew Union College.

mony, is covered. Heine only speaks of an ordinary napkin,
but in older times an artistic touch was given to the cover.
Embroidered ones with long fringes (Fig. 44) and even
costly pouches with three separate pockets were used. On
these covers or pouches the other symbolic foods were then
placed. The design of the Passover dishes was often
prompted by the particular foods which they contained. For
instance, the brown mixture of raisins and spices, called
charoses, was served now and again in a miniature wheelbarrow pushed by a farmer (Fig. 40). It is supposed to remind us of the clay from which the Hebrew slaves made
bricks for their Egyptian masters. The wheelbarrow is divided into two parts, one for serving the charoses and the
other for the bitter herbs, which are likewise reminders of
the sufferings of the Israelites in Egypt.

40. CONTAINER FOR CHAROSES
AND BITTER HERBS
*19th century. New York,
Jewish Museum.*

Fellmann Photo Service

In recent times, probably not before 1800, a convenient combination of Seder plate, Seder dishes, and matso cover was invented. We include an illustration of a contemporary dish (Fig. 41) which shows the advantage of this arrangement. A circular base contains the three matsos. Over this is a plate with six identical dishes for the symbolic foods. In the center the goblet for the prophet Elijah is placed. The very modern artistic effect is achieved by the contrasting use of glass and metal, and by the horizontal and vertical design of the piece.

Besides the matsos used at home, a special matso was kept

41. COMBINATION MATSO
CONTAINER, SEDER PLATE,
AND SEDER DISHES
Made by Ludwig Wolpert

42. PLATE FOR THE
CEREMONY OF ERUVE CHATSEROS
1770. Strassburg, Alsatian Museum.

in the synagogue to fulfil the ceremony of eruve chatseros.[14] This matso was put on a plate, usually made of wood in the shape of the Star of David, and it was hung over the heads of the worshippers. It usually had a simple design, but now and then became more elaborate (Fig. 42). The corners of the star in our illustration are filled with flowers and the center is taken up by a double-headed eagle, while the Hebrew letters give the date, 1770.

Returning to the Seder table, there is still one important item to be discussed, the Pesach Haggadah. It is the book which is read by the family on this evening. The variety of its contents inspired a variety of illustrations and ornaments in the writer-artists. Here they were at liberty to disregard the Second Commandment, because the Haggadah was not used in the synagogue and no fear of idol-worship came into consideration. Finally, the Haggadah was meant to interest the children, whose attention is best attracted by pictures.

It would be impractical to list here all the mere decorative motifs employed in the ornamentation of various Haggadahs. We refer briefly to the reproduction of a page from the Darmstadt Haggadah, which is perhaps the most exquisitely designed and colored Haggadah known to us (Fig. 128). We can, however, give an outline of the types of illustrations most frequently used. They sometimes originate from the literal interpretation of a few words of the text taken out of their context. For instance, the Haggadah quotes the metaphor of the prophet Ezekiel who refers to Israel in this way: "And thou didst increase and grow up, and thou camest to excellent beauty: thy breasts were fashioned, and thy hair grown; yet thou wast naked and bare" (16:7). The artist takes this phrase literally and sketches a nude woman with long hair. I mention this particular example because it shows that some Jewish artists had no inhibitions about drawing a nude female figure; on the contrary, he was sensitive to the beauty of the human form.

Let us now turn to the more typical illustrations. There

are the pictures of Bible stories and legends, centering around the figure of Moses, who is the chief character in the story of Pesach. Our illustration (Fig. 43), taken from a contemporary Haggadah by Jacob Steinhardt, shows the children of Israel led by Moses, crossing the Red Sea, with the drowning Egyptians in the background. This is just as dramatic in its form as it is in its contents: the bright rays of the rising sun pierce the darkness of the night.

43. MOSES AND THE ISRAELITES CROSSING THE RED SEA

Woodcut from the Haggadah by Jacob Steinhardt

44. SEDER MEAL
From a German 15th century Haggadah.
Cincinnati, Hebrew Union College.

Occasionally earlier Biblical events are illustrated, as for instance, the story of Adam and Eve (Fig. 130), and the creation of the world. Even legendary scenes are added, because the artist and the reader never tired of new themes or stories.

A second series of illustrations is related to the sages of the early Talmudic period who are quoted in the Haggadah. They appear alone and in a group. A favorite scene shows five famous rabbis in the city of Bene-Berak so engrossed in their debate about the miracles of the Passover story, which they discussed all night, that they almost missed the morning prayers.

A third series embraces the Passover ritual and the celebration itself. It is of cultural interest because it increases our knowledge of Jewish life in the past. It is also of artistic significance because it shows the evolution of Jewish painting of domestic life. We have already shown the illustration which depicts the Jewish family decorating the matsos (Fig. 38). Another picture shows the father of the family searching for the unleavened bread before the Passover begins. The gay scene of the Seder meal is never missing. Our illustration, taken from a German Haggadah of the fifteenth century, reveals the intimacy of this scene (Fig. 44). The boy and the Seder plate in the center and the parents sitting on either side give perfect balance to the picture.

Representations of some of the dietary prescriptions, which Rabbi Gamliel has pronounced indispensable, belong to the same series. Their subjects were the pascal offering, the unleavened bread, and the bitter herbs.

The scene showing the chase of a hare, which is frequently found in Ashk'nazic Haggadahs, has a ritual origin. It represents the "Jaknhas" mnemonic for the sequence of the benedictions to be recited when the evening of the Seder and the termination of the Sabbath coincide. The Jew transformed the term "Jaknhas" to "Jagt den Has" (meaning: chase the hare). In our example taken from the same Haggadah (Fig. 45), the artist painted a hilly landscape with a hunter brandishing a large lance and pursuing two hares, who are running away from the dogs.

The picture of the "four sons" is frequently found in

45. Jaknhas (Chase the Hare)
From a German 15th century Haggadah. Cincinnati, Hebrew Union College.

Photo Jacob B. Marx

46. OMER CALENDAR
19th century. Cincinnati,
Hebrew Union College.

Haggadahs. It represents four different conceptions of the Pesach story, and the artist has therefore dealt differently with each one. Usually, the wise son is pictured as an old scholar, the wicked son as a warrior, the simple son as a fool or a peasant, and the son "who knows not how to ask," as a child.

The Passover festival is not only celebrated in recollection of the past, but also in expectation of the Messianic time. On this theme some additional pictures were based. Elijah, the forerunner of the Messiah, is shown blowing a shofor, and the Messiah himself is depicted riding on a donkey. Jerusalem is seen rebuilt in its old glory, with its Temple restored.

Fifty days elapse between Passover and Pentecost, the Festival of Weeks, and these days, called days of the omer, are carefully numbered by pious Jews. Omer originally was a dry measure of the new harvest grain which was sacrificed to God. Later on, these days were regarded as days of mourning because certain tragic events had taken place during this time. Therefore, with the exception of a few days, feasting and gaiety were forbidden. Numbering these days helped people to observe them strictly. Special omer calendars were invented for this purpose. They were sometimes shaped like a disk with a hand on a clock face, or they took the form of cases with adjustable rolls inside, as in our illustration (Fig. 46). The top figure indicates the day, the second picture the week, and the bottom section shows the number of days exceeding one week. Our illustration shows the seventh day of the first week, and consequently no figure appears in the bottom section. We can see that each figure is beautifully written and placed on a colored background, and the bottom square is decorated all over, because there are no figures on it. The edges of the case are bordered by curved ornaments in the rococo style. It is not original rococo, but a revival due to the historic trend of nineteenth century art. The Tablets of the Law are at the very top of the case. They indicate the approaching Festival of Weeks which commemorated the revelation of the Law on Mount Sinai.

Compared to the Passover festival, the Feast of Weeks lacks ritual accessories. However, in Eastern Europe it was the custom to paste silhouettes on the windows in the shape of roses, called *reiselech* in Yiddish. These are typical of folk-art, like the wooden hammer of the *Schulklopfer*. But we have also seen and discussed numerous objects which were far from belonging to folk-art. Many of them were made of silver or fine textiles, and were equal in workmanship to the best work of the time.

IV.

From the Cradle to the Grave

THE splendor of the Jewish Festivals lifted the congregation above the monotony of every-day life. The individual Jew also seized every opportunity to celebrate certain important events in his private life. These celebrations he conducted with a similar splendor.

The birth of a child had a deep meaning for the Jew. It did not only guarantee the survival of his family, but also that of his people. But the day of birth itself, as well as the days which followed, were considered to be full of dangers which, people believed, came from evil spirits. This superstition gave rise to certain rituals which were intended to counteract these baneful influences.

Special tablets with Hebrew inscriptions, with ornaments and pictures of flowers and animals, were hung in the mother's room. Figure 47 shows a very attractive example from the

47. PAPER AMULET
Strassburg, Alsatian Museum

68

Alsatian Museum in Strassburg. It is strongly influenced by the style of Louis
XVI, rich in classical forms
—vase and pillars—but it
still preserves the grace of
the previous rococo period.
The text of the Hebrew writing is taken from Psalm 121,
which expresses implicit
trust in God's help. The additional words "Almighty,
destroy Satan" are written
in large characters in order
to increase the effectiveness
of the tablet. The meaning
of the parrot remains uncer-
tain. To consider it as a bird
representing the soul as is
suggested in Psalm 124:7 is
inappropriate here. We pre-
sume that it has no significance beyond its decorative
value. Although, as we have
seen, the Jews were fond of
symbolic illustrations, we
must not make the mistake
of expecting a symbolic
meaning in every single instance. In folk-art deeply significant symbols vary with
purely decorative matter.

Mother and child fre-

Photo Th. Harburger

48. SILVER AMULET

Fellmann Photo Service

49. SILVER AMULET
*18th century. New York,
Jewish Museum.*

quently wore very beautiful amulets during the critical days.
Often, the word Shadai (Almighty), as on the m'zuzo, played
an important part. Figure 48 is an example of an amulet at-
tractively framed by beautifully carved and chiseled palm
leaves. Amulets consisting of heart-shaped capsules, inclos-
ing certain words, were also popular, because the heart was
the seat of life. The ornaments on both sides refer to the
Tent of Meeting. The Tablets of the Law and the seven-
branched candelabrum are clearly visible in our example,
which dates from the rococo period (Fig. 49).

The circumcision of the male infant eight days after his
birth is the token of his entrance into the Abrahamic covenant. In the earliest days this ceremony was performed

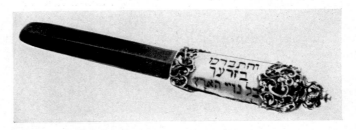

50. CIRCUMCISION KNIFE
17th century. Last at Berlin, Jewish Museum.

with a stone, which was replaced in later times by metal
knives. Their form was subject to ritual as well as artistic
considerations. The blade has two sharp edges, probably an
allusion to Psalm 149: "Let the high praises of God be in
their mouth and a two-edged sword in their hand." A
ruby is sometimes set in the top of the handle, symbolic of
blood. Our example (Fig. 50) dates from the seventeenth
century and is of exquisite workmanship. Both ends of the
amber handle show elaborate silverwork. The Hebrew
words refer to the covenant of the Lord with Abraham.

51. SILVER BOX FOR ASTRIN-
GENT POWDER
Germany

Other instruments used for the medical part of the act of circumcision were small bowls, boxes, and pincers, etc. Even these objects were ornamented beyond their practical needs. Let us take the box with astringent powder, for instance (Fig. 51). The embossed circumcision scene on the outside shows clearly that it was made especially for this occasion. The elegant shape of the box, the fine handles, and the graceful foot are particularly attractive.

Formerly, the circumcision usually took place in the synagogue. The godfather sat on a special chair holding the infant, while the mohel who performed the ceremony, knelt before him. The chair was often a bench with two seats. One seat was for the godfather, the other was reserved for the prophet Elijah, the friend and helper of human beings. In Figure 52 we see a beautiful chair which looks exactly like a secular bench of the rococo period. But the Hebrew letters along the back and the two seats indicate its exclusive use at the circumcision ceremony.

The child was specially dressed for the occasion.

52. CHAIR OF ELIJAH
*Last at the synagogue of
Deutz, Germany*

53. CIRCUMCISION
*From a Mohel Book, written in 1713
by Moses Juda Loeb.
Amsterdam, Rosenthaliana.*

At the ceremony the mohel drank some wine, with which the child's lips were also moistened. A double, rounded goblet was sometimes used, one part was filled for the child, the other for the mohel. The prayers said on this occasion were either embroidered on a curtain or were written in a special book, the so-called "mohel book." These mohel books often had a decorative title-page and some illustrations relating to the ceremony. Our example (Fig. 53) represents a charming page from a mohel book of the early eighteenth century which was still written by hand. The picture shows a typical circumcision ceremony, performed in a home this time, and is drawn in the graceful manner of the period. Here, as in certain Haggadah illustrations, a kind of religious genre-painting arose.

The first-born boy was brought to the synagogue thirty-one days after his birth. He was presented as an offering to God, but redeemed by his parents with a gift. The same rite is mentioned in the story of Jesus' childhood, as well as his circumcision, and both have often been depicted in Christian art. It may be worth while to examine pictures illustrating the New Testament when they deal with Jewish ceremonies. They sometimes supplement our knowledge of the early forms of Jewish ritual.

For the redemption of the first-born, the custom of placing the child on a costly silver platter was adopted, although we do not know exactly at which epoch. Our example (Fig. 54) of such a platter, depicting the sacrifice of Isaac, dates from about 1800. Isaac is lying on the altar in a very ungainly position, and Abraham's head is too big in proportion to his body, and the tops of the trees look like grapes. Here as so often in Jewish art, the strength of the illustration does not lie in its naturalistic accuracy but rather in the sincerity with which the artist has treated the subject. For instance, the figure of the flying angel above the altar

54. PLATTER FOR THE REDEMPTION OF THE FIRST-BORN
Last at Berlin, Jewish Museum

with his arms outstretched has power of conviction. The edge of the plate is decorated with the constellations of the Zodiac, which, according to popular belief, determine the fate of man.

In Ashk'nazic countries as we have already mentioned, a Torah binder was donated at a boy's first visit to the syna-

55. TORAH BINDER
Germany, 1842. Last at Berlin, Jewish Museum.

gogue. It contained the names of the child and of his father, the date and place of his birth. The binder was thus of some practical use to the congregation, but the desire toward decorativeness overshadowed its usefulness. The Hebrew inscription, embroidered or painted, was done in beautiful lettering. The traditional words, "May he grow up for the Torah, for the chupo (canopy of marriage) and for good deeds," were illustrated with pictures. Figure 55 shows the marriage ceremony of a young man and a girl. The rabbi, who holds the marriage contract, is taller than the couple; as in primitive and in folk-art, spiritual supremacy is represented by physical height. The bridesmaids at the left stand so close together that they seem to be clad in one dress. The pillars of the chupo are placed side by side instead of supporting the four corners of the roof; because the artist had no knowledge of perspective. Yet much imagination has been used in decorating the pillars and the embroidered chupo cover.

When the boy had reached the age of thirteen, he was solemnly accepted as a member of the congregation. The customs which were connected with this ceremony, the Bar

Mitsvo (Son of the Commandment), did not produce special ritual objects. The boy was, however, presented with the prayer-shawl, the phylacteries, and sometimes a beautifully bound prayer book.

After passing through the elementary school (cheder) and the secondary school (y'shivo) the young man received, upon his graduation, the title morenu (our teacher). His certificate, known as the morenu letter, was sometimes highly ornamented, probably in an attempt to imitate the doctor's diploma of the university. Figure 56 is the reproduction of an Italian morenu letter of 1677. At the top the crown of the Torah appears, for the study of Torah was the center of all Jewish education. The border of garlands and nude cupids is in the rich style of the times.

56. Morenu Letter

Italy, 1677. New York, Jewish Theological Seminary.

In the words on the Torah binder, "May he grow up for the chupo," we have already seen the importance which the Jew attached to marriage. It was regarded as a religious duty of every Jewish man and woman, and therefore the marriage ceremony was emphasized by a number of rituals. The first step was a gift from the groom to the bride as a visible sign of their union. Under Roman influence, in the Middle

57. BRIDAL RING
Venice, 16th century

Ages, the ring became the token of this union. Meant as a ritual object not to be worn in every-day life, the ring was of considerable size. Simple rings usually consisted of one or two bands, covered by a small plate with the words "Mazol Tov" (good luck) engraved upon it. More elaborate rings were decorated with a little house alluding to the new home of the couple. Our example (Fig. 57) shows a Venetian ring of this type from the period of the Renaissance. Venice was the place where the finest rings were fashioned. In our example, Mazol Tov has been inscribed on the ring itself in black enamel, which contrasts with the golden background. The delightful little house perched atop the band has pierced walls and a high Gothic roof.

Among the wedding presents we ought to mention a silver belt which the groom gave to the bride. It was not a specifically Jewish object, but was generally used for the purpose of carrying keys. In Jewish life it became a symbol of womanhood. We know its attractive form from the few samples which date from the seventeenth and eighteenth centuries. It was fastened with a clasp, and there was also a buckle for attaching keys, scissors, and other useful objects (Fig. 58). Sometimes groom and bride each wore a belt joined during the ceremony by a chain.

A special document set forth all the obligations which the husband took upon himself as regards his wife. K'subo was the name of this marriage contract. Today a legal document would not be ornamented, but formerly the Jews felt differently about it. They wanted to convey the impression that this contract was as much a gift as a legal document, and therefore they decorated it. We have an example of such a k'subo dating from the tenth or eleventh century of our era.[15] This one is still simple in form, but later on they were considerably elaborated. The upper edge of the example (Fig. 59) written in eighteenth century Italy, is curved in order to facilitate the unrolling of the parchment. The ornamentation is varied. Small symbolic pictures and Hebrew words are woven into a labyrinth of lines. In other types of k'subos human figures are added, either relating to the name of the groom, or picturing a married couple. Even Adam and Eve, the first couple on earth, were sometimes included in the illustrations.

A k'subo from the fourteenth century, written in Austria, shows in the margins a picture of the groom presenting the ring to the bride. The latter is wearing a crown, which should also be mentioned when speaking of the ritual objects at the marriage ceremony. Originally, the groom wore the crown (Song of Songs 3:11). Later on, both groom and bride wore them, but eventually the custom was retained only for the bride, as a symbol of dignity.[16] We do not know

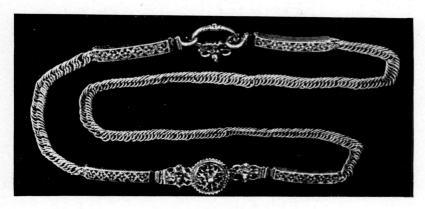

58. SILVER BRIDAL BELT
Last at Berlin, Jewish Museum

59. Marriage Contract (K'subo)
Italy, 1740

what the crowns were made of: whether of paper, cardboard, or metal. It is not possible with any degree of certainty to identify a bridal crown.

In Antiquity it was customary to erect a tent for the bride and groom; this was probably the origin of the chupo. We have already seen this kind of canopy in Figure 55, and noticed that the bridal tent was formerly far more elaborately decorated than it is today. Later it became the custom for the groom and bride to walk under this chupo from the home to the yard of the synagogue. There, outside the building itself, the wedding took place. During the ceremony, the couple had to drink some wine, but we have never seen a special cup used for this occasion. The reason may be that it was customary to employ a glass goblet which was broken immediately afterwards. This was done in order to restrain the gaiety of the feast and thus to reconcile the evil spirits. The custom is interesting for us only because it has led to the insertion of special chupo stones in the exterior of the synagogue. The stones are always placed in the north wall because this was the direction from which the demons were believed to approach. Figure 60 is a sample of a chupo stone. The letters in the circle mean Mazol Tov (good luck). The surrounding Hebrew inscription says: "The voice of joy and the voice of gladness, the voice of the bridegroom and the voice of the bride" (Jeremiah 33:11). The four letters in the corners are numbers giving the date, 1756. The design of letters and floral ornaments is pleasing to the eye.

In contrast to the joyful and happy marriage ceremonial stand the somber rituals of death and burial. As far back as Talmudic times special societies were formed whose members were at hand in the event of death. In S'fardic Judaism they were called lavadores (washers) because one of their

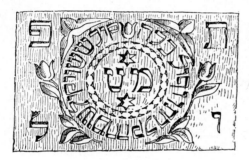

60. CHUPO STONE
Germany, 1756

duties was to wash and to clean the deceased person. A later name used in Ashk'nazic Judaism is chevro kadisho (Holy Society). Some of the old utensils have been preserved, and they are decorated in character with the occasion for which they were used. Water was poured over the deceased with a scoop as the one shown in Figure 61. It was made in Poland in the seventeenth century. A skull is embossed on the handle, and in the center is the figure of a nude man with a long beard. The frontal aspect and the strict symmetry of the figure correspond to the stern and mournful nature of death.

There were also tall silver mugs for
the annual feast of the Holy Society.
They remind one of the mugs of the
guilds which passed from mouth to
mouth during their festive repasts as
a symbol of unity. The Jewish mugs
are mostly without ornamentation.
Only the names of the members are
engraved upon them.

The coffins used today are made of
plain wood and, being black, create a
sinister impression. In death all men
are equal, so the Jew allows no differentiation in the shape of a coffin. But
this severity was not put into practice
at all periods. During the Hellenistic
period, as we shall see later on, the

61. WATER SCOOP
*For cleansing the body of
the dead. Poland, 1655.*

Jews had a more worldly outlook, and this also affected the
burial rituals. The deceased were placed on magnificent
stretchers and buried in caves, or catacombs, the interiors
of which were richly painted, whilst their exterior showed
a variety of architectural features.

Of all this only the tombstones have remained throughout
the centuries. They will be discussed later. But here it will
be sufficient to note the most striking differences between
the two types, the horizontal and the vertical tombstones.

The horizontal type is found among S'fardic Jews who,
after their expulsion from Spain, settled in France, Holland, Germany, Turkey, and other countries. Our example
(Fig. 62) is taken from the cemetery in Altona, Germany.
The slabs, all of an even size and evenly spaced, are of architectural austerity. Most of them are flat; some have a roof,
a few resemble a house.

The upright tombstones prevail among the Ashk'nazim, the Jews in Germany and in those countries to which German Jews emigrated, Eastern Europe in particular (Fig. 63). These were formerly much more uniform than the tombstones we find today, when everyone is anxious to follow his individual taste. If old stones of the vertical type are apt to give an effect of restlessness, this is due to the fact that the stones sank in the course of time and slanted. This gives them a certain melancholy touch which well befits the Jewish destiny, but was not originally intended. Only the tops of the stones differ in monuments of this kind. Sometimes they are square, sometimes pointed, and sometimes curved.

An inscription on tombstones was not always customary, probably in observance of the Talmudic words that the reading of such inscriptions might adversely affect a man's ability to study (b. Horayot 13 b) and that the righteous are remembered by their deeds, not by memorials (y. Shekalim II, 5, 47 a).

Wherever an inscription occurs, it is either chiseled in relief or hewn into the stone, and its beauty lies in the Hebrew characters.

The objects depicted on these tombstones differ according to the origin of the Jews. On Ashk'nazic tombstones the artists usually did not go beyond the use of plants, animals, and ritual symbols relating to the name of the deceased. A man named Hirsch (translated "deer") would be characterized by the figure of a deer; another with the name Israel, by a bunch of grapes, symbol of Israel (Fig. 159). A Kohen's tombstone could be identified by two hands raised in benediction; for the Levite, the Levitical pitcher was used.

In S'fardic monuments, however, the Jews ventured to use human figures. For instance, when the name of the deceased was Samuel, the scene chiseled in the stone showed

62. S'FARDIC CEMETERY IN ALTONA, GERMANY

how the Lord revealed himself to Samuel in the Temple of
Shiloh (Fig. 158). A woman named Rachel who died in
childbed, was compared to the Biblical Rachel, who is
shown on her death-bed. Both examples are taken from the
S'fardic cemetery in Ouderkerk near Amsterdam.

The memory of the deceased is also revered by the congregation. Annually, on the day of his death, a light is
burned in the synagogue. These Yahrzeit lights, as we already mentioned, are usually quite plain, consisting merely
of iron spikes upon which the candles are set.

Special tribute was paid to the memory of martyrs who
died for their faith. Their names and deeds were recorded
in memorial books and later the names of those who contributed to the welfare of the community were added. These
memorial books often have very attractive title-pages and
initials.

In our survey we have shown a large number of ornamented ritual objects evoked by the Jewish religion. The

63. Ashk'nazic Cemetery in Tarnopol, Poland

reasons for this plenitude are twofold. Firstly, the Jewish religion was able to infuse such fervor into the souls of the worshippers that the smallest object connected with its service was invested with religious significance. The beauty given to these objects was only an exterior sign of the importance accorded them. Secondly, the road towards representative art, though not entirely barred, was fraught with difficulty, particularly during the periods when the Second Commandment was strictly observed. In such times, therefore, the artist expressed himself by beautifying ritual objects. That is why these objects deserve a more detailed treatment than the religious handiwork of other communities or peoples. A thorough understanding of the form and content of Jewish cult objects will open the road to a better understanding of Jewish art.

PART TWO

THE DEVELOPMENT
OF JEWISH ART

V.

Beginnings of Jewish Art

I N THE preceding chapters we have grouped the objects of Jewish art topically. The aim of the following chapters is to find out when these objects came into being, or, more generally, how Jewish art developed in the course of time.

Our knowledge of the beginning of Jewish art is very scanty. In Palestine huge stones set up by human hands have been found. When and by whom they were erected, whether by the Israelites or by other peoples living in this country, is open to speculation. One thing however is certain: the Israelites were very familiar with such stones. They connected them with stories of their venerated ancestors and therefore held them in high esteem. There was a stone, for instance, which was considered to have been erected by Jacob over the tomb of Rachel (Genesis 35:20). Another one was supposed to have pillowed Jacob when he dreamed of the heavenly ladder (Genesis 28:10–22). On awakening, Jacob himself was said to have placed the stone in an upright position, apparently without altering its shape. He anointed the top of the stone with oil thus converting it into an altar. The Bible also tells of more elaborate altars of a later period, but it is of particular interest to learn that the Jews knew and remembered those primitive altars consisting of plain stones.

The elaborate altars of a later date did not always meet with approval. There were tendencies to simplify Jewish life as well as Jewish ritual. The following law apparently

refers to these tendencies: "An altar of earth thou shalt
make unto Me . . . And if you make Me an altar of stone,
thou shalt not build it of hewn stones" (Exodus 20:21–22).
No matter when this law was pronounced—the Bible places
it at the time of Moses, whereas modern Bible critics date it
from the time of the Kings—it proves once more that simple
altars existed before the elaborate ones appeared.

Only once in these patriarchal stories do we find mention of a religious object which extends beyond the natural
form of stones. When Rachel secretly left her father Laban
to follow Jacob to Canaan, she took with her the paternal
teraphim. Laban hurried after the fugitive in order to recapture them. But his search was in vain; Rachel had hidden them in the saddle of her camel (Genesis 31:19–35).
Apparently these teraphim were considered to have magic
powers. Because of this, Rachel took them with her, hoping
to transfer their benefits to her new abode, and for the same
reason Laban was eager to recapture them.

We learn nothing about their shape besides the fact that
they could not have been larger than the saddle under
which they were placed. But we can guess the shape of such
domestic teraphim from another reference, although this
later one dates from the time of the Kings (I Samuel 19:11–
17). When Saul sent his messengers to David's home to capture him, the latter's wife assisted her husband to escape
through the window, and placed the teraphim in the bed in
his stead. She covered the body with garments and the head
with a quilt of goat's hair. When the messengers returned to
the king, their mission unfulfilled, saying that David was ill,
Saul ordered them to bring the sick man on his bed. It was
not until then that the clever woman's trick was revealed.

We see from this narrative that the teraphim had human
form, so that, under certain conditions, they could be used to

create the illusion of a man's figure. On this illusion David's wife based her cunning and from it the narrator derived the charm of his story.

It is not possible to state a definite date for the origin of the teraphim in Israel. As they represent a superior art form we must assume that they were created later than the first unhewn stones. Furthermore it is obvious that the earlier these statues appeared, the simpler they were. This can also be gathered from the following commandments: "Thou shalt make thee no molten gods" and "Ye shall not make with Me gods of silver, or gods of gold" (Exodus 34:17 and 20:20). Thus we see that idols were cast in metal or made of gold and silver; the Bible mentions a number of such statues existing from the time of Judges to the time of the Kings. But as with elaborate altars, the use of sumptuous statues was disapproved of because the memory of the simpler ones was still alive. Consequently these early statues, although more developed than the plain stones, must be ranked amongst primitive Jewish art.

The sojourn of the Hebrew tribes in Egypt adds nothing to our knowledge of Jewish art, although we would very much like to know whether Egyptian art, already so highly developed at this period, exercised any influence upon Jewish art.

The Biblical representation of the migration of those tribes from Egypt into the Holy Land acquaints us with three ritual objects which also fall into the realm of art because of their elaborate artistic form: a Holy Ark, a Holy Tent and a candelabrum. The tent was placed in an open court, which was bordered by costly rugs hung between pillars. This court contained the altar for burnt offerings. It was made of wood and overlaid with brass. The tent itself, its entrance facing east, was not like an ordinary tent, but was more like a rectangular house with wooden walls. Although the walls were covered with rugs, the roof was made of animal skins only. The interior of this tent was divided into two separate rooms. The first one was constructed lengthwise. It contained a table for the showbread, an altar for incense offering and a seven-branched candelabrum. This last named ornament, made of pure gold, resembled a tree with a stem and branching arms, decorated with almond blossoms. There is no doubt that the number "seven" had

Photo E. L. Sukenik

64. SEVEN-BRANCHED CANDELABRUM
*Detail from the Triumphal Arch
of Titus in Rome*

a symbolic meaning, although the Bible does not mention it. The seven flames are sometimes taken to represent the seven planets.[17]

We are able to enrich our knowledge on this subject by the presence of such a candelabrum executed in marble relief on the triumphal arch of Titus in Rome (Fig. 64). Titus, the conqueror of Jerusalem, in the year 70 of our era, was honored with a triumphal procession depicted on his arch in which the booty, including the candelabrum, was carried along. This proves that this candelabrum originated in the Herodian Temple in Jerusalem. It was most probably constructed by order of Judas Maccabeus [18] but taken from an earlier model as can be seen by its old, oriental style. The double, polygonal base must be subtracted. The style of the base (eagles with wreaths and dolphins) could be attributed to Roman art of the period of Titus. We suppose that the broad base was added to facilitate the handling of the heavy candelabrum, which was carried on a stretcher.

Behind the room containing the seven-branched candelabrum was a smaller room, the breadth, height and length of which were equal. This cube form in its severe regularity, no doubt, had a religious significance, although the Bible gives us no clue as to its meaning. The room was particularly holy. It was protected by a costly veil and the Ark which was placed behind this veil, served as a shrine for sacred objects and as a seat for divine revelations.

The Ark was made of acacia wood, the exterior and interior overlaid with gold. Over the gold top still another plate of pure gold was placed. On the opposite ends of this plate were depicted two winged cherubim, facing each other. These cherubim are generally imagined in the form of angels, because angels seem to us today the adequate expression of so noble a thought. To be sure, oriental art knows composite figures which resemble angels, but it also knows hybrid figures, the bodies of which represent animals. This latter form was not considered less dignified than the former. We read in the Bible that God rode on a cherub (II Samuel 22:11; Psalm 18:11). This particular cherub certainly had the body of an animal.

The Bible does not tell us clearly in what manner these cherubim were placed on the gold plate. In one place we read that they were "of beaten work" and "of one piece with the ark-cover" (Exodus 37:7–8). This would indicate that they were hammered out of the plate as reliefs. Following this, we read "the cherubim spread out their wings on high, screening the ark-cover with their wings," which points to figures carved in the round. Probably two separate

65. Two Cherubim Facing a Tree Column
Ivory plate from Arslan Tash, Northern Syria

versions were combined, and the compiler wished to preserve as much of the stories as possible, even at the risk of
contradiction.[19]

Let us first discuss the cherubim as reliefs on the gold
plate. This version is strongly supported by Biblical stories
as well as by works of art handed down to us. On the walls
of the Temple of Solomon, according to Ezekiel, two-
headed cherubim, alternating with palm trees, were carved
in relief (Ezekiel 41:18–20).

As to works of art which have been preserved, we insert
the picture of a small ivory plate excavated in Arslan Tash,
northern Syria (Fig. 65). Fragments of a similar plate were
found on Palestinian soil in Samaria, dating from the time
of the Kings.[20] The plates depict two winged rams, facing
each other. Between them are the fragments of a structure
showing a combination of a tree and a column. This use of
the tree as the central motif in the design brings to mind
the description of the walls of the Temple of Solomon, and
it should be added that in oriental religions, trees were
highly venerated objects.

There is no indication in the Bible that the plate of the

ark-cover had any centerpiece. It only mentions the cherubim placed on the edges. Should we assume that the center
remained blank, although the walls of the Temple of Solomon as well as the above-mentioned ivory plates carry a
central design? The spiritual significance of a composition showing a centerpiece flanked by two cherubim has
been preserved in the Bible: the Lord makes His appearance between the cherubim (Exodus 25:22). This is the
reason for their presence: they are His court, they serve
Him, and they protect Him.

But what about the second Biblical version which shows
the cherubim carved in the round? The Biblical expression,
"the Lord sitteth on the cherubim" (I Samuel 4:4, and elsewhere), always mentioned in connection with the Ark, has
been interpreted by scholars to mean that the cherubim
were used as supports of a throne, similar to other oriental
thrones [21] (Fig. 69). In this case the Biblical description
would have changed the original form by omitting the
throne and by placing the cherubim at the ends of the Ark,
facing each other.

No matter whether the cherubim on the plate over the
ark-cover were reliefs or were carved in the round, they are
described in the Bible as magnificent works of art and so
is the seven-branched candelabrum and the Tent of Meeting with its colorful carpets. Modern Bible critics have har-
bored doubts as to whether such great splendor really
existed in the time of Moses or whether it was only attributed to that period in later times in order to glorify the
venerated past. How was it possible, say these critics, that
at the time of the wandering in the wilderness the Israelites
were able to obtain the costly materials mentioned in the
Bible? How did they know the complicated arts of weaving,
founding, and embossing? The excavations of recent times

have shown us that the oldest settlements of the Israelites in the Promised Land were far inferior to those of the native Canaanites. The treatment of their walls was cruder and their ceramics were technically and artistically more primitive. This is easily explained if we assume that the Israelites only gradually acquired the artistic skills of the native population, but it is not conceivable if we suppose that they already possessed a high degree of artistic maturity before invading the Promised Land. Furthermore, when the golden altars and the elaborate idols made their appearance in the Promised Land, the Israelites themselves, as mentioned before, remembered their simple past, and treasured it because of its association with Moses. How then could they treasure simplicity, if they had already produced such costly altars, such a precious candelabrum, and such a magnificent Holy Ark?

On the other hand a seven-branched candelabrum existed at some time. Furthermore the plate above the Holy Ark in the Tent greatly resembled some works of art in the Temple of Solomon, and the small ivory plate shown in our illustration. A final point: the description of the Tent of Meeting reveals the names and the tribes of two artists, Bezalel, the son of Uri, the son of Hur from the tribe of Judah and Oholiab, the son of Abisamach, from the tribe of Dan. These names could have been invented, but it seems more probable that these men lived, and their fame, as so often with artists, was carried on from generation to generation.

There is one solution to these difficulties. The Tent of Meeting may once have possessed such splendor, though not at the time of Moses, but later on in the Promised Land when the Israelites turned from a nomadic life to a life of agriculture, and gradually became acquainted with the highly developed culture of the Canaanites. We read in the Bible that the Tent of Meeting still existed in the Holy Land and the Holy Ark also is frequently mentioned. As to the latter, it was brought by David to Jerusalem and was placed in a special tent. It is possible that this tent, as well as the Ark and the seven-branched candelabrum, received their rich ornamentation at this time. A sacred tent and ark and some kind of lamp may have existed at the time of Moses, but like the early altars and statues, they showed great simplicity at first and only later developed greater richness.

VI.

In the Days of Judges and Kings

I GAVE you a land whereon thou hadst not laboured, and cities which ye built not, and ye dwell therein; of vineyards and olive-yards which ye planted not do ye eat." These words uttered by the Lord to Joshua (Joshua 24:13) reflect a historic fact. The Israelites did not enter the Holy Land as pioneers, they became the beneficiaries of a culture created by others. The Ras-Shamra tablets, recently discovered, have given us astonishing information concerning this Canaanite culture: the complicated world of deities, and the mythological poems and hymns created for their worship. Furthermore, excavations have brought to life some of their settlements, including temples, palaces, and houses. Remnants of the walls still exist and prove that the builders possessed a large degree of technical knowledge. The houses are solidly constructed, the floors paved, the cities surrounded by massive walls, and the city gates flanked by towers. In contrast, the houses and walls of the early settlements of the Israelites unearthed in Shiloh, in Bethel, in Mizpah, in Gibeah, and in Beth-zur are of inferior construction and comfort. The potteries are also more primitive. The Israelites had much to learn, and they quickly assimilated much of the foreign culture.

In the domain of religion as well, the Israelites adopted many features peculiar to the Canaanites, for instance, the cult of Baal, of the Asherah, and of the goddess Ashtoreth. This does not mean that old traditions were completely forgotten. We have assumed that the Tent and the Ark were already in existence at the time of Moses and remained as objects of veneration in Canaan. But the Israelites did not limit themselves to the use of these objects alone. Just as the Canaanites, "they saw every high hill, and every thick tree, and they offered there their sacrifices, and there they presented the provocation of their offering, there also they made their sweet savour, and there they poured out their drink-offerings." These are the words used later by the prophet Ezekiel (Ezekiel 20:28).

Whether the tradition of the Israelites moved on parallel lines with the new beliefs or mingled with them, belongs to the history of religion. In either event, we are interested in the material objects necessary for their religious services. We hear of altars to the god Baal and the goddess Ashtoreth, although there is no mention of their shape. Baal was probably represented as a bull. As to Ashtoreth, small plaques and figurines were found on almost every site in Palestine, dating from before and after the immigration of the Israelites. They depict nude goddesses with arms either hanging down or supporting their breasts or holding lotus flowers (Fig. 66), all very Egyptian in character.

We hear furthermore of an Asherah standing beside the altar. This word denotes a goddess as well as the object erected in her honor. This object could be a tree or a wooden post, probably similar to the treelike column shown in our illustration of an ivory plate (Fig. 65). As late as in the time of the Kings, Queen Maacah made an "abominable image for an Asherah" (I Kings 15:13). It would be interesting to know if this Asherah was made of wood or of a more precious material and what was its shape, but the Bible says nothing about it. Stone pillars belonging to the cult of the Canaanites were used by the Israelites as well.

66. Goddess with Lotus Flowers
Jerusalem, Archaeological Museum

We became acquainted with such stones in the stories of the patriarchs. These had no definite forms but it is likely that they gradually acquired a more artistic shape. Later, when the Jews fought against the use of images, in human or animal form, these stones were most likely destroyed, whereas some of the shapeless ones have survived.

A large portion of the Israelite-Canaanite religious service took place in the open. But it appears that the Israelites possessed sacred edifices besides the Tent of Meeting. Judges tell us about a House of God in Shechem, a center of the Jewish tribes since the time of Joshua (Judges 9:27). The Holy Ark at the time of Samuel was in Shiloh in a temple, at least the doors mentioned in this connection lead us to this conclusion (I Samuel 3:15). When Saul and his servant visited Samuel in order to find the lost asses, the prophet led them to a high place and "brought them into the chamber, and made them sit in the chiefest place among them that were bidden, who were about thirty persons" (I Samuel 9:22). We gather that this was, as usual, a sanctuary in the open, to which was added a hall of large dimensions in which a sacrificial repast was held.

The Israelites also possessed images made of gold and silver, and we may take for granted that they learned this technique from the Canaanites.

In a private house of worship at the time of Judges, a man named Micah had erected an idol of silver (Judges 17:5). The ephod ordered by the judge Gideon in Ophrah was apparently also an idol (Judges 8:24–27). Generally the word "ephod" is meant to denote a garment used for oracles, but the Bible relates that the ephod of Gideon was of gold and "all Israel went astray after it there, and it became a snare unto Gideon, and to his house." One would not refer so scornfully to an object which was legally considered necessary for the cult of Yahweh, but such words were used in the combat against idols.

This is all we know about the artistic activities of the Israelites in the first centuries following the immigration into the Promised Land.

The advent of the kings in the life of the Israelites gave art a strong impetus. The political unification of the different tribes increased their strength, and the power of a king aroused a desire for pomp and circumstance. As the kingly line became hereditary, tasks could be undertaken which needed lengthy preparations. It took two generations to build the Temple of Solomon, from its first planning by David to its completion by his son.

The life of King Saul was too full of wars to allow of many peaceful occupations. His architectural achievements were confined to the construction of fortifications. In the capital Gibeah, such a fortification, or at least a corner of it, was discovered, which enables us to reconstruct the ground plan. It is a rectangle, with a double row of walls and massive towers placed at the corners.

David's reign was also primarily a warlike one, but after having made a capital of the newly conquered Jerusalem, he began to beautify this city. He first planned a palace and then approached the Phoenician king for assistance in the fulfilment of his purpose. The latter furnished him not only with cedar wood but also with carpenters and masons (II Samuel 5:11). Apparently the Israelites were insufficiently experienced to carry out a task of such magnitude. The Bible tells us nothing more about this edifice but that it was a "house of cedar" (II Samuel 7:2). This probably refers only to the interior, which was paneled with wood.

To strengthen the religious fervor of the capital, David transferred the Holy Ark to Jerusalem and as the Bible says "set it in its place, in the midst of the tent that David had pitched for it" (II Samuel 6:17). In this instance he clung to the old tradition in erecting a tent instead of a house. Very probably this tent was more elaborately decorated than the previous one and so were its implements as we have already assumed when interpreting the description given in Exodus. Later on David planned to substitute a temple for his tent. He procured cedar wood from Phoenicia; he collected gold, silver, copper and iron; he engaged trained artisans and worked on plans and models. He may even have made these plans and models himself. Tradition knows him to be a poet and musician; he may also have had some talent for the plastic arts.

David himself chose the site of the Temple, on a hill, similar to the high places of the Canaanites. He never began the construction of the edifice himself, but left all his plans and the material to his son King Solomon. The latter added a brass-founder to the staff of artisans, the half Phoenician Hiram, as this art needs particular skill.

The Temple, which was completed after seven years' work in 959, is described in I Kings and II Chronicles. Ezekiel has given us an additional and somewhat idealized picture of the Temple, which he saw in a vision when living in the Babylonian Exile. After the much dreamed of return of his people to Jerusalem, Ezekiel would have liked to see the Temple even more embellished and particularly more isolated as befitted its holiness.

In spite of all these detailed sources, it has not been possible to obtain an exact picture of the Temple, and we have
to be satisfied with a general outline of it and its ancient cult
objects.

The precincts were bordered by walls and doorways,
segregating an outer as well as an inner court, the latter on
a higher level than the former. Steps led to the Temple itself. The entrance faced eastward. This orientation was not

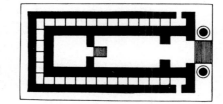

67. THE TEMPLE OF SOLOMON
Ground plan

mere chance, but had a religious significance. We naturally
first think of the rising sun and rightly so; as late as in the
Talmud, admiration is expressed for the fact that the eastern doorway of the Temple was constructed in such a way
as to allow the sun to enter at the start of winter and summer
(y. Erubin 5, 22 c).[22]

To come back to the Temple itself (Fig. 67): first, one
entered a porch through a particularly high and wide portal.
This porch was twenty cubits in width and ten cubits in
depth. The height, mentioned only once in Second Chronicles (3:4), was given as 120 cubits. If this were true, the
facade would have been six times as high as it was wide and
would have conveyed the impression of a high tower. It is
generally assumed that this figure is incorrect. In no other
oriental temples can one find a similar proportion between
height and width.

The porch led through a narrower and lower doorway
to the main hall. It was a long room, forty cubits deep,

twenty cubits wide, and thirty cubits high. These proportions were simple and pleasing to the eye. From this room
one penetrated through a still smaller doorway and most
likely by a stairway, into the last room, the Holy of Holies.
Here the measurements were of extreme regularity—twenty
cubits in all directions. The lack of windows added to its
calmness and solemnity. In this darkness the Holy Ark was
placed.

The stones which were used for the foundation were
given their form already in the quarry; "and there was
neither hammer nor axe nor any tool of iron heard in the
house, while it was in building" (I Kings 6:7). This passage
brings to mind the unhewn stones, used for ancient altars,
which we have already discussed. Apparently the architects
took pleasure in employing well-carved stones for the
Temple, but because there was a restriction as to the use of
iron tools, they evaded this difficulty by preparing the stones
in the quarry.

We have no conception as to the appearance of the exterior of the Temple and it is useless to attempt a reconstruction. No doubt it was dominated by the high facade of the
porch. The sides and the back were bordered by three-
storied wings divided into rooms, probably used for ritual
purposes. The main hall rose above these wings and could
therefore be provided with windows.

The interior derived its beauty from the well-planned
proportions as well as from its decorated walls—wood panels
richly carved. Here one could see the palm trees between the
cherubim which we have mentioned when we discussed the
cover of the Holy Ark.

The ritual objects are elaborately, if not always quite
clearly, described in the Bible. The inner court contained
the altar for the burnt offerings, which no longer had the

old simplicity, characteristic of the early period. It was of brass and probably accessible by steps.

In this court were ten brass lavers furnished with wheels so that they could be moved about. In these the animals for sacrifice were washed. The borders of the lavers were adorned with cherubim, lions, oxen and palm trees. Such a laver, though smaller in size and of simpler ornamentation, has been discovered on the island of Cyprus, a country strongly influenced by Phoenician art. This laver must furnish the illustration of the lost lavers of the Temple (Fig. 68). In this picture the cherubim do not flank palm trees, but columns, which, as we have already seen, are interchangeably used as objects of worship. A laver used by the priests for their own ablutions was a magnificent piece of brass founding. This laver, considerably larger than the above-mentioned ones, stood on the ground and was not transportable. The Bible calls it "the molten sea." It is questioned whether this name was given because of its size or whether it had a symbolic meaning. The Bible is silent on this subject, but similar vessels denoting the sea are known to have existed in Sumerian and Babylonian temples. If this be so, what is the meaning of the twelve brass oxen which supported the bowl? We would like to believe that this is also sym-

68. LAVER ON WHEELS
From Cyprus. Berlin, Altes Museum.

bolical. We previously mentioned that Jewish art must not always be interpreted symbolically, but the ancient East was full of such symbols and each object represented an idea. According to the Bible, three of the above-mentioned oxen faced north, three west, three south and three east. It is generally assumed that these were in four groups with vacant areas between each group. More likely this description is intended to convey that the oxen faced in every direction and were placed at equal intervals. This recurring rhythm is characteristic of oriental art.

As artistic as the "molten sea" were the two brass columns of the Temple of Solomon. It was formerly believed that these columns belonged to the Temple structure itself, until it was discovered that similar monuments in a number of oriental temples were placed in front of the entrance. They have no architectural but only ritual importance. The proof of this is that one column is called Jachin, "He shall establish," and the other, Boaz, "In Him is strength." To judge by these names, the columns may have been symbols of the Lord. We have no clear picture of their appearance. The top was decorated with pomegranates and "network," and surmounted by "lily work." Apparently not only hybrid beings, but also hybrid plants were used in art work in the ancient East.

We do not know what kind of implements, if any at all, stood in the porch. The main hall shone with a number of holy accessories. There was one altar of gold, obviously for incense offerings, and a second one for the twelve showbreads. Furthermore there were ten golden lamps, decorated with blossoms. There is no record that they had seven arms. Possibly the Temple possessed a seven-branched candelabrum which may have originated in the Tent of Meeting which David erected.

The Holy of Holies contained only one ritual object: the ancient Holy Ark. In front of it stood two cherubim placed on the ground, carved in wood and overlaid with gold, facing the main hall. With their wings outstretched, their height and breadth were the same. Thus in their regularity, they corresponded to the cubic room in which they stood. The outer wings touched the walls and the inner ones each other. In this way they formed a golden chain, protecting the Ark. These cherubim carved in the round, do not exclude the presence of other cherubim on the ark plate. We have already seen that the walls were decorated with them as well. Oriental art owes its solemnity to the perpetual recurrence of the same subjects in contrast to modern art which prefers variety.

The Holy Ark was not carried into the Temple until the day of dedication. "And it came to pass," the Bible relates, "when the priests were come out of the holy place, that the cloud filled the house of the Lord, so that the priests could not stand to minister by reason of the cloud; for the glory of the Lord filled the house of the Lord" (I Kings 8:10–11). The Ark and God are bound to each other; it is the Lord himself who is carried into the Temple with the Ark and thus enters His costly abode.

It is possible that the song sung at this or a later festival, has been handed down to us in the verses of the Psalm 24:

> Lift up your heads, O ye gates,
> And be ye lifted up, ye everlasting doors;
> That the King of glory may come in. . . .

Such words help us to realize why the portal of the Temple was far above human proportions. This portal was not meant for the priests alone; its first purpose was to admit the Lord.

It is easy to see that the Temple of Solomon was related
to the Tent of Meeting. In this tent the altar also stood in
front of the entrance, which faced eastward. Here as well,
a table for the showbread and a lamp, but only one, was
placed in the main hall. The Holy of Holies had the same
cubic form and was the abode of the Holy Ark. The modern explanation given for this similarity is generally based
on the assumption that the descriptions of the Tent of Meeting are derived from the Temple. It seems just as probable
that the tent, which was in existence in some form or other,
served as model for the Temple. One is nowhere more
conservative than in religion.

We have finally come to the question as to whether the
Temple of Solomon was an original building, or whether
its architecture was influenced by earlier temples. In former
times, when our knowledge was limited to the Bible and
we knew little about other oriental peoples, the Temple was
considered an unique structure. Today we have an ex-
tensive knowledge of Egyptian, Babylonian, Assyrian, Phoenician and Canaanite temples, and we know that the whole
Orient was a world closely bound together, as are the civilized countries of today. As with us, so with them there was
a continual exchange of ideas and forms.

We have already noticed the relation between various
ritual implements in the Temple in Jerusalem and those in
other oriental temples, as, for instance the "molten sea" and
the two columns. Similarly the Temple itself was closely
related to temples of neighboring states. The graduated
entrances leading from a secular outer world to realms of
increasing holiness, culminating in the Holy of Holies, is
a common oriental feature. The only difference was that
the Israelites, according to Biblical records, developed the
idea that the Deity was not represented by a statue but was

given a place in which to make His appearance. Isaiah has recorded a magnificent description of how such a vision came into being (Isaiah 6).

Next to the Temple, Solomon erected a palace of hewn stone, which took thirteen years to construct. It was also an oriental custom to place temple and palace side by side, because the monarch was, at the same time, the religious leader who consulted the oracle before important events.

The palace of Solomon did not consist of one building, but of several, which were grouped around two courts. We are told without any further details of a dwelling place of the king as well as of an abode for his favorite wife. Another building was called the "House of the Forest of Lebanon" (I Kings 7:2), either because it was paneled with cedar wood like the Temple of Solomon or because four rows of wooden columns supported the ceiling of the main hall and gave it the appearance of a forest. In Egyptian architecture such halls in temples and palaces were frequently constructed with similar columns. In this particular palace, golden targets and shields were stored away (I Kings 10:17). It was an arsenal and possibly the king's body-guard was housed there. Another hall of columns of smaller dimensions is mentioned (I Kings 7:6), and finally a hall in which the king held his audiences and sat in judgment (I Kings 7:7). This hall contained a magnificent throne made of gold and ivory. These were considered to be the most valuable materials in Antiquity and the contrasting effect of shining gold and dull ivory enhanced each other's beauty. Six steps, which were flanked on either side by statues of lions led to the throne. The arms were also decorated with lions. "There was not the like made in any kingdom" (I Kings 10:20). These words indicate that other thrones were known to exist and in fact, a few, similar in shape, have come down to us. The following example (Fig. 69), executed in miniature, dates from the late Egyptian period but has preserved older traits. The throne, supported by lions, stands on a base, and the back is decorated with two cherubim as if they were protecting a king or a deity. In this case, we see only two animals flanking one step leading to the throne.

69. Miniature Throne
Late Egyptian. Berlin, Altes Museum.

To conclude, in the Song of Songs we find a vivid description of Solomon's bed (Song of Songs 3:9):

> King Solomon made himself a palanquin
> Of the wood of Lebanon.
> He made the pillars thereof of silver,
> The top thereof of gold,
> The seat of it of purple,
> The inside thereof being inlaid with love,
> From the daughters of Jerusalem.

This charming love song is certainly no authentic description, but it is an echo of the splendor prevailing at the court of Solomon. This Israelite king, the first one who, after many years of war, was able to reign in peace, dreamed of imitating the style of the far older and mightier oriental courts. To give a modern analogy we need only think back to the small German rulers of the eighteenth century, who brought the magnificence of Versailles to their own courts.

Solomon no doubt had the means to carry this out. The copper was brought from his own mines,[23] and gold, silver and ivory were imported by his own ships, which had joined forces with the Phoenician fleet. "He exceeded all the kings of the earth in riches," the Bible relates (I Kings 10:23), and although this is without doubt an exaggeration, it denotes that Solomon understood how to accumulate great riches and to spend them profusely for his artistic achievements.

*   *   *

During the reign of Rehoboam, Solomon's son, the kingdom was already split in two—the northern kingdom of Israel and the southern kingdom of Judah. This naturally brought a weakening of political power as well as of economic strength. On the other hand, this separation was of some advantage to art, inasmuch as it increased the artistic needs and created competition between the two kingdoms.

Solomon himself had already erected architectural works outside Jerusalem: palaces, government buildings and stables. He attached great importance to the latter because of his ardent love for horses, and it is interesting to learn that in recent times the ruins of a number of such stables were unearthed in Megiddo.[24]

Rehoboam, following in his father's footsteps, built several cities in the southern kingdom and fortified them against attack (II Chronicles 11:5–12).

Naturally the newly established northern kingdom was in very great need of edifices for its secular and religious requirements. The number of these buildings reached a climax in the ninth century when the dynasty of the Omrides came into power. Omri, the founder, transferred his residence from Shechem to a new site which he called

Samaria, and he and his son Ahab built magnificent palaces
there. We can gather from the word "ivory house" (I Kings
22:39) what precious materials were used in their decoration. Recent discoveries testify to the truth of this statement.
The mention of summer and winter palaces is further evidence of the growing differentiation in architecture.

Now let us turn to the religious art of these kingdoms.
According to popular belief the Temple of Jerusalem was
the only one of this period and in this sanctuary only one
Deity was always worshipped—the Lord who had appeared
to Moses on Mount Sinai. Another popular belief is that
the Lord was never represented in plastic form. An inten-
sive study of the Bible has brought us to modify these opin-
ions. At one time the Temple of Jerusalem certainly did
become the sole sanctuary and Yahweh the sole God and
no image was needed for His worship. But this was the outcome of many centuries of development.

We have mentioned once before that after their immigration, the Israelites made a sanctuary of most every hill and
that this habit persisted after the erection of the Temple of
Solomon. Furthermore we have seen that the immigrants
adopted the deities of their new country, or at least mingled
the religion of the Canaanites with their own. This custom
was also adhered to, even intensified, at the time of the
Kings, sometimes for political reasons. Solomon himself
worshipped other gods—Ashtoreth, Milkom, Chemosh,
Moloch—and built separate temples for them. According
to the Bible he was induced to do this by his foreign wives,
who wanted to continue the cult of their own deities. Moreover, his own heart "was not whole with the Lord his God,
as was the heart of David his father" (I Kings 11:4). The
God Yahweh was not the only one worshipped by the aged
Solomon.

The architectural activity during the reign of Solomon was consequently greater than has been described thus far, because temples had to be erected in the honor of these foreign deities. These temples had one characteristic which the Temple of Solomon lacked, the image of the deity stood in the place of the Holy Ark.

Even Yahweh seems to have been worshipped occasionally in the form of an idol. After the division of the kingdom into two parts, Jeroboam, the first king of the northern half, feared that the worship of Yahweh in the Temple of Jerusalem would endanger his reign. The masses of his people who made pilgrimages to Jerusalem on certain holidays could easily be influenced to a desire for a reunion of the separated kingdoms and thus his power would be at an end. Therefore he thought it advisable to cast two golden calves which he placed at the northern and southern frontiers of his kingdom, in Dan and in Bethel. They are, he said to his people, "thy gods, O Israel, which brought thee up out of the land of Egypt" (I Kings 12:28). This proves that they were to take the place of the Lord in the Temple of Jerusalem.

We learn, furthermore, that a later king of the northern kingdom, the above-mentioned Ahab, built a temple in Samaria for his Phoenician wife, Jezebel, in honor of the Phoenician Baal, and erected a statue of the Asherah (I Kings 16:31–33).

The conditions were no different in the southern kingdom of Judah, although the Temple of Solomon stood there. The Asherah was worshipped there as well, and Queen Maacah for instance, consecrated a statue in its honor (I Kings 15:13). The cult of the Phoenician Baal penetrated into this country as well. In the ninth century Jehoram built, or at least tolerated, a temple for him in Jerusalem;

in the seventh century King Manasseh constructed altars for him. "And he built altars for all the host of heaven in the two courts of the house of the Lord" (II Kings 21:5). From this we see that even the grounds of the Temple were used for the worship of other gods.

The people still adhered to this polytheistic conception at the time of Ezekiel, that is to say, during the period of the collapse of their kingdom and its temple. The prophet saw on one of the gates of the Temple an "image of resentment which arouses resentment" (Ezekiel 8:3); apparently he meant an image which arouses the resentment of the Lord. On the northern gate, he saw women who worshipped the god Tammuz; in the forecourt he saw men who worshipped the sun. It is particularly interesting, from the standpoint of the history of art, to read his words condemning a chamber in the forecourt. He saw depicted on the wall "every detestable form of creeping things and beasts, and all the idols of the house of Israel" (Ezekiel 8:10–16). Not only statues existed, but walls were decorated with representations of deities, in relief or in paintings. There were such mural decorations before in the Temple of Solomon—the palm trees and the cherubim previously mentioned.

This splendor in religious art was matched by similar riches in the applied arts of every-day life. In the menacing words of the prophet Isaiah, we have a vivid report of the luxury indulged in by the women. He saw the day coming in which the Lord would take away "the bravery of their anklets, and the fillets, and the crescents; the pendants, and the bracelets, and the veils; the headtires, and the armlets, and the sashes, and the corselets, and the amulets; the rings, and the nose-jewels; the aprons, and the mantelets, and the cloaks, and the girdles; and the gauze robes, and the fine linen, and the turbans, and the mantles" (Isaiah 3:18–23).

70. Capital
*From a Palace in Megiddo, Palestine. The Oriental Institute,
University of Chicago.*

The excavations in Palestine confirm these reports, but
only give a feeble hint of the rich art of the period. In
Megiddo, in Taanach, in Samaria, in Jericho, in Tell Beith
Mirsim (Kiriath-Sepher), in Ezion-geber, etc., the ruins of
settlements have been unearthed which give us some information about the art of that epoch. The stone houses formed
a rectangle and their rooms, small in number, opened onto
a court, connected to the street by a narrow passage. Occasionally these houses were two-storied. If this were so a stairway on the outside led to the upper rooms. Because the roofs
were flat the inhabitants were able, on hot days, to enjoy the
coolness of the evening air. The floors of the rooms of these
houses were paved with tiles and the inner walls were covered with wood.

The palaces and administration buildings were constructed of stone, hewn with care. These huge stones needed
no cementing because they were held together by the accuracy of their measurements. At regular intervals, stretchers (stones placed lengthwise) were followed by headers

(stones placed at right angles) which held the edifice together, and at the same time gave variety to the whole structure. Sometimes the front part of the stone was left unfinished, sometimes it was smoothed down. Large buildings
as well as small houses were grouped around open spaces,
the former needing several courts. Occasionally the courts
of the large buildings were preceded by a hall supported by
columns. There were also anterooms supported by columns.
Towers were constructed, their height contrasting agreeably
with the flat design of the buildings themselves.

Only small remnants of the outer ornamentations of such
palaces have been preserved; capitals of pilasters, found
in several places, must suffice to give us an idea of what has
been lost. The Oriental Institute in Chicago possesses one
from Megiddo (Fig 70). It depicts the blossom of a lily in
conventional design. The petals of the flower are rolled
downwards, so that straight and curved lines form an agree-
able contrast. Needless to say this form was not invented by
the Israelites, but is characteristic of the Orient in general.
It was this kind of capital which inspired the art-loving
Greeks in the evolution of their own Ionic capital. We may
conclude from this detail, that the important buildings of
the epoch of the Kings had a very pleasing exterior.

Recently we have been able to obtain some knowledge
about the interior decorations of these edifices. Small ivory
tablets have been found in Samaria, the capital of the
northern kingdom. The material itself is very beautiful and
the warm tone of the ivory is sometimes enhanced by colored inlays of glass, by pastes, and by gold-leafed ornamentation. The tablets probably belonged to the palaces of Ahab,
one of which was an "ivory house," as we have mentioned
before. They may have adorned the throne, the beds and
the small toilet accessories if we assume that the subjects

depicted on them—deities, animals, and trees—which are
of a religious character, were also suitable for secular use.
As an example we have chosen a fragment representing a
hybrid being standing beside a plant (Fig. 71). There was
most likely a similar figure on the other side of the plant.
It is the old design which we have so often noticed: two
cherubim flanking a plant. The human head in profile and
the eye full-face are strongly reminiscent of Egyptian art, as
well as the double crown over the wig and the garment
covering the breast. Detailed analysis, however, has shown
us that small differences occur between the tablets and genuine Egyptian art. Furthermore, the letters found on these
tablets are not Egyptian, but are either Hebrew, Phoenician
or Aramaean. Most likely the tablets were executed in
Palestine. This is borne out by the fact that some were void
of ornamentation or only half finished. Had they been imported, they would surely have been completed beforehand.

71. HYBRID CREATURE
Ivory plate from Samaria, Palestine

The artists may have
been Israelites, or trav-
eling artists from Syria.
Several details in head-
dress and clothing can
be traced to that coun-
try.

In any case, those tab-
lets show highly devel-
oped workmanship. We
have already spoken
about the delicately col-
ored additions to the
ivory. The technique of
the relief is no less delicate. Occasionally, as in

our illustration, the background is carved out, giving the impression of a fine network. We have to bear works like this in mind, to fully appreciate the elegance of this "court art."

A limestone lamp, found in Megiddo, is just as delicate in shape and workmanship (Fig. 72). Only the upper part has been preserved. It consisted of two rows of leaves turning downwards on which was placed a bowl for oil or perhaps for incense. This bowl was decorated with lotus buds and blossoms, which are reminiscent of a frieze in the Temple of Solomon described in the Bible: "And the cedar on the house within was carved with knops and open flowers" (I Kings 6:18). The floral ornamentation of the shaft of the seven-branched candelabrum, with leaves facing downwards (Fig. 64), also comes to mind. This would prove the aforementioned assumption, that this candelabrum, in its original form, dates from the period of the Kings. It is another example of the richness and delicacy of style cultivated at the courts of the Jewish kings.

Bronze lamps were also found in Megiddo, one of which

is supported by a narrow pedestal in the shape of a woman blowing a flute. Vessels made of faience in the shape of animals and used as receptacles for salves and perfumes have also been unearthed. A beautiful silver spoon, the handle of which represents a nude girl looking into the scooped-out part as into a mirror, was found in southern Palestine (Tel-el-Fara), as well as the silver basin, which we have chosen for our illustration (Fig. 73). Narrow pointed leaves, growing out of

72. LIMESTONE LAMP
From Megiddo, Palestine

73. SILVER BASIN
*From Tel-el-Fara,
Palestine*

a round kernel at the center, shape the basin. The motifs of these works of art are mostly of Egyptian origin and some of the articles may even have been imported. Nevertheless they show the taste of this period for elegant styles and fanciful conceptions.

The refinement of the art of the upper classes is a long way from the crudeness of some primitive works originating at the same period. Figure 74 may serve as an example of this kind of work. As clay was the material used, it could have been an oven, but it may also have been an altar. This would explain the religious objects depicted on it as well as the horn at the top which is familiar to altars. The carvings show winged cherubim with heads of animals and human beings alternating. The bodies are in relief whereas the heads, as is so often the case in oriental art, are carved in the round. These distorted, rudely executed figures lack the careful workmanship of the ivory tablets. Apparently, folk-art existed side by side with court art.

74. OVEN OR ALTAR
*From Taanach, Palestine. Jerusalem,
Archaeological Museum.*

In conclusion, the art of the period of the Kings may be
illustrated by some seals which were discovered and are still
to be found in Palestine. Seals are common to the oriental
world. They were employed for the sealing of documents
as well as pitchers, chests, and so forth. They, therefore,
identified the owners of these objects. An inscription would
have sufficed for this, but in several cases figures were added
or substituted. These seals have various forms. In Egypt

75. SEAL OF SH'MA
Jasper

76. SEAL OF JAAZANIAH
Onyx

preference was given to the form of the scarab whereas in
Babylonia seals of cylindrical form were used. These were
rolled over the wax which allowed more room for ornamentation. Both methods were employed in Israel, but an
engraved stone, oval-shaped, was the most popular. The
pictorial motifs consist mostly of plants, animals or hybrid
creatures, but here and there human beings are represented
in the act of praying or offering sacrifices. The artistic value
of these seals differs greatly. Here also we can distinguish
between a more cultivated form of art and a primitive one.
One of the finest examples (Fig. 75) belonged most significantly to a high official of a royal court: the court of
Jeroboam I or II. A roaring lion, his fore and hind legs

planted firmly on the ground, with ruffled mane and tail
raised in anger, is carved in a stone of jasper. Lions are common in oriental art; sometimes they are depicted in conventional design, sometimes as in Assyria, very naturalistically.
The lion in our seal follows the naturalistic tendency. The
artistic manner in which the available space is utilized by
the lion and the inscriptions is worthy of note. This seal,
owing to its outstanding qualities, was attributed to a foreign
artist, but recently another seal has been found, of a later
date, about 600, and of equal artistic value (Fig. 76). The
owner was also a high official of the king. His name was
Jaazaniah, probably the one mentioned in the Bible as governor of Mizpah (II Kings 25:23). In the same realistic style
as the lion, a cock is placed under the inscription. He is running, head outstretched, beak open. Apparently he has
seen some food and hurries to seize it. This second seal suggests that the art of seal engraving in Israel had attained a
high standard during the reigns of the Kings. There is little
reason to doubt that native artists contributed to this florescence.

*   *   *

If we summarize all we have said and shown about Jewish
art during this period, bearing in mind temples, altars, statues, seals and the applied arts, then it would seem as if Jewish art of this period were no different from the art of the
other oriental peoples. But there is a difference. These peoples regarded their art as so much a part of themselves, that
it never occurred to them to discuss it or argue about it. The
Israelites on the other hand, gradually developed an increasing opposition to certain forms of art in their midst.

In the ninth century, not long after the erection of the
Temple of Solomon, consecrated in the year 959, a sect

emerged, which in one of its manifestations bears out the above statement. This sect, known as the Rechabites, after their founder, Jonadab ben Rechab, refused all the acquisitions of sedentary life: agriculture, wine growing, as well as walled houses. They preferred, as their nomadic ancestors did, to occupy themselves with cattle-raising, to forgo wine drinking and to live in tents (Jeremiah 35:3–10).

It is this last point which is important for us, because it shows a decided aversion to houses and palaces so elaborately constructed at the time of the Kings. We do not know how great the following of this sect was, but we can assume that these tendencies were the underlying influence which gave rise to or at least emphasized the laws demanding the utmost simplicity in the construction of altars and in the erection of statues. As we have seen, Jewish art was very primitive in its beginnings, and there were many who wished to adhere forever to these old, venerated habits.

In addition to this reactionary trend, a second one arose which, rather than the traditional, stressed the ethical point of view. The spokesmen of this movement were the prophets of the eighth century, Amos, Hosea, and Isaiah. They were opponents of the luxurious life and rich art of their time, because all this splendor drew the people away from the Lord and His laws. When Hosea exclaims: "Israel hath forgotten his Maker and builded palaces" (Hosea 8:14), he voices the thought that in their wealth the people turned away from the worship of God. Amos chastises those who "lie upon beds of ivory," who "drink wine in bowls" (Amos 6:4–7). He is evidently thinking of costly drinking vessels. The prophet tells how the wrath of God is inflamed against all these extravagances. "I will smite the winter house with the summer house; and the house of ivory shall perish and the great houses shall have an end, saith the Lord" (Amos

3:15). As to the prophet Isaiah, we have already quoted his scornful words condemning the "daughters of Zion," who were painted, powdered, richly overdressed and covered with jewels.

A third movement, the fight against images, had the most far-reaching effect on the plastic arts. This fight was instigated by some of the kings themselves, since it was part of their function to decide which cults should be permitted and which forbidden. About the year 900, only a few decades after the death of Solomon, Asa, king of the southern empire, rose up against the idols erected by his predecessors. Even his mother Maacah, who "had made an abominable image for an Asherah" was deprived of her sovereignty and the idol cut down (I Kings 15:11–13; II Chronicles 14:2). In explanation of this iconoclasm, the Bible relates that Asa was a devoted servant of the Lord. His fight against the foreign idols was a fight against the strange gods which had found favor in Israel. The success of his struggles was of short duration and again and again, we hear of similar reformatory movements. We have mentioned once before that in Jerusalem the cult of the Phoenician Baal gave rise to the erection of a temple and a statue of this deity. Both were destroyed during a revolt against Queen Athalia, the protectress of this god (II Kings 11:18).

In the northern empire the struggle began somewhat later, not before the middle of the ninth century. Here the worship of the Phoenician Baal also aroused resistance and King Jehoram eliminated the "pillar of Baal" erected by his father Ahab (II Kings 3:2).

"Nevertheless," the Bible complains, "he cleaved unto the sins of Jeroboam," which means that he left the golden calves unmolested, no doubt because he considered them to be images of the recognized Deity. We hear the same about

his successor Jehu. He destroyed the entire sanctuary of
Baal, but also left the golden calves untouched (II Kings 10:
26–29). We can conclude from this that the first phase of the
fight was only directed against foreign deities. Their temples
and statues destroyed, they could no longer be worshipped.

The second phase began in the eighth century, inaugu-
rated by the prophets Amos, Hosea, Isaiah, and followed up
by their successors. They did not only denounce the statues
of foreign deities, but also the images of their own God. In
the first place they accused the idols of lacking the power
ascribed to them by their worshippers. Let us remember the
story of Rachel who robs her father of the teraphim to transfer them to her new home because of their magic power.
The general oriental belief was that an image not only was
the likeness of a god, but had at the same time supernatural
power. The prophets had the courage to dispute this belief.
"The craftsman made it, and it is no god," Hosea says, referring to the golden calves in Israel (Hosea 8:6). "Every one
worshippeth the work of his own hands," says Isaiah (Isaiah
2:8). "Be not afraid of them (the images), for they cannot do
evil, neither is it in them to do good," Jeremiah exclaims
(Jeremiah 10:5), and Habakkuk expresses the powerlessness
of the idol by the following words: "There is no breath at
all in the midst of it" (Habakkuk 2:19).

This thought acquires greater depth through the Second
Isaiah, who places the greatness of God in contrast to the
smallness of human achievements (Isaiah 40:18):

> To whom then will ye liken God?
> Or what likeness will ye compare unto Him?
> The image perchance, which the craftsman hath melted?

And in contrast he describes the greatness of the Lord
(Isaiah 40:22):

It is He that sitteth above the circle of the earth,
And the inhabitants thereof are as grasshoppers.

This God cannot be conceived of in conjunction with any
other god, for He is the sole regent of the universe. And this
God, dwelling in heaven, transcends every pictorial representation. The might of God and the immensity of His worship, as developed by the Israelites, exclude once and for all
the possibility of representing Him in an earthly form.

Many centuries elapsed before this goal, the destruction
of foreign idols as well as of the images of the Lord, was
reached. An important step in this direction, was the discovery of a book in the Temple during the reign of King
Josiah, towards the end of the seventh century. This book
may have been in substance what we know today as Deuteronomy. The prohibition of images is here most definitely
expressed, as in the Second Commandment which forbids
the creation of any image that might lead to a false worship
of God (Deuteronomy 5:8). This book also includes the prohibition against worshipping God at different sanctuaries or
"high places." There was to be but *one* center of worship
(Deuteronomy 12:5–14). At
the time of the discovery of
the book this could only
mean the Temple of Solo-
mon.

77. COIN FROM JUDAH
*Representation of Zeus. London,
British Museum.*

The king, deeply moved
by the injunctions in this
book, undertook a campaign
of destruction against the
"high places," against the
images, and against the foreign cults which were still
worshipped in the Temple.

In spite of this determination, we learn from the prophet Ezekiel that such cults were still practiced in his time. We have aready dealt with his records.

At this point we would like to mention a coin made, according to its inscription, in Judah, probably in the fifth or fourth century, that is to say, after the time of the reconstruction of the Temple. The obverse shows a helmeted head, the reverse (Fig. 77) depicts a bearded man sitting on a winged wheel and supporting an eagle on his left hand. The motif corresponds to certain representations of the Greek god Zeus. It has been assumed that this figure of Zeus represents Yahweh in the guise of the Greek deity. If this be so, it would prove that, at least on coins, Yahweh was tolerated in a pictorial representation at such a late date.

But whatever place and date be ascribed to this coin, there can be no doubt about the following: images of many gods permeate the whole period of the Kings, although a contradictory movement prevailed at the same time which in the end triumphed over the images and led to their destruction. The heights to which the religion of the people of Israel soared, unique in its magnitude, obliged them to sacrifice a considerable part of their art.

VII.

In the Days of the Second Temple

THE prohibition of images was a severe but not a deadly blow to Jewish art. Nor did the political disasters which overcame first the northern and later the southern kingdom make an end to the people's striving after beauty. When the Israelites were forced into Babylonian captivity, "the craftsmen and the smiths a thousand" were taken along as well (II Kings 24:16). This proves that Jewish handiwork stood in high repute. Without a doubt they not only continued their work in Babylonia, but as was the custom, passed their skills on to their sons.

Many of the exiles attained greater wealth than would have been possible in their own small country, Palestine. Consequently, a great number preferred to remain in Babylonia even after they were able to return to Palestine. Probably this prosperous Jewish group had some artistic aspirations, at least in the expression of its religious worship. We shall refer to this later on.

The Temple of Jerusalem was burned by Nebuchadnezzar in the year 586 B.C.E. The loss of their only legal sanctuary was a climax to the destruction of the images by the Jews themselves. But the Babylonians in their turn were conquered by the Persians and the Persian King Cyrus permitted the Jews to return to their own country (538 B.C.E.). The accessories belonging to the Temple which had been taken away by the Babylonians were returned to them: "Thirty basins of gold, a thousand basins of silver, nine and

twenty knives; thirty bowls of gold, silver bowls of a second
sort four hundred and ten, and other vessels a thousand"
(Ezra 1:9–10). On reading these words we realize once again
how rich was the Temple in the period of the Kings. It is
possible that the seven-branched candelabrum was among
the treasures given back to the Jews.

It was Cyrus also who not only allowed the Jews to re-
build their Temple, but even provided them with funds for
that purpose and had plans furnished by his own court architects. This is not only a definite proof of the tolerance
shown by the Persians, but also a sign of the similarity of all
oriental temples. How otherwise would it have been possible to plan the construction by Persians?

Zerubbabel, the governor of the newly-founded province
of Judah, and the high priest supervised the construction of
the new Temple.

The first step was the erection of an altar in the open for
burnt offerings. In the beginning this was sufficient for the
worship of the Lord. Then in the year 537, the foundation-
stone was solemnly laid. It is very moving to read with what
intense emotion the people participated in this ceremony:
"Many of the priests and Levites and heads of fathers'
houses, the old men that had seen the first house standing on
its foundation, wept with a loud voice, when this house was
before their eyes; and many shouted aloud for joy; so that
the people could not discern the noise of the shout of joy
from the noise of the weeping of the people; for the people
shouted with a loud shout, and the noise was heard afar off"
(Ezra 3:12–13). Whenever have a people shown such deep
love for their Temple as did the Jews?

In spite of this auspicious beginning, the construction of
the Temple was not continued. This was due to the quarrel
which arose between the inhabitants of Judah and the Sa-

maritans living in the northern province of Israel. This
province, after its fall, had become the home of a mixed
population, which had grown out of the amalgamation of
the native Israelites and the peoples brought into the country by the Assyrian king who had conquered it. The Samaritans wanted to take part in the rebuilding of the Temple,
but the newly returned Jews prevented them from doing so
because they did not consider the Samaritans to be sincere
in their religious faith. The Samaritans complained to the
Persian king with the result that he forbade the Jews to continue the work. It was not until after his successor Darius
came to the throne that the Jews received permission to take
up the construction of the Temple again. This was in the
year 520, seventeen years after the laying of the foundation-
stone; several years later the edifice was completed. The Samaritans, who had been excluded from this work, were
forced to erect their own place of worship on Mount
Gerizim.

We know very little about the Temple of Zerubbabel.
The old plan of dividing the structure into a porch, main
hall and Holy of Holies no doubt was adhered to. As to the
superstructure, only a measurement ordered by Cyrus, has
been handed down to us: "the height thereof threescore cubits, and the breadth thereof threescore cubits" (Ezra 6:3).
This probably only refers to the facade of the porch, which,
according to the above quotation, was square. We know
from our study of earlier sanctuaries, that measurements
were inclined to be very regular as a symbol of the Divine
Order.

Was the Holy Ark still in the Holy of Holies? We hear
nothing about it in the Bible, but the Mishnah tells us that
it was taken into exile to Babylonia (b. Talmud Yoma 53 b).
The Mishnah (Midot 113) tells us also that the Persian capi-

tal, the city of Shushan, was depicted on the eastern gate of
the forecourt. This work, perhaps done in relief, was no
doubt executed during the Persian reign in Palestine, in
honor of the king. The Temple of Zerubbabel was a much
simpler construction than the old Temple, due to the deterioration of the economy of the Jewish state. Compared to
the old Temple it was "as nothing," said the prophet Haggai, who remembered the Temple of Solomon from his
childhood (Haggai 2:3).

We have already mentioned that the Samaritans had their
own place of worship and later on, perhaps in the fourth
century, this became the site of a temple. Yet another temple was erected by Jewish mercenaries in Elephantine in
Egypt, probably in the sixth century. It is interesting to note
that it was dedicated to Yahweh as well as to two goddesses.[25]
As so often in the time of the Kings, here also several deities
were worshipped in the same building. Monotheism was not
yet firmly established.

Still later, in the third or second century before our era,
another temple was built in Leontopolis in Lower Egypt.
The founder was a high priest by the name of Onias who
fled from Jerusalem to Egypt. The records of the temple
which have been handed down to us are contradictory.
When did Onias live, when did he leave Jerusalem, what
was his object in founding the temple, and what part did this
temple play in comparison with the Temple of Jerusalem?
These questions cannot be answered and we have just as little correct and accurate information about its appearance.
Josephus mentions, the temple was, "not like to that of Jerusalem, but such as resembled a tower" (Jewish War VII, 2,
3). But on another occasion he tells us that the Temple of
Onias was like the Temple in Jerusalem (Antiquities XII,
3, 3). All of which proves that the law allowing for only one

central place of worship to which burnt offerings might be brought was not strictly obeyed everywhere. It seems that in the countries too far distant from Jerusalem for the inhabitants to visit the Temple, the deuteronomic law was disregarded.

These countries, remote from Palestine, were also probably the starting point for another more legal institution: the synagogue. Needing a special place for their devotion and not wishing to interfere with the Temple of Jerusalem, the Jews of the Diaspora, that is of Babylonia, Persia, Syria, Egypt, and elsewhere, began to assemble in order to read the Torah, to interpret its contents, to pray and to carry out the law according to its regulations. These activities were of greater spiritual depth than the sacrificial acts performed in the Temple. This was in line with the development of the Jewish religion which showed a tendency to ever greater spiritualization.

It was at first more important to have adequate room for these different functions than to care about their outward appearance. If no special edifice could be constructed, a large room or hall in a public building was best adapted to these purposes. Jeremiah once mentions "houses of the people" (Jeremiah 39:8), and these may have been used frequently for religious services. A sentence in the Talmud points to this: "It was taught, R. Ismael ben Eleazar said: 'On account of two sins ignorant men die, because they call the Holy Ark a chest and because they call a synagogue a house of the people' " (b. Sabbath 32 a). These words were uttered when the expression "house of the people" for synagogues was looked upon with disdain. Apparently no one cared to be reminded of the secular origin of their beloved synagogues.

We have no knowledge of the exact date of the beginning

of the new form of worship, neither do we know exactly
when special buildings were erected for them. The first records about synagogues do not date farther back than the
third century before our era, the first remains are even half
a millennium later.[26] It would therefore best serve our purpose to discuss synagogue architecture at a period from which
some tangible remains of buildings have come down to us.

Nor do we have much information concerning the construction of secular buildings of this period, but we must
assume that they can in no way compare with the splendor
of the time of the Kings. The Persian governors in Palestine
probably had no desire for any rich display. Later on when
the power of the Persian empire diminished and the position of the Jewish high priest increased, the latter was certainly more concerned with his religious duties than with
secular ambitions. The ruins of only one large edifice, probably a palace dating from the sixth or fifth century, have been
discovered. These ruins were found in Tell ed Duweir (La-
chish) on a hill in the Shephela.[27] An open court was surrounded by some small rooms and by two large halls, one
supported by two columns, the other by two pillars. Among
the ruins, an archaic Greek vase was unearthed, which dates
the edifice as of the Persian era. This vase indicates that
Greek works of art were imported into Palestine not long
after the Babylonian exile.

Greek influence was greatly increased when Palestine was
taken from the Persians by Alexander the Great, the Mace-
donian king, in 332. This king was also the conqueror of
Greece, but at the same time an ardent admirer of Greek
culture. His reign and the founding of his empire mark the
beginning of what is known as the Hellenistic epoch. This
means that Greece, although a conquered nation, was able
to spread its influence over the whole of the civilized world

of that time. The Jews also took part in this Hellenistic culture. Previously they had only been influenced by oriental art, but from now on the Jews turned their attention to the Occident as well.

This influence was felt particularly in a new city founded by Alexander the Great in conquered Egypt, and named Alexandria after him. This city attracted vast numbers of Jews who were largely responsible for its rapid development into a metropolis. Its advantageous position on the sea, its situation centered between the Occident and the Orient, was conducive to making Alexandria a place of exchange, not only for merchandise, but also for the spiritual and cultural ideas of the two worlds. Greek culture dominated, but oriental ideas influenced the city's culture. The Jews of Alexandria made use of the Greek language and even composed Greek epics and dramas, but the subject matter was taken from their Bible. It is not surprising that the desire arose to translate the Bible into Greek. The Jews began to forget their native language. Non-Jews became interested in the Jewish religion. One of the kings, Ptolemy II Philadelphus (308–246) is said to have sent one of his officials, an Egyptian Jew, to Jerusalem to bring a Pentateuch and several competent translators to Alexandria. The history of this translation, which is known as the Septuagint, is also of interest in the history of art. The Jews presented the Egyptian ambassador with a magnificent Torah Scroll written with gold letters. This seems a trifle indeed, but it may have been the starting point of a long evolution destined to lead to the adornment of all venerated manuscripts. Was the embellishment of this scroll an original Jewish idea or was it the imitation of a Greek custom? At any rate, it showed an increasing desire for beauty, which may easily be attributed to Greek influence.

Antioch, the Syrian city, attracted the Jews no less than
Alexandria. This city was founded about 300 before our
era by Seleukos I (358–280), the sovereign of Syria, in honor
of his father Antiochus. The number of Jews in this city
eventually surpassed those of the Egyptian capital. Here
also they became imbued with Greek culture. We know that
the synagogue of Dura Europos, the Syrian frontier town,
was decorated in the third century of our era with Biblical
murals and there is no doubt that the roots of such pictorial
decorations were not to be found in Palestine, but in the
Hellenistic cities of the Diaspora.

Palestine itself was the country which showed the greatest
resistance to the Greek mode of life. After many wars between the successors of Alexander the Great, in the year 198
before our era, it fell into the hands of the Syrians. One
of their kings, Antiochus IV Epiphanes, attempted to introduce Greek customs as well as the worship of the Greek god,
Zeus, into the Holy Land. In the year 168, he penetrated
into the Temple of Jerusalem, carried away its costly accessories, for instance the seven-branched candelabrum, and
dedicated the Temple to Zeus, no doubt by erecting a statue
to him. A similar treatment was meted out to the temple of
the Samaritans on Mount Gerizim. It is most probable that
those synagogues already extant also became the victims of
this campaign. The words of Psalm 74, "They have burned
up all the meeting-places of God," are attributed to this
epoch.

This desecration aroused the wrath of the heroic Maccabees. After a severe struggle, they succeeded in driving the
Syrians out of Palestine and rededicated the Temple to its
rightful God. The first book of Maccabees (I Maccabees
4:48–57) gives us a vivid description of these events, which
are also of artistic importance.

Hereupon they restored the holiness of the Temple and consecrated the forecourts. They renewed the holy vessels and brought the candelabrum, the altar for the burnt offerings and the incense offerings and the table (for the show breads) into the Temple. . . . They adorned the facade of the Temple with gold wreaths, restored the gates and cells, and provided doors for them.

In the Talmud (b. Rosh ha-Shanah 24 a) the construction of the candelabrum is described in still greater detail. According to this version, it was first fashioned of wood placed on an iron stand. As the wealth of the sovereigns increased, silver and finally gold was substituted. Even though this account be legendary, it is evident that the old candelabrum was renewed. It may have been the one found later on in the Temple of Herod, robbed by the Romans and depicted on the triumphal arch of Titus (Fig. 64). As we have already stated, the base was added later. The Maccabees who clung faithfully to tradition would not have tolerated such an addition. They probably did not care about contemporary art, but wished to preserve the venerated past in all its purity.

The victory of the Maccabees resulted in a renewal of the kingdom in Palestine. This necessarily gave a certain impetus to material civilization. Thus we learn that a citadel was built in Beth-zur to protect the approach to the city of Jerusalem from the south (Josephus, Jewish Antiquities XII, 4, 71).

According to the same author (XII, 4, 11), John Hyrcanus (reigned 135–106 B.C.E.) erected in Transjordan a "strong castle and built it to the very roof entirely of white-stone; and had animals of a prodigious magnitude in relief upon it." There are some ruins discovered in Araq el Emir which can be identified as the castle mentioned by Josephus. These ruins were not white but of red sandstone; apparently Josephus only knew of this edifice from hearsay. Otherwise the description is correct as can be seen by the view of the reconstruction of the main entrance (Fig. 78). Immense stones formed the four walls enclosing a center court. At both narrow sides flights of steps led to entrance halls which were supported by Corinthian columns. Thus, despite the strong resistance of the Maccabees to Greek influence, Greek architecture, in all its serenity, appeared in their own constructions. The Greek element however did not entirely domi-

78. PALACE OF JOHN HYRCANUS
In Araq el Emir. Reconstruction.

nate. A broad frieze ran around the walls. On this "animals of a prodigious magnitude" met face to face above the entrance, similar to the cherubim on the Ark of the Covenant. In this way Greek and oriental art were beautifully interwoven.

There was still another structure erected by the Maccabees, but of this building we have only literary evidence (Book of Maccabees I, 13, 27 ff.). This refers to a tomb erected by Simon Maccabeus (143–135) for his closest relatives in Modin, the birthplace of his family. It is an old Jewish custom to bury all members of one family in the same grave; "to be gathered to thy fathers" is the Biblical expression. We have never heard that the graves in early times were marked in any way, with the exception of the stone

which Jacob erected over Rachel's grave because she died on
a journey and could therefore not be interred in the family
tomb. On the other hand, the Egyptians during a certain period built immense rigid pyramids over their graves. Hellenism took over this custom but elaborated it by a richer
architecture and the use of sculpture. We find both Egyptian and Hellenistic motifs united in the above-mentioned
tomb of the Maccabees. A stone structure was crowned with
seven pyramids which represented Simon's parents and five
brothers. Carved trophies and ships were used for ornamentation. Such picturesque and naturalistic groupings were
well known in Hellenistic art.

This period also claims some coins minted by the Macca-
bean kings. These also followed Hellenistic patterns, but in
such a way as not to disregard the Second Commandment.
Heads of sovereigns and even of animals were avoided. The
coin minters had to content themselves with plants, architectural forms and sacred implements. For these objects,
coins from neighboring countries were studied. Anchors
and crossed cornucopia, as on Syrian coins,[28] came into use
at this time and were augmented by specifically Jewish
motifs—esrog, lulov, sacrificial goblets, even the seven-
branched candelabrum.

Similar coins with those motifs as well as new ones were
fashioned in later times. This always occurred when a new
political independence was attained; during the First Revolt
(66–70 of our era) and during the Second Revolt (132–134).
Our example is taken from the latter period (Fig. 79). The
reverse depicts the lulov in a finely curved goblet and beside
it a small esrog. The obverse shows us a magnificent structure containing the Holy Ark. This is no doubt meant to
represent the Temple of Jerusalem. At the time our coin
was minted this edifice was lying in ruins, but its reconstruc-

tion by Simon, the leader of the Second Revolt, was eagerly anticipated. He was named Bar Kochba, son of a star, and this accounts for the star over the Temple.

If we compare this coin with the seals shown in the preceding chapter (Figs. 75, 76), the difference in the dates can be clearly noticed. The dominating note of the seals at the time of the Kings was one of strength and fervor, whereas the Jewish coins of a later date breathe an atmosphere of gentleness and peace.

The reign of the Maccabees which had begun so success-

79. COIN DATING FROM THE SECOND RE-
VOLT UNDER SIMON BAR KOCHBA

fully came to an inglorious end owing to the weakness and the disunity among their leaders. In the year 63 before our era, the country was placed under the care of a Roman governor and remained for many centuries an integral part of the Roman Empire.

This new government did not bring about any change, artistically speaking, as the Romans themselves were ardent disciples of Greek culture. On the contrary, Hellenism was still more widely spread over Palestine during this period. The reason for this lies in the fact that the Romans extended their great architectural activities over this province. All over Palestine new cities sprung up with streets framed by columns, with heathen temples, palaces, theaters, stadia,

court-houses, and market halls. It is not necessary to discuss
these structures, because they not only lacked Jewish forms
—this would not be sufficient to exclude them from the history of Jewish art—but also because they were devoid of the
Jewish spirit. Such structures spread over the whole Roman
Empire and appeared in Rome as well as in Trier, in Alexandria, and in Jerusalem, Samaria, and Gerash (Gerasa).

On the other hand, it is necessary to deal at some length
with an edifice such as the newly-constructed Temple of
Jerusalem, firstly because it was intended solely for Jews and
secondly because it upheld the old traditions in spite of its
Roman disguise. It was built by Herod the Great (reigned
37–4 B.C.E.), who was king of Judah, Samaria, Galilee, and
Idumaea under Roman sovereignty.

The motive for this reconstruction was hardly a religious
one. It was rather the desire of a vain king for splendor and
his wish to make his capital a center of attraction.

To begin with, the site on which the Temple stood was
enlarged by massive foundations and provided a base of 300
by 480 meters, a sight which even today fills visitors with
amazement. This enabled the architect to add to the two already existing courts, a third and larger one. This outer
court had no ritual significance; everyone, Jew or non-Jew,
was permitted to enter by means of one of the mighty gates.
It was looked upon as a public square, surrounded by colonnades in Corinthian style, and probably had no more connection with the Temple than the Square of San Marco in
Venice has today with the church of the same name.

The entrance to the second court was forbidden to non-
Jews under penalty of death, whereas the third court was
accessible only to priests. In here, the huge square altar for
burnt offerings was placed. In keeping with the oldest tradition, horns were attached to its four corners.

The Temple itself had retained its original partitions: porch, main hall, and Holy of Holies. An immense portal led to the porch, a smaller one, from which hung a Babylonian curtain, led to the main hall. A large bunch of golden grapes, a costly work of the goldsmiths, was suspended from this second doorway, a symbol of Judaism.

The main hall contained the seven-branched candelabrum, the same one as depicted on the arch of Titus. The golden table for the showbread, likewise carved on the arch, stood here as well and finally the altar of incense. Two valuable curtains separated the main hall from the last room. "In this there was nothing at all. It was inaccessible and inviolable, and not to be seen by any, and was called the Holy of Holies," Josephus says (Jewish War V, 5, 5), and in these words we can feel the mysterious thrill which the emptiness of this room aroused.

The facade of the Temple was meant to be the most striking part of the edifice. The width and height, as in the Temple of Zerubbabel, were of equal dimensions, but whereas the latter was only 60 cubits square, the new Temple was 100 cubits in width and height. The measurements of the Temple of Solomon, 120 cubits in height as related in Chronicles (II, 3–4), were certainly in the architect's mind during the construction of this Temple, although we have stated that these measurements are not authentic.

We have no literary report as to how this immense facade was constructed, but we can refer once again to the coin dating from the Second Revolt, which doubtless shows us the front of this very Temple (Fig. 79). According to this coin, four immense pilasters or half columns in Greek style arose from a socle which divided the facade into a broad center part and narrower sides. A straight cornice finished off the structure and emphasized the squareness of the facade.

In conclusion, let us once more allow Josephus to speak.
He describes the splendor of the Temple as it appeared to a
spectator (Jewish War V, 5, 6): "It was covered all over with
plates of gold of great weight and at the first rising of the
sun reflected back a very fiery splendor, and made those who
forced themselves to look upon it to turn their eyes away
just as they would have done at the sun's own rays. But this
Temple appeared to strangers, when they were coming to it
at a distance, like a mountain covered with snow, for as to
those parts of it that were not gilt, they were exceedingly
white. . . ." This is certainly no accurate description, but
it shows the overwhelming impression which the Temple
made upon the Jews.

As is well known, the days of the Temple were numbered.
Barely half a century later when the Jews rose up in an un-
successful revolt against the Romans, the city of Jerusalem
and the Temple were destroyed. The valuable ritual objects
were brought to Rome, carried around as trophies in a triumphal procession and finally stored in the Temple of the
Goddess of Peace. From this moment on they can no longer
be traced.

The destruction of Jerusalem in the year 70 of our era,
with the short interval of the Second Revolt, brought the
political life of the Jews to an end. But religious and cultural
life in Palestine still persisted for centuries. In the seventh
century, when the Mohammedan Arabs conquered the Holy
Land, this came to an end as well. The Jews of the Diaspora
were less affected in their cultural and domestic life by the
fall of Jerusalem. They mourned deeply for the loss of their
sanctuary, and dreamed of its reconstruction, but at the
same time they enjoyed the liberty accorded them under
Roman rule.

VIII.

From 70 C.E. to the Middle Ages

F WE undertake to discuss Jewish art in the five centuries
following the destruction of the Temple of Herod, .we
must consider this period as a whole. The material at
our disposal is too meager to differentiate between the countries and the centuries. We will content ourselves with giving a general survey of the opportunities which the Jews had
for expressing themselves artistically.

Let us begin with the synagogue. As we have previously
explained, a new form of worship without animal sacrifices
may have arisen already during the Babylonian exile and
this new form led sooner or later to the construction of special edifices. We know nothing of the form of these oldest
synagogues. Later on, when Hellenism placed its marks on
Judaism, the basilicas, built by the Greeks and Romans for
bazaars, stock exchanges, and law courts, could serve as most
appropriate models for the synagogue. The aim of these
structures was to afford halls large enough to accommodate
public gatherings. The interior of the basilicas contained
galleries supported by columns which provided still more
space for the masses and added beauty to the edifice. In an
adjoining room in the building itself or in a domed semicircular recess, a so-called apse, stood the platform from
which the head of the judicial court administered the law.
The Jews needed similar accommodation for their own
large gatherings and their legal activities which, as we have
seen, also took place in the synagogue. The impression cre-

ated by these early synagogues was probably very worldly. We must remember that the Temple still existed for centuries, side by side with the synagogue and it symbolized the concentration of the highest religious devotion.

Without doubt, the religious atmosphere of the synagogue was changed after the Temple was destroyed, but it does not mean to say that the architecture of the Temple was completely transferred to the synagogue. Such an imitation was excluded by the high reverence in which the Temple was held. This was the reason why the Talmud forbade any reproduction of the Temple as a whole, in part, or of any of its implements (b. Rosh ha-Shanah 24 a).[29]

But there were other means of giving the synagogue a more ritual character, and these were influenced by memories of the Temple. For instance, the synagogue was often placed on a hill. This was certainly a reminder of the site of the Temple. Furthermore, a walled court with a fountain in the center for ritual ablutions stood in front of the building. This again reminded one of the Temple with its forecourt in which ritual ablutions took place.

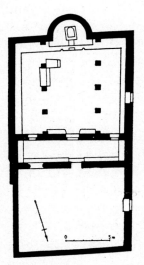

80. Synagogue at Beth Alpha, Palestine
Ground plan

Finally, the synagogue was constructed at a prescribed angle. The Temple was also placed at a certain angle—its gates faced the Orient from which the sun arose. This was sometimes a requirement for the synagogue as well (b. Talmud Megillah IV, 22). After the destruction of the Temple, however, this custom was modified. Jerusalem, the lost, the city to which the Jew looked back with a holy long-

81. FRONT VIEW OF THE SYNAGOGUE IN K'FAR BIRIM, PALESTINE

ing, became the focal point towards which the doors of every synagogue were turned.

Later on, but still in ancient times, another change took place. It was no longer the gates, but the wall opposite the entrance which was made to face the Holy City. This probably resulted from the desire to place the Torah shrine in an immovable position. Until then the Torah Scrolls were kept in an adjoining room and were carried into the synagogue when they were to be used for the service. When the Torah Scrolls were first stored in the synagogue itself, the shrine was placed against the entrance wall, apparently because it was just this wall which faced Jerusalem. This proved to be impracticable because it partly blocked the entrance. Therefore the obvious thing was to place it against the opposite wall which then became the holy one.

The galleries were used for the women only. In the second forecourt of the Temple of Herod, women had been given a special section and this segregation from the men was taken over by the synagogue. The staircase leading to the galleries was placed outside the synagogue.

82. Synagogue in K'far Birim, Palestine
Reconstruction

A few very large synagogues possessed not two, but four rows of columns, dividing the hall into five aisles. The largest one of this type was erected in Alexandria and the Talmud exclaims with great pride that it could hold twice as many people as were led by Moses from Egypt into the Promised Land (b. Sukkah 51 b). We know that such another one existed in Tiberias in Galilee.

The synagogue could be enlarged still further by the addition of a porch, or a vestibule, another reminder of the Temple.

In order to illustrate the above, we show you some Palestinian synagogues, erected between the second and the sixth centuries of our era. The ground plan of the synagogue in Beth Alpha is a good example of the partitions prevalent in such an edifice (Fig. 80). We first come to a forecourt surrounded here by plain walls, then to a vestibule and finally to the hall divided by pillars into a nave and two aisles. At the back we see the apse, which here forms a semicircle.

The synagogue at K'far Birim in Galilee, shown in ruins

and also reconstructed, gives us the front view of one of the more elaborate buildings (Figs. 81 and 82). The ruins show only one column of the porch still intact. There were originally six, supporting a triangular gable. The straight line of the entablature is broken above the two middle columns and forms an arch. This is an attractive motif familiar to eastern Hellenism. The three doorways leading from the porch into the interior are easily recognizable in Figure 81. The middle one is the highest and widest. A wreath decorates the lintel which supports a semicircular window and thereby emphasizes the center. The windows over the side entrance are rectangular and more simply executed. Their only ornamentation is a delicately carved gable with rosettes.

All these exterior as well as interior details—cornices, friezes, gables, capitals, keystones, consoles—were decorated

83. CONSOLE
*From the synagogue
in Capernaum, Palestine*

with the utmost care. Floral motifs, animals, cupids, centaurs, and such ritual implements as the Holy Ark, the Torah shrine, the seven-branched candelabrum, et cetera, were used. The example (Fig. 83), taken from the main portal of the synagogue in Tell Hum (Capernaum), shows us a date-palm depicted very naturalistically. The scaly stem, the palm leaves and the fruit are true to life. Most likely the palm tree had a ritual significance; the Temple of

84. Cross-section of the Synagogue in Capernaum, Palestine
Reconstruction

Solomon was already ornamented with palm trees alternating with cherubim.

As an example of the interior of a synagogue, we choose the edifice from which the above-mentioned console with the palm tree was taken. The illustration (Fig. 84) shows a cross-section of the reconstruction. The court in this case was placed at the side instead of in front on account of the location of the site, and was more imposing than the one in Beth Alpha. This court was bordered by colonnades, probably also a reminder of the colonnades in the Herodian Temple. The Corinthian columns in the interior supported a gallery upon which another row of columns was erected, which held up the beams of the roof.

In the entrance wall we see a semicircular window similar to the one already described in the ruins of Figure 81. The door beneath it is closed up by a stone Torah shrine, of which remnants were found. Originally a fixed Torah shrine did not exist in this synagogue. Later on, when the shrine was erected it was placed against the entrance wall, that being the one which faced Jerusalem. When the synagogue in Beth Alpha was constructed in the sixth century, the previously mentioned change had already taken place and the Torah shrine was placed against the opposite wall, probably in the apse.

In some synagogues stone lions were discovered (Fig. 85). They probably stood in pairs in front of the Torah shrine and are reminiscent of the cherubim placed in the Temple of Solomon in front of the Ark of the Covenant. If this be so, then one may consider the Torah shrine as a substitute for the Ark of the Covenant, a further proof of the great influence which the lost Temple exercised over the synagogues.

What these old Torah shrines looked like can be seen by reproductions in stone reliefs, mosaics, glasses and plates, as well as from the ruins of the above-mentioned one in Tell

85. Basalt Lion
From the synagogue in Chorazin, Palestine

Hum. The gold design on the bottom of a drinking glass (Fig. 86) is very instructive. Steps led up to the Torah shrine; steps also led up to the Holy of Holies in the Temple of Solomon. The shrine itself was like any other chest intended to hold scrolls. Let us refer once again to the Talmud: "On account of two sins, ignorant men die; because they call the

86. GILT GLASS
Berlin, Kaiser Friedrich Museum

Holy Ark a chest and because they call a synagogue a house of the people." Now we can understand why it became a sin to call the Ark of the Law a chest. Originally it was a chest, but in later times when it had become a sacred Ark, no one wanted to be reminded of its secular origin. The scrolls in these shrines were laid aside like secular scrolls, without mantles and metal ornaments.

The platform from which the Torah was read was constructed on simple lines in the synagogues of Antiquity. The only one which has been completely preserved dates from the sixth century of our era and was found in a mosque (formerly a synagogue) in Aleppo in Syria (Fig. 87). It is of basalt and the only decorative motifs are a few columns.

A special seat, facing the congregation, was provided for the leader of the synagogue. Since it was his duty to designate the different readers of the Pentateuch and to preserve order during the services, he sat with his back to the Torah shrine. Among

87. BIMO
From the synagogue in Aleppo, Syria

88. SEAT OF MOSES
From the synagogue in Chorazin, Palestine

the ruins of the synagogue of Chorazin in Galilee, such a "Seat of Moses" was found which we have already mentioned (Fig. 88). It is also of basalt and preserves the massive aspect of this stone. The front is engraved with an Aramaic inscription, expressing gratitude towards the donor of the synagogue who was doubtless the leader as well. The low arm-rests are hollowed out; the curved back is ornamented with a rosette. The floors were elaborately decorated with mosaics, depicting geometrical patterns, plants, animals, even human beings.

Apparently there were at this period various tendencies regarding the interpretation of the Second Commandment. We read, for instance, that Josephus, the oft-mentioned historian of the Jews who lived in the first century of our era, reproached King Solomon for decorating the "molten sea" with bulls and his throne with lions (Jewish Antiquities VIII, 7, 5). This rigorous trend may have lent opposition to any but the very abstract designs. Such a floor mosaic has been unearthed in the synagogue of the Greek Isle of Aegina. On the other hand, some Jews agreed to the use of plants and animals for their motifs. The pavement of the synagogue in Hammam-Lif in northern Africa may serve as an example. This pavement was taken to pieces and today parts of it are to be found in the Bardo Museum in Tunis and in the Brooklyn Museum. Our illustration (Fig. 89a) shows the pavement in its original state. It is divided into

89a. Mosaic Floor
From the synagogue at Hammam-Lif, Africa

three unequal panels. The sides are designed with tendrils, the spaces of which are filled with all kinds of animals and birds, which appear very true to life. The center is again divided into two parts by a dedicatory inscription. On the lower section a fountain is placed between palms with two

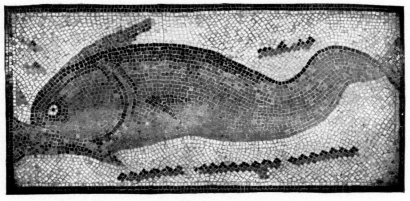

89b. Detail from the Mosaic Floor of Hammam-Lif
Courtesy, Brooklyn Museum

peacocks on the rim. Maybe the fountain denotes the "fountain of life," an old oriental symbol. The upper half, partly destroyed, depicts waves and a large and a small fish (Fig. 89b). Possibly they represent the legendary Leviathan with spouse, promised as food for the righteous in times to come. The wheel may also have a symbolic meaning as it is often taken to represent the sun. In contemplating the mysterious significance of this mosaic characteristic of the late period of Antiquity, let us not forget to note its artistic value: the ease with which the spaces are filled, the flexible curve of the fish, the graceful attitude of the peacocks, and the silvery color.

There was also another trend of thought which allowed still greater freedom in the choice of motifs; an example of this can be found in the Targum of Pseudo-Jonathan to Leviticus 26:1. The Targum written during this period interprets the prohibition concerning idols in such a manner that scenes depicting human beings on synagogue pavements became permissible, provided they did not become objects of worship.

A mosaic in the synagogue of Gerash in Transjordania still shows that there was a certain reluctance to accept this interpretation. The departure from the Ark after the deluge is depicted, but animals in rows play the most important part; Noah and his sons are pushed into a corner. On the other hand, in the mosaic of the synagogue of Beth Alpha (Fig. 90) we notice nothing of this timidity. Near the entrance we see the sacrifice of Isaac on Mount Moriah. The center panel depicts Helios in his sun chariot surrounded by a circle of the twelve constellations, and the corners are filled with allegorical figures picturing the four seasons. The third division nearest to the Torah shrine consists of a representation of the Temple containing two seven-branched candelabra, the Ark of the Covenant, and other ritual ob-

90. MOSAIC FLOOR
From the synagogue at Beth Alpha, Palestine

jects. The lions and the birds are obviously a reminder of
the cherubim standing in front of the Holy Ark in the Temple of Solomon and decorating the golden plate over the
ark-cover.[30] But we have also seen statues of lions apparently protecting the Torah shrine in synagogues, and the
picture of the Ark of the Covenant resembles the Ark containing the Torah Scrolls. Thus the Temple and the synagogue merge anachronistically into one. They all express
the longing of the Jews for the lost sanctuary. The sacrifice
of Isaac which took place on Mt. Moriah points to the same
desire; as the Bible relates "Solomon began to build the
House of the Lord at Jerusalem in mount Moriah" (II
Chronicles 3:1).

The Greek god Helios appears somewhat out of place in
this otherwise Jewish milieu. It can be put down to the in-
trusion of Greek elements in Jewish life.

How unfortunate that this well prescribed mosaic pavement, made in the sixth century of our era, dates from a period of artistic decay. The sacrifice of Isaac shows the
human figures in infantile distortion. The classical sense of
proportion has completely disappeared. In the picture of
Helios, the chariot and the horses are devoid of perspective
and the conventional face on the long neck of the Greek
god rises like a mask above the chariot.

In the third panel everything appears on one plane. The
lions, supposed to be in front of the Ark, are placed right at
the side; and the two candelabra, instead of standing in front
of the lions, seem to be above them. The whole picture is
not a natural representation, but composed of isolated objects, which we can interpret only in the light of our knowledge of the subject. Only the colors, warm shades of yellow,
brown and red, with an occasional tint of green, still possess
something of the beauty of the classic period.

91. MURALS IN THE SYNAGOGUE AT DURA EUROPOS
Damascus, Museum

Given the mosaic pavements which represent human figures in the synagogues, the question arises as to whether the
walls were decorated with murals. Not so long ago this
question would have been answered definitely in the negative. Up to then no murals had been discovered nor was it
considered likely that they existed. But lately, in the year
1932 in Dura Europos in Syria, the walls of a synagogue
were dug out of the sand in the desert and were found to be
covered with paintings (Fig. 91). This edifice is also archi-
tecturally remarkable. It belongs to a simpler type than the
ones shown before and consists only of a hall built hori-
zontally on to the entrance without columns and galleries.
The seat of the leader is placed against the opposite wall,
which faced Jerusalem. Next to it is a niche flanked by

columns. The Torah Scrolls were kept there, not in a shrine, but probably only during the services.

When they began to decorate the synagogue, the arch over the entrance to the niche was the first thing to be adorned. The sacrifice of Isaac, the seven-branched candelabrum and the Temple were depicted on it showing once again in which direction the thoughts of the people lay. The sacrifice of Isaac has a peculiarity. The figures are seen from the back, the heads indicated by black spots. The desire for pictorial representation struggles against the scruples imposed by the law on prohibiting all images. Not until all the walls of the synagogue were to be decorated, in the year 244–45 of our era, were all restrictions discarded. The figures of four men were painted on the wall over the niche. It has not been ascertained whom they represent, but they are considered to be the finest part of the ornamentation. The artist has nobly depicted one of these holy men (Fig. 92), sometimes called Moses, sometimes Ezra, unfolding the Torah Scroll. He is clothed in a white garment with rich folds; his leg, placed lightly to one side, gives the body a slightly curved attitude. The horizontal, opened scroll contrasts vividly with the upward striving figure of the man. He is not reading from the scroll he is holding, but his gaze extends dreamily into the distance. It is easy to recognize the Greek statues of poets and orators from which the artist has taken his inspiration. The statue of Demosthenes (Fig. 93) not only shows the similarity of the position and the garment, but also of the scroll and its container.

Besides these four male figures, the walls are decorated with scenes from the stories of the patriarchs, of Moses, of Samuel, of the early Kings, of Elijah, of Ezekiel. Orpheus and his animals appear, demonstrating again Greek influence. The underlying idea governing these paintings is still

92. MAN WITH SCROLL

Mural from the synagogue at Dura Europos

subject to debate, and the difficulty of interpretation is increased because not all the murals have been preserved. Only one fact is certain: they do not create an historical chronological narrative, but rather depict the hope for the restoration of the Jewish state and Temple.[31]

Some of the individual paintings are as difficult to interpret as the entire cycle. This is often due to the fact that the figures are placed next to each other without any definite connection. Besides, the same figure appears several times in the same scene. Our illustration (Fig. 94) clearly shows this "continuous style." Human bones lie on the ground and above them the same figure appears in three different attitudes. It depicts the prophet Ezekiel as he visualizes the resurrection of the dead (Ezekiel, Chap. 37). The hand of the Lord has seized Ezekiel and transported him to the valley of the dead. This hand appears a second time over another figure of the prophet, as though the Lord was saying to him, "Prophesy over these bones." Once again we see the hand above Ezekiel—"Prophesy unto the breath," the Lord says to the prophet and this breath brings the bones to life again, as can be seen in the right part of the painting, missing here. Ezekiel is attired in a Persian costume, and his movements are so restless and agitated that one can again feel the oriental touch amalgamating with Grecian dignity.

93. Demosthenes
Marble Statue. Rome, Vatican.

As the religious life of the Jews was at this time greatly affected by the beauty-loving tendencies of Hellen-

94. Ezekiel's Vision of the Resurrection of the Dead
Mural from the synagogue at Dura Europos

ism, so was their secular life enhanced by means of art. Marriages were celebrated in great magnificence. The bride was beautifully clothed, a crown was placed on her head and she was seated on a special bridal chair, probably of particularly beautiful craftsmanship. She then left the parental home in an elaborate sedan chair and was carried thus into the bridal tent, which was made of purple cloth and adorned with jewels. As we have already mentioned, the bridal canopy, the chupo, was a development of this tent.

At this period even death was robbed of its sinister appearance. The body of the deceased was anointed, wrapped in beautiful garments and placed on a magnificent bier. Special attention was paid to the grave. The Maccabees already had erected a tomb over their family grave. It was an architectural construction adorned with sculptures. Originally intended only for families of the highest rank, the custom gradually became more and more general, causing the Talmud to complain that the splendor of these

95. TOMBS IN THE KIDRON VALLEY NEAR JERUSALEM

monuments excels that of the palaces of Nebuchadnezzar
(b. Sanhedrin 96 b). One of the most magnificent tombs was
probably the one erected over the grave of Helena of
Adiabene, Queen of the Parthians, who was converted to
Judaism in the year 43 of our era and was buried together
with her son in Jerusalem. According to Josephus (Jewish
Antiquities XX, 4, 3), the superstructure of this imposing
monument was crowned by three pyramids, similar to the
motif used for the tomb of the Maccabees.

Some of the smaller superstructures, hewn out of the
natural rock, have been found in the Kidron Valley near
Jerusalem. The so-called "Tomb of Zechariah" (Fig. 95),
standing on this spot, also has a pyramid over the cubelike
structure, the latter decorated with Ionic half columns.
Once again we see the combination of Occident and Orient.
More elaborate still is the so-called "Tomb of Absalom"
(Fig. 96). We find the same Ionic half columns, but here

they support a richer entablature which in its turn supports
a stone superstructure. A short, round turret with a curved
roof culminating in a point towers over the whole edifice.
Formerly a chalice of stone adorned the point.

The caves which served as graves were also lavishly decorated. The entrance was sometimes accentuated by a forecourt and a porch. In our illustration (Fig. 95) to the left of
the Tomb of Zechariah, we find such a porch consisting of
columns. Occasionally it developed into a two-storied facade. Not so very long ago in the north of Jerusalem, the
remnants of a facade were unearthed which could easily be
reconstructed into a two-storied edifice.

In early times the dead were placed in graves hollowed
out of the floor of the caves. Hellenism changed this custom.
Shelves were carved into the walls and the stone tablets
covering them were inscribed and adorned with Jewish
symbols. A more complicated method consisted of hollow-
ing out a semicircular niche.
The corpse was laid on the
floor of the niche or a grave
was dug in the niche for the
body of the deceased. This
niche was decorated with
paintings. Often the entire
walls of the cave were covered with murals.

In Palmyra, Syria, richly
adorned caves were found,
which are sometimes attributed to Jews because Jewish
names were inscribed on the
walls. The motifs of the
paintings do not bear out

96. Tomb of Absalom
Jerusalem near Kidron Valley

this conclusion. Portrait medallions held up by winged figures, and full length figures of mothers with children could
possibly be considered Jewish, but the scene, which depicts
Achilles discovering Ulysses in female clothes amongst the
daughters of Lycomedes, has certainly nothing to do with
Judaism. These caves, as we know, did not come into the
possession of the Jews before 191 of our era, consequently
we may assume that the paintings dated from before that
time.

But specifically Jewish paintings have been found in
catacombs in northern Africa and in Italy, particularly near
Rome from which our illustration (Fig. 97) is taken. It
shows a ceiling of a chamber in the catacombs under the
Villa Torlonia in the Via Nomentana. In the center of the
cross-vaulting, a seven-branched candelabrum is depicted,
a favorite motif in funeral art. It is meant apparently to
express the hope of the deceased for the coming of the
Kingdom of God, which will bring about the resurrection
of the dead and the reconstruction of the Temple with its
candelabrum. The shofor as well as the esrog and lulov in
the small circles allude to the same desire. The charm of this
painting lies in its delicacy and the lightness of its touch. It
ranks amongst the finest examples of decorative Roman art
of that time.

Besides the shelves and niches hollowed out of the walls,
sarcophagi were placed against walls. Such stone coffins
were found in the Orient as well as in Italy. The illustration
(Fig. 98) is taken from the tomb of Queen Adiabene in
Jerusalem. The sole ornamentation of the coffin and the
curved lid consists of elaborate and sharply outlined rosettes.

The Italian sarcophagi show a greater variety in the
choice of decorative matter. The seven-branched candelabrum also appears here either as the only decoration or, as

97. Ceiling of a Room in the Catacomb under the Villa Torlonia at Rome

98. Sarcophagus
From the tomb of Queen Adiabene in Jerusalem. Paris, Louvre.

we see in illustration 99, flanked by a number of figures.
The ring surrounding the candelabrum is supported by
winged figures wearing fluttering garments and making
lively gestures. On either side of them allegories of the four
seasons are depicted, impersonating the passing of time.
Only the figure of Autumn has been preserved. It is shown
as a beautiful nude youth carrying two dead birds and a
filled cornucopia, for the autumn is the season for hunting
and gathering fruit. Below the candelabrum three naked
boys are pressing grapes in a tub with their feet. This is a
symbol of death, for human beings, too, lose their outer
shape, and only the soul or spirit remains. Similar sarcophagi are also found in the heathen world. On these, the center
is often filled out with a bust of the deceased, whereas the
Jews avoided portraiture by substituting symbols.

Nevertheless, in a very few instances, tombs with portraits
did make their appearance. The Lateran Museum in Rome
possesses such a sarcophagus on the cover of which a boy
lies (Fig.100). He is stroking a dog, but his face bears a

99. SARCOPHAGUS
Rome, Museo Lateranense

melancholy expression. A Jewish tombstone depicting a mother with her child was found in the Roman province Pannonia, today a part of Hungary. We see from this latter example that upright tombstones were also used then. They are the origin of the type of stones still executed today.

In the vicinity of Jerusalem small chests were found. They were first thought to be sarcophagi for children, but later on their true use was recognized—they were destined for the conservation of bones. There were two reasons for constructing these "ossuaries." The bodies were exhumed and the bones placed in the chests, to make more room in the cemetery. The second reason was the desire of some Jews, living outside Palestine, to be buried in the capital of the Holy Land. The bones were easily transportable and were placed in the small chests when they reached Palestine.

These chests were made of wood or of limestone, but of the former nothing has remained. The ornamentation on the limestone chests reminds us of the Palestinian sarcoph-

100. JEWISH BOY
From the cover of a sarcophagus.
Rome, Museo Lateranense.

agus which we described in Figure 98. Rosettes again form the main motif of our example (Fig. 101). But, these rosettes are differently treated. They are not carved *out* of the stone, but *into* it and the contrast of light and shade adds to their beauty. This "scallop" technique is probably derived from the wooden ossuaries. The glitter or vibration of this work is characteristic of the period just before the beginnings of the Middle Ages.

We should still mention the various utensils of domestic life which were placed in the graves beside the deceased person. At this period death was not considered the end of all things, but simply an interim between life and resurrection in the Kingdom of God. Consequently lamps, bowls, plates, jugs, glasses, bracelets, and amulets were placed in them, and most of these objects are artistically adorned. The

101. OSSUARY
In the possession of the Archaeological
Society, Jerusalem

Torah shrine depicted on the bottom of a glass (Fig. 86) which we have already described, was found in such a tomb. It is a fragment of a "gilt glass" so called because the design was cut out of a fine gold leaf and placed between two thin glass plates. It includes various other Jewish symbols and the Latin inscription, "May they remain in good health, Vitalis, his wife and their two children Felix and Venerius." Apparently this glass was given to Vitalis during his lifetime and was considered valuable enough to be placed in the grave with him.

As to lamps which were found in tombs, our illustrations show us two examples, a simple one of clay and a more valuable one of bronze. Both are decorated with the seven-branched candelabrum, which in Figure 102 ornaments the

102. (Left) JEWISH LAMP. Jerusalem, Adolph Reifenberg.
103. (Right) JEWISH LAMP. Bronze.

flat surface, but in Figure 103 forms the handle. On both, a shofor has been designed which alludes to the coming of the Messiah presaged by Elijah, who announces the event by blowing his horn. We see how all these objects point to one and the same thought: the restoration of Jerusalem and the Temple in the Kingdom of God.

The question arises whether the abundant works of art of this epoch were executed by the Jews themselves. Handiwork, including applied arts, stood in high esteem. It was not slaves, as in Greece and Rome, who labored at these crafts, but free men who considered them as essential to their livelihood. The Talmud says: "He who does not teach his son a craft, teaches him brigandage" (b. Kiddushin 29 a). Even the sages were at the same time craftsmen; even so were the Jewish founders of Christianity. Jesus was a carpenter and Paul a tentmaker.

The Talmud gives us a vivid record of Jewish craftsmanship in Alexandria (b. Sukkah 51b). In the great synagogue, the craftsmen "did not occupy their seats promiscuously, but goldsmiths sat separately, silversmiths separately, metal workers (or perhaps seal engravers) separately, and weavers separately, so that when a poor man entered the place, he recognized the members of his craft and applying to that quarter, obtained a livelihood for himself and for the members of his family." We may gather from this that the craftsmen formed separate guilds and each one was so fully occupied that even a stranger could find employment.

An inscription on a tombstone found in Hierapolis in Phrygia, which since the second century of our era had a strong Jewish colony, gives us an insight into the Jewish textile trade. The deceased artisan expressed the wish that the guilds of purple dyers and carpet weavers ornament his tomb on the Passover and on the Feast of Weeks and he left a sum of money for this purpose.[32] He might as well be referring to Jewish guilds as to the general guilds in which Jews and non-Jews may have worked in harmony. Certain textiles into which fabulous beasts had been woven were so well known at this time, that a Roman poet of the fourth century A.D.—Claudius Claudianus—writes of them as "Judaica Vela"—Jewish Veils (in Eutropium I, 350 ff.).

In the second century B.C.E., in Ecclesiasticus (38:27), we find particular praise for the Israelite seal engraver and the care and lifelike quality shown in his work:

His diligence is to make variety
He setteth his heart to make his likeness true
And his anxiety is to finish his work.

Human figures were no longer permitted on these seals
(Tosefta, Abodah Zarah, ed. Zuckermandel, p. 486), therefore, animals were probably the principal motifs. In this
craft the Jews already excelled during the time of the Kings.

The art of constructing pavements of mosaics was known
to them. On the above-mentioned pavement in Beth Alpha,
the names of two masters of this art are perpetuated in a
Greek inscription: Marianos and his son Chanina. They
may have come from Alexandria. This would explain the
Greek motif of the sun god Helios. Judging by this one
example, it is possible that all the other synagogue mosaics
were executed by Jews as well.

The name of an artist was also found in a catacomb.
"Here lies Eudoxios, the painter. May thy slumber be peaceful" is the inscription on his tomb in the catacomb of the
Vigna Rondanini in Rome. From this we may assume that
the catacombs were also decorated by Jews.

The Jewish building trade is referred to in a passage from
the Talmud. The artisans were forbidden "to build a
basilica, scaffold, stadium or judge's tribunal"; this means
buildings of an outspoken heathen character. They were
allowed "to build public baths or bath-houses." But, the
Talmud adds, "when they have reached the vaulting where
they set up the idol, it is forbidden to build" (b. Abodah
Zarah 1, 7).

Probably the Jews were also stone masons carving sarcophagi and ornamenting the synagogues, for both show an
abundance of Jewish symbols.

Were they architects as well? Numerous inscriptions have
been found in synagogues, which could be interpreted as

referring to builders. The "Seat of Moses," shown in Figure 88, contains the following Aramaic inscription: "May he be remembered for good, Judan, son of Ishmael, who made the synagogue and its staircase. As his reward may he have a share with the righteous." This sounds on first reading, as if the architect was implied, but the plea for spiritual reward makes it more probable that the donor was meant. Other inscriptions convey a similar impression. Be this as it may, we may assume that the Jews constructed all or most of the synagogues themselves. Active in all the arts, why should they have neglected architecture?

In conclusion, the reader may well bear in mind that Jewish art of this period played a very important part in influencing the daughter religions, Christianity and Mohammedanism. To be sure, Islam, which arose 600 years later than Christianity, did not always look directly to Judaism, but took Christianity for its model. Nevertheless, these traditions which were first taken over by the Christians and passed on to the Mohammedans must be credited to their original owners.

Christianity and Mohammedanism inherited one negative trait from Judaism—their refusal to accept pictorial representation. This reserve was very noticeable in the first centuries of Christian art. It bursts out afresh in the Byzantine iconoclasm of the eighth and ninth centuries and grew with renewed vigor when Protestantism arose.

On the other hand, the Christians learned from the Hellenistic Jews how to interpret the Second Commandment in a very liberal manner. The sarcophagi ornamented with figures of human beings, the pictorial mosaic pavements, and the murals like those found in Dura Europos may have encouraged them to decorate their tombs and churches in the same way. It was not until later when the rift between

Jews and Christians had widened, that the Christians threw off all these fetters.

Mohammedanism invested this pictorial prohibition with still greater and more lasting severity, although here also exceptions were made, especially in the decoration of palaces and in the field of manuscript painting. But all in all, the abhorrence of the representational art is a definite characteristic of Mohammedan art. It has turned this art away from nature and thereby created an abundance of abstract forms in architecture and in the applied arts, imbuing it with a particular charm and grandeur.

To turn to the positive influences of Jewish art, we see that Christianity as well as Islam erected sacred structures which were not intended as the abode of a deity, but rather as gathering places for the members of a congregation. Christianity as well as Judaism adapted the Hellenistic basilicas with their columns, their galleries and their apses, to their own use.

Christianity and Islam also added some ritual features to the heathen constructions as the Jews had already done. A colonnaded forecourt stood before the church as well as before the mosque, and both had fountains for ritual ablutions. Those who have seen the Square of St. Peters in Rome, with its colonnades and two fountains, will realize that all this is derived from the forecourts of the synagogues or to go further back, from the Temple of Jerusalem.

Christians and Mohammedans built their churches and mosques to face in a specific direction just as the Jews did. At first, the direction was toward Jerusalem. Later on the churches substituted the supposed location of Paradise for the Holy City, whereas the mosques faced toward Mecca because the Kaaba, the Holy Stone, stood there.

The Mohammedans marked this wall by a niche, the

Mihrab, to which the worshipper turned. A similar niche for the Torah Scrolls was mentioned in our survey of the synagogue of Dura Europos (Fig. 91), and we can assume that such a Mohammedan niche was derived from the synagogues.

The church as well as the mosque inherited the raised platforms found in the synagogues and these were also used for reading the Holy Scriptures. When the Jews of the Middle Ages lived in Spain in the proximity of the Arabs, they took the word al-mimbar and adapted it to their own use, making the word almemor out of it, by which the reading platform is still known today.

The seat of the leader of the synagogue became the seat of the presbyter or the bishop in the church. The Jews had already endowed this seat with special importance (Fig. 88) and the Christians increased its artistic value by elaborate decorations.

The Christians also took over the "perpetual light" from the synagogue, and adopted the form of a suspended bowl which the Jews had acquired in Hellenistic times.

A chest for the scrolls may also have been prevalent in the early Christian churches, but as far as we know never had a definite place there as had the Ark of the Law in the synagogue. The holy place in the synagogue where the Ark stood was reserved in the church for the altar on which the communion was observed.

The scrolls to which the Jews have clung with such tenacity, made room for books in Christianity and Mohammedanism. But the wish to adequately adorn these sacred Scriptures, was probably inherited from the Jews. We have spoken about a Pentateuch in gold letters which the Jews wrote in the third century before our era for the Egyptian king. It was not unique. A man named Alexander who probably lived in Alexandria in the first century of our era possessed a similar Pentateuch.[33] It is quite possible that the Jews did not content themselves with this one mode of ornamentation. As pavements and walls were decorated with Biblical scenes, why should not Biblical manuscripts have been treated in the same way, at least when used for domestic purposes? Attention has been drawn to the fact that the Christians, when first illustrating their manuscripts, mostly used scenes from the Old Testament. Furthermore the earliest examples of this art known to us came into existence in the east, particularly in Alexandria and in Antioch, where Jews had large colonies. All this leads to the conclusion that also in manuscript paintings, Christian art had its prototype in Jewish art.

In funeral art likewise, Jewish customs found their way into Christianity. The Christian catacombs are nothing more than variations of the Jewish caves, and have the same shelves, niches and sarcophagi. Similarly the mural decorations of the Christian catacombs may be derived from the Jewish ones. Here as well the scenes of the Old Testament play an important part, particularly in their early days.

Utensils belonging to the deceased were also placed in Christian tombs, and it was only necessary to substitute Christian symbols for Jewish ones in their ornamentation. In the place of the candelabrum, a cross was used.

In spite of all this, we must never forget that the exterior form and style in which the Jews clothed their ideas were taken from Hellenism. But the Jews adapted these forms to their own belief, and when this belief gave birth to two new religions, they accepted the Jewish art forms as well. Jewish art of this period was the link which connected Hellenism with the Christian and Islam art of the Middle Ages, and this lends it special significance.

IX.

The Middle Ages

O N THE day when the sacred implements of the
Temple of Jerusalem were carried in triumph
through the streets of Rome, no one would have
believed that in conquered Palestine a new religion had
already been born, one which was eventually to destroy the
religion and culture of the heathen Romans. Still less was
it possible to guess that the rock on which the Temple stood
would once again become the foundation of yet another
House of God, which was not Jewish nor heathen, nor
Christian. The Mohammedan religion, in a mighty sweep,
spread over large parts of the Roman Empire, through Africa
and as far west as Spain.

The manner in which the Christians and Mohammedans
adapted and transformed the rich heritage of pagan art to
their own beliefs constitutes the history of mediaeval art.
We have seen the part which Jewish art played in this
process. To some degree, it became the mediator, bearing
this heritage of pagan art to the new religions. This only
took place at the beginning. Later on Christianity and Islam
tended the seeds planted by Judaism and eventually created
magnificent cathedrals and mosques, excelling that which
their teachers had produced.

No new religious movement inspired the Jews sufficiently
to further develop their own artistic forms. No new blood
flowed into their veins, as with the Christians and Mohammedans, and we know well how great was the influence,

particularly on Christian art, exerted by new peoples which came under the domination of this faith.

After Palestine was definitely lost, and the hope of ever regaining it faded, the Jews became a people without a home. It is true that the number of countries open to them for immigration had increased. They settled in Spain, in Italy, in Germany, France, England, as well as in parts of Eastern Europe, in fact everywhere where civilization was growing, but they always remained a religious minority. Their presence was, at best, only tolerated, their rights were limited and they were often persecuted and expelled.

These are doubtless not the best conditions for establishing a flourishing art. Art requires security, power and self-reliance.

There is still another factor which limited the artistic activities of the Jews of the Middle Ages. Previously they had lived as Roman citizens in a world full of beauty, and just as they became assimilated in language, in names, and in customs, so they adopted to a certain degree, the pagan love of art. In the Middle Ages they lived among peoples whose religion also imposed restrictions on pictorial art. This was especially so in Islam which, as we have already mentioned, had accepted the prohibition of representational art sometimes more severely than the Jews themselves.

The Christians had adopted the Second Commandment but, with few exceptions, had gradually rid themselves of this fetter. In the meantime, however, the gulf between Jews and Christians had become so apparent that the artistic liberties which the latter had acquired caused a reaction in Jewry which drove the Jews to a yet severer interpretation of the Second Commandment.

As we have shown before, in the period of late Antiquity

many Jews nourished the belief that mosaic pavements or
murals with figures of human beings were compatible with
the Second Commandment. But, when in the twelfth century, the Jews adorned a stained-glass window in the synagogue of Cologne with lions and serpents, Rabbi Eljakim
ben Joseph objected to it. The Talmud, he argued, only
allows painting for practical purposes and for acquiring
perfection in that art, and not for creating permanent works.
In the same way Rabbi Isaac ben Moses of Vienna (1180–
1260) in his old age condemned the trees and birds which
he had seen as a boy in the synagogue of Meissen in Germany.[34]

Others were more lenient in their judgment, but one
thing remains certain: human figures were no longer portrayed, at least in the synagogues.

In view of the economic as well as the religious restrictions imposed on the Jews of the Middle Ages, it is not so
astonishing that their art lagged behind that of late Antiquity; we can only wonder that they were able to produce
works of art at all. To be sure, conditions varied somewhat,
according to the time and place, and some proved more
favorable than others. In Christian countries the Jews were
limited in their vocations, persecuted because of their belief and often expelled from the country in which they had
settled. Mohammedanism in Babylonia, in North Africa,
and in Spain, to cite a few countries, gave them greater
freedom. Consequently in these countries their artistic life
could become much more active.

As to the Christian countries the first millennium passed
in comparative peace and it was only with the Crusades that
the persecution of the Jews became violent. The rise of the
Christian guilds at that time doubtless did great damage
to Jewish craftsmanship. These guilds were not only profes-

sional unions, but at the same time religious brotherhoods under the protection of a certain saint. Consequently the Jews were excluded. This prevented them from learning a trade under a Christian master and selling their products to Christian consumers. But the Jews somehow still found it possible to learn one trade or another within the narrow confines of the ghetto and disposed of their work among their coreligionists. Whether they engraved pewter plates for Purim and Passover, or embroidered Torah curtains, or illuminated books, at least the thread of Jewish art was never completely severed.

Moreover, even during the period of the bloody persecutions, which followed on the first millennium of Christian tolerance, the attitude of the Christians varied in different countries. For instance, at a time when Jews were burned at the stake in Germany and fled the country in great masses, in Poland they were welcomed. In Germany they were driven out of the craftsmen's trades and became almost entirely dependent upon money-lending or peddling for a livelihood, but in Poland they were needed as artisans because the Poles had few craftsmen of their own. Here the Jews became strong enough to organize their own guilds similar to the Christian ones from which they were excluded.

The material at our disposal, in an appraisal of Jewish art during the Middle Ages, is too scant to warrant a division of the subject either as to century or country. We would do well to consider this epoch as a whole. There is a paucity, or even a complete lack of art material from certain countries. We have no record of mediaeval works of art from Palestine, Arabia, Persia or Babylonia. This is particularly regrettable as concerns Babylonia because, as late as the eleventh century, the Jews possessed academies of learning there which were visited by students from all parts of the world. These institutions were most likely housed in stately edifices, and the synagogues connected with them were probably of proportionate distinction. The expulsion of the Jews from France, England, Germany, Spain, Portugal, and Sicily was responsible for the loss of many objects of art.

There is also a blind spot in the history of Jewish art because of the lapse of centuries without record of artistic achievement. It is most unfortunate that there is no Jewish work of art extant which dates from between the synagogue of Beth Alpha in the sixth century to the illuminated manuscripts discovered in the synagogue of Cairo, the oldest of which is from the ninth century. This gap of three centuries prevents us from following chronologically the course of Jewish art at a very important period: the gradual development from Antiquity to the Middle Ages. It will therefore be necessary to content ourselves with a description of the principal themes of Jewish art of the mediaeval period.

The main artistic effort of the mediaeval Jew was centered on the construction of the synagogue. We must not think, however, of the magnificent synagogues which we have described in the preceding chapter. These were often erected on hills with colonnaded forecourts, with porches and facades consisting of three portals, a semicircular window and an elaborate gable. With few exceptions the mediaeval synagogues were much simpler, at least on the exterior. A synagogue towering above a city was suitable for a people who played an important part in that city, but not for minority communities forced into narrow quarters. The Jews were taught that a synagogue must rise above the roofs of a city (b. Talmud Sabbath 11 a), but they had to be content with building their houses of worship just a little higher than the houses in which they lived. If even this was

104. SYNAGOGUE OF TRANI
Southern Italy

impossible, a pole was placed on the roof. This pole symbolized the desired height of the whole edifice.

Courtyards in front and around the synagogues were still used, as law courts, for market-places, for marriages and for the celebration of the new moon, but their dimensions grew smaller and smaller and the surrounding columns were entirely dispensed with. The three portals were reduced to a single one and it was placed in an inconspicuous position. The entrance was no longer built into the facade facing the Torah shrine so that the passer-by could watch the service, but was now installed at the side of the building. This eliminated the possibility of beautifying the facade with a vestibule. When mediaeval synagogues have vestibules, they are generally found at the side and were added later as the size of the congregation increased. It became customary to seat the women there, emphasizing their separation from the men, as there were usually no galleries. The vessels for ritual ablutions, formerly situated in the open forecourts, were placed there as well.

The rectangular form of building was generally adhered to, particularly in Christian countries where the churches of the city served as models. In Mohammedan countries, mosques often exercised a great influence on the construction of the synagogue by favoring the "central structure" type of architecture, in which length and width are equal. We learn from an old record that a synagogue in Palermo,

Sicily, was erected on a square ground plan, measuring forty
cubits in each direction.[35] This synagogue also had courts
surrounded by colonnades, showing that, under particularly
favorable conditions, the spaciousness of Antiquity was retained. Another synagogue, built also on a square foundation, forty by forty meters, still exists in Trani, lower Italy.
We know it was the work of a Jewish architect, although
his name on the inscription stone has been modestly
omitted.[36] The edifice built in 1247 has been preserved
because when the Jews were expelled from Trani, it became
the church of St. Anna. The square form is emphasized on
the exterior. Above the walls a polygonal structure arises,
topped by a flat cupola (Fig. 104).

The interior of the synagogues of the Middle Ages was
reached by a few steps leading downwards. The reason for
the descent into the building was explained by the Talmud,
which interpreted verse 1 of Psalm 130 very literally: "Out
of the depths have I called
Thee, O Lord" (b. Ta'anit
23 b). This interior usually
consisted of a simple hall.
We have occasionally come
across this type of synagogue
in Antiquity as well, for instance in Dura Europos.
During the Middle Ages,
however, we find only a few
interiors decorated with columns. To begin with an oriental example: the syna-
gogue of Bagdad, Iraq, was
"constructed with many colored columns, which were

106. CAPITAL
*From the synagogue of Toledo, Spain,
twelfth century.*

105. SYNAGOGUE OF TOLEDO, SPAIN

inlaid with gold and silver. Verses of the Psalms were inscribed on them with gold letters." These are the words of Benjamin of Tudela, the well-known Spanish-Jewish traveler of the twelfth century, who visited it.

A still more elaborate interior can be seen in a synagogue in Toledo, Spain (Fig. 105), consisting of four rows of columns, similar to the ones in Alexandria and Tiberias which we mentioned in the previous chapter. This synagogue was erected in the twelfth century and owes its preservation to its conversion into a church—Santa Maria la Blanca. The exterior is extremely simple in line, there is not even an apse jutting out of the rectangular construction. This simplicity is counterbalanced by the richness of the interior. Twenty-eight columns divide the big hall into five aisles. The short octagonal pillars support exquisitely carved capitals (Fig. 106) with designs which may have been inspired by the description of the two columns in front of the Temple of Solomon (I Kings 7:20). In both capitals fruits were used, pomegranates on the ancient columns and pine cones on the Spanish ones, and the "network" entwining the fruit is common to both. The horseshoe arches which crown the pillars are derived from mosque architecture. The triangular spaces between the arches and the frieze above them with their abstract geometric forms likewise point to Islamic influence. The gallery for the women is situated above the frieze of the entrance wall. It recedes into the wall and does not stand free as the balconies in the synagogues of ancient times.

We do not know who the architect of this exquisite synagogue was, but the five aisles, which were mentioned in the Talmudic report about the synagogue in Alexandria and the capitals influenced by the description of those in front of the Temple of Solomon, lend credence to the suggestion

107. FRIEZE
From the synagogue of Samuel Abulafia in Toledo, Spain

that he was a Jew. The Jews of Spain during the mediaeval period were very favorably situated and all the artistic professions may well have flourished there.

Still another synagogue exists in Toledo, preserved because it was converted into a church: el Transito. This edifice dates from the middle of the fourteenth century and was founded by Samuel Abulafia, the rich treasurer of Peter the Cruel. It is also of rectangular construction but has no columns. As in the other synagogue, the galleries are built into the walls and lattice windows look on to the interior (Fig. 107). These windows are framed with delicate arcades. The double columns support richly carved capitals which in their turn carry cusped arches, a familiar feature in Islamic art. The broad frieze under the windows is more elaborate than the one in the older and larger synagogue. Instead of the geometric motifs, we find lifelike tendrils, the leaves of which are sometimes protruding. This is a touch of the youthful naturalism of French Gothic art. The combination of Islamic and Gothic art first took place in the Christian churches of Spain, but the Jews also accepted this merging of styles, and this frieze can be considered one of the most perfect examples.

A few other synagogues have been preserved in Spain and Portugal, but they add nothing to the story.

Only two synagogues of mediaeval France have come down to us and even these have been rebuilt in the style of Louis XVI. They are situated in Carpentras and in Cavaillon, both in Provence. These synagogues contribute something new in architecture, but we do not know if this departure from the older characteristics dates from the Middle Ages or is a later addition. The balconies are not only reserved for the women, but carry the bimo, so that everyone could look up to the readers of the Torah. The Jews were driven out of the crown possessions of France during the fourteenth century and were only allowed to remain in such small districts as Lorraine, la Franche Comté, Savoy and Provence—lands free of the crown sovereignty. This naturally restricted the number of synagogues and caused the destruction of those which already existed, excepting the two just described.

The Jews were also driven out of England in the year 1290, shortly before they were expelled from France. As they were so few in number, their synagogues were probably unimportant. The only one which has been preserved was nothing more than a large room in a house built of stone. It belonged to Aaron of Lincoln (*ca.* 1123–1186), one of the richest Jews of his day. This, as well as a few neighboring buildings in the Jewish quarter, are supposed to be the oldest stone houses in England.

Compared to the dearth of Jewish mediaeval buildings in

England and France, the synagogues of Germany, Bohemia, and Poland were much greater in number as well as in size and beauty. The oldest of these, preserved until its destruction by the Nazis in the year 1938, was the synagogue of Worms. It was begun in the twelfth century, at the same period as the great one in Toledo, but was much smaller in

108. SYNAGOGUE OF WORMS

size, clearly showing the difference between the rich Jews of Spain and their poorer brothers in Germany. The building consisted of a small rectangular hall. A century later a second hall for the women was added at right angles to the main building. The exterior was very simple and decorated with one portal only, characteristically placed at the side. This portal, according to romanesque style, consisted of converging sides supporting an arch.

The interior (Fig. 108) boasts a special feature which makes this synagogue outstanding. Here, for the first time, the flat ceiling is replaced by stone vaultings. In the main hall, six cross-vaultings are supported by two columns, whereas the "Frauen-Schul" has only one column in the center. The beautiful capitals in the main hall, with their carved palmettes were, according to the inscription, fashioned by a Jew. We do not know if the construction of the building itself was in the hands of a Jewish architect. Conditions in Germany were so unfavorable for the Jews that they may well have abandoned the science of architecture, because of the technical skill and special knowledge and training required. The style of the synagogue of Worms approaches that of the romanesque churches of Worms, but lacks the elaborateness of the latter with their apses, transverse aisles and towers. Judaism renounced all these imposing features and contented itself with nothing but columns, forming a double-aisled hall. The division into three aisles, which was customary in the Palestinian synagogues of the late period of Antiquity was not used in the Middle Ages, no doubt intentionally. The Jews had to avoid too great a resemblance to the churches, all the more so because the number "three" was symbolical of the Trinity. The two-aisled form of construction was not unknown to the Christians, but was not generally employed by them for churches. They used it only for the halls of municipal buildings, castles and monasteries.

The double-aisled synagogue, after it appeared in the venerated community of Worms, became the model for a number of others. The beautiful synagogue in Ratisbon, Germany, built in the thirteenth century, was destroyed during a pogrom in the sixteenth century, but two etchings by Albrecht Altdorfer made shortly after it was destroyed con-

109. THE ALTNEUSCHUL AND THE JEWISH TOWN HALL
IN PRAGUE, CZECHOSLOVAKIA

vey an impression of the interior. The synagogue was romanesque, but the side vestibule, added later, already had
the pointed Gothic arch.

The Altneuschul in Prague is purely Gothic. It is an edifice of the thirteenth century, which brings the double
aisled construction to Bohemia. The exterior (Fig. 109) is,
as usual, a solid rectangular building, but the Gothic tendency is clearly seen in the buttresses and the steeply rising
gabled roof. The entrance, as in Worms and Ratisbon, was
placed at the side and was ornamented in a like manner. According to Gothic style, the doorway was narrow and high,
terminating in a pointed arch (Fig. 110). The space over the
lintel is beautifully carved in relief: vine tendrils are growing from a hill, although depicted with Gothic naturalism.
The vine is a symbol of Israel; a bunch of golden grapes, as
will be remembered, hung over the inner portal of the

Temple of Herod. On entering, one is struck primarily by the height of the hall. Tall pillars strive upwards and carry Gothic arches with their finely profiled groins (Fig. 111).

In Poland, which received the main stream of German exiles in the Middle Ages, we find the largest synagogue of

110. DOORWAY OF THE ALTNEUSCHUL
IN PRAGUE

Ashk'nazic Jewry, the old synagogue in Cracow. The exterior was reconstructed in the sixteenth century in Renaissance style, but the interior, probably built about 1400, still shows Gothic characteristics (Fig. 112). As in Prague and in Worms, two pillars divide the hall into two aisles and carry Gothic vaultings. The bimo, which is in late Gothic style is placed in the middle of the synagogue between the two pil-

111. INTERIOR OF THE ALTNEUSCHUL IN PRAGUE
From a drawing

lars. Its particular charm inclines us to describe more fully
the ritual accessories of this period.

In the past the bimo, as we may gather from the only
one remaining (Fig. 87), was but a sparsely decorated plat-

112. SYNAGOGUE OF CRACOW, POLAND
Notice the iron bimo

form set near the Torah shrine. In the Middle Ages the
bimo was frequently placed in the center, "so that he who
reads from the Law or he who speaks words of exhortation to
the people, may stand upon it and all may hear him," according to the words of Maimonides (Mishneh Torah, Hilkot Tefillah 11, 3). This more exposed position may have
gradually given rise to the desire for embellishing the bimo.
In the Altneuschul in Prague (Fig. 111) the bimo takes up
the space between the two pillars, its height emphasized by
a tall, iron-wrought fence, with staves like lances pointing
upwards. In Cracow the bimo, also made of iron, is even

more elaborate (Fig. 112). The fence, in this example, has twelve sides and terminates in a point like a tent.

As to the Torah shrine, in Antiquity it was still modest in size, resembling the secular scroll chests (Fig. 86). In the Middle Ages it became larger and more richly decorated. When the shrine receded into a niche, this niche was sometimes crowned with a beautifully chiseled gable. There is a particularly fine example in the above-mentioned synagogue in Prague; the decorative motifs, consisting of vine leaves in relief, are similar to those on the doorway.

When the Ark stood freely against the wall, as in Italy, great pains were taken to beautify it. Our illustration (Fig. 113) shows an Italian shrine of wood, dating from the year 1472. It demonstrates the richness and refinement with which a Torah shrine could be decorated towards the end of the Gothic period.

Inside the shrine a change took place regarding the position of the scrolls. In Antiquity, at least in the European countries, they were placed in a horizontal position so that they were inconspicuous (Fig. 86), whereas in the Middle Ages, they were given a vertical position. In a Spanish Haggadah of the fourteenth century, the picture of an open Torah shrine, showing this new arrangement, has been preserved (Fig. 114). The three scrolls are wrapped in differently colored and differently woven mantles. Rimonim of gold are placed on the top of them.

113. TORAH SHRINE
From the synagogue of Modena, Italy.
Paris, Musée Cluny.

This development in the artistic decoration of ritual objects is just what this epoch was striving for. We have seen that the synagogue was derived from the secular basilica and the Ark of the Law from the secular scroll chest. After the destruction of the Second Temple the Jews had already essayed to emphasize the sacred character of the synagogue. The Middle Ages continued along this path. No matter how small a synagogue of this period compared to the size and splendor of those of Antiquity, the bimo and the Torah shrine were continually enhanced in importance by gradually increasing their dimensions and the beauty of their decoration. This added to the ritual character of the synagogue.

The richly carved capitals of the synagogues of Toledo and Worms, the delicate friezes in the Spanish synagogues, the wrought-iron fences around the bimos, and the elaborate Torah shrines bring us to the subject of the applied arts, and we wonder what part the Jews played in the craftsmanship of this period. Popular belief pictures the mediaeval Jew only as a merchant or a money-lender; a man who knows how to use his head but not his hands. It is certainly true that at this period the Jew did become a successful business man. His knowledge of languages enabled him to act as mediator between Christian and Islamic countries in the exchange of merchandise. He was successful also as a money-lender because Christians were not allowed to loan out money. But it is a mistake to assume that the Jews of the Middle Ages had no inclination toward handiwork.

We know that the Jews were skilled craftsmen already in Biblical times and they remained so during the whole period of Antiquity. As late as the sixth century of our era, a Christian writer, Cosmas Indicopleustes, living in Alexandria, speaks about the variety of crafts mentioned in the Bible, such as the work of gold and silversmiths,

bronze workers, stone masons, wood carvers, weavers and
dyers and ends with the phrase: "even today we find most of
these occupations followed by Jews."

This was in the sixth century and it was not much different in the twelfth century, especially in the eastern countries, in Spain and in Sicily, where the Jews remained unmolested. Benjamin of Tudela, the Spanish traveler, who

114. MEDIAEVAL SYNAGOGUE
From the Haggadah of Sarajevo.
Sarajevo, Library.

visited many parts of Europe, Asia, and North Africa, en-
countered Jewish artisans everywhere. He meets Jewish
glass-blowers in Tyre "who make that fine . . . of Tyrian
glassware which is prized in all countries." In Thebes he sees

silk weavers and purple dyers "who are the most skilful in all Greece."

The Crusaders, traveling eastwards and returning westwards, and traders between the Orient and the Occident, were the means of bringing the technique of many crafts from the older oriental countries to the younger ones of Western and Northern Europe. The Jews played their part in this. The Roman monk, Heraklios, in his book *The Colors and Arts of the Romans* written not later than the tenth century, mentions "Jewish lead glass"; [37] apparently the Jews possessed the secret of the manufacture of this glass. During the Crusades when the Venetians came to Phoenicia, they doubtless learned a great deal from the Jewish glassblowers, whom Tudela mentions having seen there. This inspired them to found their own glass works in Venice, famous to this day.

The influence of Jewish weavers and dyers on the Occident was equally important. In the time of Herod, a Jewish weaver by the name of Baruch was said to have been called to Spain by the Roman prefect there. This story was handed down by Spanish-Jewish families, who claimed to be the descendants of this Baruch. In the tenth century, two Spanish Jews, Jacob and Joseph ibn Gan, attained such renown as weavers of silks and flags, that they worked for the Caliph Hisham (976–1013). In the twelfth century, the Norman King Roger II brought a number of Jewish silk weavers from Thebes in Greece to Sicily as prisoners of war after a victorious campaign. They were employed in the royal factories of Palermo and thus brought their technique into that country.

The Jews were also recognized as coin minters in the Middle Ages. Owing to their international connections, they had the means of obtaining the necessary metals, and applied

their knowledge of the technique acquired in ancient times
to this skill. In France, as early as the Merovingian dynasty, coins were minted, inscribed with the name Priscus.
This was a Jew, an agent and jeweler of the King Chil-
perich I (561–584). In the seventh century, a Jew by the
name of Sumair minted coins for the Arabian Caliph Abd-al
Malik (646/47–705),[38] who was the first to mint his own
coins instead of using those of other countries. Such cases occurred again and again in the following centuries; they are
too numerous to cite.

Jews were also skilled in the kindred art of seal engraving.
The head of the Academy (Gaon) in Pumbedita, Babylonia,
Hai b. Sherira (939–1038), had a seal on which a lion was engraved.[39] When we bear in mind the lion seal of the time of
the Kings (Fig. 75) we realize the strength of a tradition unbroken from Antiquity to the Middle Ages.

We do not know whether these seal engravers worked for
non-Jews, but it is certain that Jewish goldsmiths were popular with the peoples of the Orient as well as of the Occident. King John of England (1167–1216) employed a Jew,
Leo, at his court. The Augustinian Eremites in Barcelona,
Spain, in 1399, commissioned a Jewish goldsmith by the
name of Salomo Barbut to fashion a silver reliquary.[40] This
was not an exception in the Christian parts of Spain. On the
contrary, Jews were so often employed by Christians that
Pope Benedict XIV in 1415, as we stated, forbade them to
manufacture Christian ceremonial objects—goblets, crucifixes and so on.

The same bull forbade the Jews to bind books in which
were the names of Jesus or Mary. It appears that the Jews
were masters in the art of bookbinding as well. A Spanish
Jew by the name of Mahir Salomo bound the records of the
Royal Treasury from 1367 to 1389. We even come across

Jewish bookbinders in Germany, in the fifteenth century, who bound some books for the councils in Nuremberg and Noerdlingen.

The art of lacemaking was known to the Jews in Barcelona, Toledo and on the Isle of Mallorca, and some of these

115. JEWISH CARPET
Detail. Berlin, Kaiser Friedrich Museum.

laces, interwoven with gold and silver threads, were so costly, that special laws, forbidding the manufacture of luxuries, were passed.

In Spain, we even find Jewish sculptors and painters in the service of Christians. When Francis of Assisi visited Spain in the year 1214, a Jewish sculptor made a figure of him. Two Jews, or more correctly, two descendants of Jews appear in connection with altar paintings: Juan de Levi and Guillem de Levi, who worked for Christian churches about the year 1400.[41] There must surely have been other Jewish altar painters during the fifteenth century because, as we pointed out, Queen Isabella of Spain in 1480 appointed a court painter, whose duty it was to see that no Jewish or

Mohammedan artist painted holy subjects. The penalty was a heavy fine.

Did these above-mentioned artists only work for Christians? Did they go as far as to use the figures of human beings when working for their fellow Jews? In this connection, the words of Profiat Duran, Spanish-Jewish grammarian of the fourteenth century, are worthy of note: "The House of Learning should be beautiful and pleasing in structure. This increases the desire for learning, and strengthens the memory because the viewing of pleasing forms and beautiful reliefs and drawings rejoices the heart and strengthens the mind." Does this quotation only refer to sculptured and painted ornaments or did the Jews of Spain also deviate from the Second Commandment? One thing is certain, Jewish art of the Middle Ages like Jewish poetry reached its peak in Spain.

Unfortunately, due to the expulsion in 1492, very little of all this splendor has come down to us. We have already mentioned a few synagogues, transformed into churches, and consequently deprived of their Jewish features: the Torah shrine, the bimo and other accessories. Quite by chance a carpet was recently discovered in the Berlin Museum in the section of Moslem art (Fig. 115). It was considered to be of

Mohammedan origin, until the woven design was recognized as depicting Torah shrines. Most probably the rug decorated the eastern side of a synagogue, as Torah shrines generally face the direction of Jerusalem.

116. SEAL OF TODROS HALEVI
Spain, 14th century

117. BRONZE ALMS BOWL
Oxford, Ashmolean Museum

Among the small number of mediaeval seals still preserved, we also find some Spanish ones. The one here illustrated (Fig. 116) belonged to Todros Halevi who lived in the fourteenth century in Toledo. The outline of the design and the lilies (*fleurs de lis*) point to French-Gothic influence, the same influence as was seen in the frieze of the synagogue of Samuel Abulafia (el Transito) which also dates from the fourteenth century. The center, showing three turrets, is framed by a Hebrew inscription, giving the name of the owner of the seal.

From other countries as well, only a few objects of applied art have come down to posterity. A bronze vessel was found in England (Fig. 117) which, according to the Hebrew description encircling it, was donated by Joseph, son of Rabbi Jechiel. This was probably the same rabbi who emigrated from Paris to Palestine in the year 1257 in order to found an institute of learning there. The bowl was used for collecting alms for the Jews in Palestine. From the artistic point of view, it is very pleasing to our modern eyes because of its clear-cut functional shape. The three hoofs are planted firmly on the ground. The belly of the vessel is well rounded in anticipation of the gifts to be poured in. The neck is narrow to prevent money from falling out too easily and the handles seem to invite us to grasp the bowl.

Compared to the massiveness of the alms bowl, the bronze Chanuko lamp shown in our next illustration (Fig. 118)

seems particularly light and delicate. The eight oil containers are attached to a shield. This shield is a development
from the short handle of the late period of Antiquity (Fig.
103). It has now acquired a triangular Gothic shape. Over
the burners, intersecting arches have been designed and the
upper part of the shield is decorated with two lions, probably cherubim, and a salamander, the symbol of fire. The
lamp may date from the fourteenth century and may have
come from France or Spain.

A number of tombstones from the Middle Ages have been
preserved, particularly in Germany and southern Italy.
Compared to the funereal art of the late period of Antiquity,
with its monuments, its richly painted catacombs, and

118. BRONZE CHANUKO LAMP
14th century

119. TOMBSTONE
From about 1314.
Worms, Cemetery.

its elaborate sarcophagi, the plain tombstones of the Middle Ages are striking in their utter simplicity. This may be partly ascribed to Christian influence. We know that catacombs and sarcophagi disappeared in Christian art as well, and that cemeteries with individual tombstones replaced them. Furthermore the Jews took to heart the saying of the Talmud: "we need not erect any monuments to the righteous, their deeds are their memorials" (Jer. Sh'kolim II:5, 47 a), and conformed with this injunction.

Inscriptions on tombstones, which in late Antiquity were executed in Greek and Latin in the countries of the Diaspora, were written in Hebrew in the Middle Ages: a hostile world forced the Jews back upon their own traditions.

On tombstones of the early Middle Ages, we still find small engravings of the seven-branched candelabrum so characteristic of late Antiquity. Later on these disappeared and nothing but unadorned stones remained. It was not until the twelfth century that the desire was felt to give the stones a more pleasing outline. A tombstone dating from the year 1314 (Fig. 119) reflects a further step in this direction. The surface with the inscription recedes behind a design of cusped arches. It is worth while noting that this motif was used here, because Gothic art had taken it over from Islam; it was a pattern familiar to the Jews.

If Jewish funereal art in the Middle Ages reverted to greater simplicity, the contrary can be said of the art of manuscript illumination. The rich development of this art is not peculiar to the Jews, but common to Christians and Mohammedans of the Middle Ages who shared with them their devotion to their respective Holy Scriptures.

On one point however Jewish book art differs from that of other religious groups: it is of a more private character. The decorated manuscripts of the Holy Scriptures of Christians and Mohammedans were often intended for use in their houses of worship. There were, therefore, always ample time and means available for the preparation of the manuscripts. Judaism clung to the traditional use of scrolls for their synagogue services and did not tolerate any elaboration of the manuscripts themselves. There was, however, no objection to the use of ornamented books in the home. It became the task of the individual to adorn his own books; the results were, consequently, simpler.

The Jews' first care was naturally the binding. We have

120. LEATHER BINDING FROM A PENTATEUCH
Made in 1468 by Meir Jaffe. Munich, State Library.

already stated that in this craft the Jews were so skilled that
they were in demand even by non-Jews. A leather binding
of a Hebrew printed Pentateuch has been found. It was
made in 1468 for the council of Nuremberg by a Jew (Fig.
120). He has proudly inscribed his name around the edge of
the front cover: "Meir Jaffe, the designer." The main motifs
are the coat of arms of the city and a deer entwined with thin

121. PAGE FROM A PENTATEUCH
Written in 930 by Salomo Halevi Barbujah.
Leningrad, State Library.

tendrils. The back cover is decorated entirely with thicker
tendrils terminating in human heads. The technique applied in this case is a very complicated one. The design is cut
into the moistened leather, which by a certain process gives
the effect of a relief. This tooled leather technique was also
familiar to non-Jews; however, it is to their credit that
Jews acquired a high degree of perfection in this difficult art
in the fourteenth and fifteenth centuries, and that their volumes are among the best examples of that period.

There is no doubt that the above-mentioned Meir Jaffe

was the same man who wrote and decorated a beautiful Haggadah to be found today in the Hebrew Union College in Cincinnati, Ohio (Figs. 44 and 45). This was not exceptional. The writer and illuminator of a book frequently bound it himself in order to insure an adequate cover for his work.

This art of illumination was already an ancient heritage. We have learnt that Pentateuchs in gold script were

122. Page from a Bible
Written in 1010 in Cairo.
Leningrad, State Library.

written in late Antiquity. Probably, already at that time, the Jews did not stop at mere decorative writing, but illustrated their rolls as well. One can do no more than guess this because no illuminated Jewish manuscripts of that period have survived. The earliest decorated Jewish manuscripts which are known to us date from the ninth to the eleventh century of our era. They were found in the synagogue of Cairo (in the so-called Geniza). Most of these fragments are at the present moment in the State Library of Leningrad. Luckily a portfolio of colored reproductions exists, which enables us to judge their beauty.[42] Gold is the dominant color of these illuminations and lends a lofty beauty to the pages. The designs themselves are solemn and dignified. Our illustration (Fig. 121) is taken from a Pentateuch written in 930 by Salomo Halevi Barbujah. The leaf border is reminiscent of the tendrils of Antiquity, but already very conventional in its conception. The main motif has nothing naturalistic about it. It is a quadrangle framing a circle and bordered by four semicircles. The lines of the design appear to be straps

123. Mosaic Floor Panel
From the synagogue in Beth Alpha

which form knots at various intervals. Similar motifs are to be found in the art of Islam, and it is in an Islamic country that these Hebrew manuscripts were executed. This need not lead us to believe that these illuminations were entirely under the influence of Mohammedan art. Both Islamic and Jewish art are derived from that of late Antiquity but the Jews had the advantage of many centuries of previous artistic activity in this field.

Another page, taken from a Bible of the early eleventh century (Fig. 122), clearly shows its dependence upon pagan art. This design consists of verses from the Bible, so assembled that they form a portal with a post in the center. Pagan Antiquity already made use of this fanciful idea in poetical works; *carmina figurata*—poems in pictures—they were called by the Romans, and they take the form of an egg, an altar, a double axe, a shepherd's flute or a cupid's wing.[43] To this source, the above-mentioned portal can be traced, but it acquired a more abstract and complicated geometrical form following the tendency of the Middle Ages.

A third page taken once more from Barbujah's Pentateuch (Fig. 124) depicts real objects: at the bottom, the Tent

124. THE HOLY IMPLEMENTS
Page from a Pentateuch written in 930.
Leningrad, State Library.

of Meeting, above it the seven-branched candelabrum, and at the top, among other ritual objects, the Holy Ark with the two tablets of the Law. The two columns of different sizes at the sides represent the two columns in front of the Temple of Solomon. All this reminds us of similar motifs on glasses, lamps, stones, murals and mosaics of Antiquity. The mosaic pavement of the synagogue of Beth Alpha (Fig. 123) also comes back to our memory, in connection with this page. This pavement, originating from the end of Antiquity,

struck us because of its conventional forms and lack of perspective. These tendencies increased in the Middle Ages, as
may be seen in our illustration. The sides of the Tent of
Meeting are opened up and spread flat, so that it is difficult
to conceive it as a tent. The candelabrum has sharp angles
instead of being rounded. The Ark in the design of the Beth
Alpha mosaic was flanked by lions and two birds, which
were meant to represent the cherubim in front of and above
the Ark. In our Pentateuchal page, animals are omitted and
the cherubim on the ark-cover are reduced to two wings,
barely recognizable. The restrictions imposed by the Bible
on pictorial representations are, at this period, taken far
more literally than they were before.

The further development of the art of illumination can
be seen in manuscripts of the twelfth to the fifteenth century, which were written in Spain, France, Italy, and Germany. The scope of literature chosen for illumination had
gradually increased. The Biblical Scriptures were augmented by the prayer book for week-days (siddur) and for
festivals (machzor). A special book for the Seder evening,
the Haggadah, grew out of the prayer book. We have seen
that this book was the object of particular artistic interest.
To this can be added a number of books written by mediaeval authorities, as for example, the Bible commentary by
Rashi, the Mishneh Torah of Maimonides and the Arbo-o
Turim of Jacob ben Asher. Occasionally secular writings appear among these religious ones: the animal fables of ibn
Sahulah, and the medical works of the celebrated Arabian
physician Avicenna, which were translated into Hebrew.
An enumeration of all the decorated manuscripts belongs to
a special history of Jewish manuscript painting, still to be
written. We shall limit ourselves here to a presentation of
some general tendencies in this branch of art.

125. PAGE FROM THE FARHI BIBLE
14th century. London, David Solomon Sassoon.

To begin with, much of that which was found in the above-mentioned manuscripts from Egypt was developed in the following centuries. The abstract forms are to be found in more elaborate designs in some Spanish manuscripts. The Farhi Bible of the fourteenth century consists, for instance, of purely ornamented pages, very complicated in design

126. INITIALS AND MASORAH
From a German Bible.
Karlsruhe, Germany, Library.

(Fig. 125). The tranquillity of the Egyptian motifs has given way to a restlessness noticeable in the thick, knotted straps. This abstract style, under Islamic influence, lasted until the end of Spanish manuscript painting. The peak is reached in the Kennicott Bible No. 1 of the Bodleian Library in Oxford, dating from the year 1476. The design as well as the coloring of the ornamented pages are of extreme refinement and delicacy.

The *carmina figurata* of Antiquity were likewise in use in later manuscripts. In Bibles, the margined notes vouching for the correctness of the traditional text—the so-called masorah—often took the shape of figures. This method was

popular, particularly in Germany, although already in the
twelfth century Rabbi Juda ben Samuel of Regensburg objected to it. Our illustration, taken from a German Bible
(Fig. 126), gives an example of this playful form of decoration. The first word of the Book of Exodus, the letters of
which are filled up with animal figures, shows the masorah
in the form of tendrils, ornaments, and animals.

These old motifs are augmented by two new ideas which
are derived from Christian sources. The one is the treatment of the initial letter or word, which surpasses the others
in size and beauty. The attraction of the Greek, Latin and
Hebrew writing of Antiquity was to be found in the succes-
sion of letters of equal height and spacing. They were placed
side by side, we might say, like the columns of the ancient
temples. This custom was still retained in the Egyptian-
Jewish manuscripts as can be seen in the dedicatory page of
the Pentateuch previously described (Fig. 127).

Christian mediaevalism developed an entirely different
pattern. Instead of the regular lines, a few letters stand out
prominently from the others. Comparing this with architectural forms as well, we are
reminded of the turrets of
mediaeval churches, rising
above the rest of the edifice.

The Jews acquired the art
of the ornamented initial letter some centuries after the
Christians, probably not before the twelfth or thirteenth
centuries, but then it became very popular. It con-
curred with their own growing desire to show their de-

127. PAGE FROM A PENTATEUCH
Written in 930.
Leningrad, State Library.

votion to Hebrew lettering, which was a part of their
glorious past. As an example, we show a page of the
Darmstadt Haggadah, so called because it is in the Library
of Darmstadt, Germany (Fig. 128). This manuscript originated in western Germany about 1430 and represents the
climax of Jewish art in the decoration of initials. Our illus-

128. PAGE FROM
THE DARMSTADT HAGGADAH
Germany, 15th century.
Darmstadt, Landes-Bibliothek.

tration unfortunately only gives a very feeble idea of its
beauty, because one cannot see the magnificent colors. For
those who are unable to see the original, we recommend a
facsimile edition, recently published, which faithfully reproduces every page of the manuscript.[44]

The first word of our illustration, *or* (light), is written
with gold letters placed on a blue background with a design
of fine red tendrils, framed with a golden-green ribbon. The
whole page is bordered by tendrils, which shimmer in blue,

green, brown-red, mauve, and golden colors. On closer observation, one discovers that the border has not been confined to floral decorations alone. In the lower left-hand corner there is a deer; on the right-hand side, immediately below the frame of the initial, a tiger crouches, and small human figures climb up and down the tendrils. It would be

129. PAGE FROM A FRENCH BIBLE
13th century. British Museum, Add. 11639.

a mistake to ascribe a symbolic meaning to all this; as so often in Jewish art, the design is merely the expansion of a playful imagination.

In this decorated page, we can already discern the second innovation in the European-Jewish manuscripts: a more faithful imitation of nature. Let us not forget that this naturalism may have existed in Jewish manuscript painting in Antiquity, corresponding to the motifs of the mosaics and murals, which we have already described, but if so it became

lost in the early Middle Ages. In the Egyptian Pentateuch of
the tenth century, the sacred Tent of Meeting and the ritual
implements were so conventionally treated, that they were
often barely recognizable. The later Middle Ages continued

130. THE STORY OF ADAM AND EVE
From the Sarajevo Haggadah.
Sarajevo, Library.

to depict these sacred implements in their Bibles and Bible
commentaries, but they gradually regained a more natural
shape. Our illustration for instance, taken from a French-
Hebrew Bible of the thirteenth century (Fig. 129), goes so
far as to add a human figure to the seven-branched candelabrum. It portrays the high priest pouring oil from a
flask into the containers. The figure of the priest in French-

Gothic style seems to float rather than stand and it lacks depth, giving it a flattened impression. That the figure of a human being has been included at all is a great innovation.

Generally speaking, human forms were gradually introduced into the illustrations. In Spain in the fourteenth century, a Haggadah was written, which was later called the Haggadah of Sarajevo because it was discovered in the library of that Yugoslavian town. In this document not only has that part of the story of Moses, which pertains to the Passover festival, been related pictorially, but the illustrator goes back as far as the Creation and the story of Adam and Eve. Our illustration (Fig. 130) shows Eve emerging from the rib of the sleeping Adam, then the Temptation, the expulsion from Paradise, on which both cast a longing backward glance, and finally Adam and Eve working, Eve with a spindle and Adam with a spade. These figures are also influenced by the French-Gothic style, which had penetrated into Spain. To this influence can be attributed the slim forms, the curved body of Eve with the spindle and the flat carpet-like background where we would expect a landscape, a subject which no illuminator up to this time had attempted to depict.

Conventional tendencies gradually disappear during the following centuries. The Jewish-Italian manuscript illuminations of the fifteenth century, executed under the influence of the Italian Renaissance, are the most progressive in this respect. To give one example, we show the Code of Jewish Law, called Arbo-o Turim (Four Rows) of Jacob ben Asher, copied in Mantua in 1436. Each of the four parts of this work begins with an elaborately decorated page. The third section from which our page is taken (Fig. 131), contains the marriage laws and is introduced by a picture of a wedding scene. The artist faithfully reproduces the rich cos-

tumes of the time, and tries to give depth to the scene and
create an impression of a crowd. Let us not forget the magnificent wreath, consisting of leaves and flowers with tiny
figures, similar to the Darmstadt Haggadah of approxi-
mately the same date.

In Germany, the tendency towards naturalism also dominated, but in a different way. Contrary to the Jewish-Italian
illumination which is aimed at giving the effect of a framed
picture, the Jewish-German artists preferred to sketch their
subjects nonchalantly around the margin. This is clearly
demonstrated in the so-called Second Nuremberg Haggadah
preserved in the German Museum of Nuremberg together
with another earlier Haggadah. Once again the story of
Moses is depicted but augmented with legendary scenes.
According to one of these legends, Moses in his youth was
Emperor of Ethiopia; he was taken prisoner there, but re-
leased with the help of the clever Sephora, whom he then
married out of gratitude. Our illustration refers to this story
(Fig. 132). At the side we see the prison tower, surrounded
by water, and Sephora approaching with food. At the bottom of the page, the artist with a few strokes of his pen has
drawn the wedding scene. The subject is the same as in the
Italian illustration just shown, but in this case, the figures
sprawl loosely around the edge, instead of being grouped as
in a painting. The art of the illustrator lies in his ability to
give life to the individual figures: the bride and bridegroom
under the prayer-shawl, the man with the large mug, and
the musician standing with legs spread, furnishing the music
for this festive occasion. As much as our Italian-Jewish
manuscripts are influenced by Italian paintings, so the
German-Jewish illuminations can be traced to the graphic
arts which came into fashion in the fifteenth century, but
flourished particularly in Germany.

131. MARRIAGE SCENE
From the Book Arbo-o Turim of Jacob ben Asher. Rome, Vatican Library.

In conclusion, let us say a few words concerning the illuminators themselves. Their work is so closely knit with the
art of the countries from which they come, that at first sight
one is inclined to believe they are not Jews at all. We must,

132. PAGE FROM THE
"SECOND NUREMBERG
HAGGADAH"
*Nuremberg, Germanisches
Museum*

however, bear in mind that in the Middle Ages, as in earlier
times, Jewish art was strongly dependent upon surrounding
influences, and even if the separation between Jews and non-
Jews gradually became more and more intensified and the
Jews were enclosed in ghetto walls, the seeds of art were able
to pass over them and descend on fertile soil. Therefore,
the similarity between Jewish manuscript painting and the
art of the respective countries is no argument against Jewish

craftsmanship. To this may be added that we know with certainty that a number of beautiful manuscripts were illuminated by Jewish artists. In the magnificent Mishneh Torah of the year 1296, today in the Academy of Sciences in Budapest, a man by the name of Nathan ben Simeon Halevi from Cologne gives thanks to the Lord, "that He has made him worthy to write, to complete and to furnish with painted pictures the book of Ibn Maimon" (Maimonides).[45] In the same way Joel ben Simeon, called Phoebus, mentions himself as the designer of a Haggadah now in the Jewish Theological Seminary in New York and in a second Haggadah at the present moment in the British Museum in London (Add. 14762).

Where names are not mentioned we may, from certain characteristics, infer that the artists were Jews. Let us turn once more to the Haggadah of Sarajevo (Fig. 130). The sequence of scenes moves definitely from right to left instead of from left to right, as in Christian art. The reason for this can only be that the artists followed the same method as is used in Hebrew writing, which, as is well known, goes from right to left. In some Haggadahs we find that words taken out of the context have given rise to illustrations placed in the margin. For instance, out of the sentence, "Go and learn what Laban, the Aramaean, designed to do to thy fathers," the artist has taken the words "go and learn" and has drawn a wandering youth holding a book, as we can see in the Cincinnati Haggadah. Surely only a Jew, perfectly familiar with the Hebrew text as well as with the preference for such literal interpretations, would explain these words with marginal drawings.

In Portugal in the thirteenth century, a writer by the name of Abraham ben Jehudi ben Chayyim wrote a Hebrew treatise on the preparation of colors, and particularly, of the gold needed in the decoration of miniature manuscripts. This proves that he was acquainted with this art himself and wanted to teach it to his coreligionists.

In this, as well as in the manuscripts before mentioned, the writer was at the same time the illuminator. He was an expert in Hebrew writing, which in itself he considered an art, and which, occasionally, he beautified with ornamented initials. From this point on the road was short to the illustration of whole pages of these manuscripts.

We only know of one instance on which two men, a writer and an artist, both Jews, worked on the same manuscript: the Spanish Kennicott Bible No. 1 in Oxford, which we mentioned previously. This is significant in a country saturated with art and artists as Spain was at that time, but it is an exception. Generally, the writer was his own illustrator and often his own bookbinder.

At the opening of this chapter, we discussed the limitations imposed on Jewish artists and craftsmen in Christian countries, particularly in the late Middle Ages. Under the pressure of persecution and exile, a great deal of the rich heritage of Hellenistic-Roman culture which the Jews brought to their new homes became lost. But the art of writing, illuminating and binding remained unmolested. This makes it possible and important to study these arts more deeply. It is the one branch of art in which Jewish creative genius was allowed full reign.

X

The Modern Era to the Emancipation

THE opinion is frequently voiced, and with a measure of truth, that the Middle Ages lasted, for the Jews, until the Emancipation of the nineteenth century, whereas the Christian peoples of Europe started a modern era in the fifteenth century with the Renaissance and Humanism. This argument is based on the fact that both in outward living conditions and in the direction of their cultural and spiritual lives, the Jews remained unchanged until the Emancipation. Forcibly separated from the surrounding Christian world, looked down upon as inferior beings, suffering innumerable restrictions, they were consoled in their isolation by their religious faith, the tradition of Bible and Talmud. The whole of their spiritual life centered around the interpretation of these sources. This mode of life lasted until they were freed from the ghettos and could take their part in the world about them.

It is well known that the Modern Era exercised a decisive influence on the art of the Christian countries. The greatness of Antiquity was rediscovered and brought with it a return to the use of classical subjects and forms, and a comprehension of the beauty of the human body.

Scientific eyes sought to penetrate the wonders of the world, and the scientific spirit was also applied to art. The human body was studied anatomically, and the laws of perspective, just discovered, made it possible to reproduce space with scientific exactitude.

The human being was looked upon as an individual personality and this recognition gave an immense impetus to the art of portrait painting. To paint and sculpture a man in detail showing his characteristics, his good and bad traits, became one of the chief aims of art.

This discovery of the individual also favored the development of the artist as a personality, and consequently brought forth a number of great artists such as Michelangelo, Dürer, El Greco, Rembrandt, Poussin, to mention only a few.

With all the possibilities at hand, it is interesting to note which the Jews utilized for their own artistic development. More concerned with ethics than with beauty they refused to accept the art of heathen Antiquity with its cult of the nude. A few Jews may have been interested in scientific research, but they made no use of it in art. They were willing to study the human body from the medical point of view, but in art they were unwilling to go beyond the limits set during the Middle Ages.

The trend toward the development of the individual personality may have produced great naturalists and philosophers among them but not artists. There was too little demand for art and the scope of activity in that field was too small to encourage the development of a great personality.

Is it therefore correct to say that modern Jewish art did not come into being before the period of Emancipation? Yes and no: yes, because Judaism as a whole clung to its mediaeval concepts; and no, because we must take care not to generalize too much. In some countries, the new ideas succeeded in infiltrating into the traditional beliefs and in influencing art to a certain extent.

Before discussing them, let us consider some events which affected not only the lives of the Jews, but their art as well. At the end of the fifteenth century, the Jews were expelled from the Iberian Peninsula. Even those converted to Christianity, but who had secretly clung to their former faith—the Marranos—were continually menaced with the horror of the Inquisition and emigrated in great numbers. As had happened before, these wanderings resulted in a scattering of Jewish culture over other lands. We hear of Spanish Jews who brought the art of lacemaking to Saloniki, and others who, as armorers, were of great service to the Turks, who in their turn were pressing forward towards other European countries. Spanish-Jewish majolica workers settled in Italy and founded their own factories in this craft. We will refer to them later on.

From the end of the sixteenth century on, many Marranos settled in southern France, Holland, a few north German cities, and later in England and the Scandinavian countries. The development of those who settled in Holland is of particular interest from our point of view, not only because they were received with great kindness and in time became wealthy citizens of that country, but also because Holland then already was a country rich in art. Consequently, the Jews were able to fulfil their cultural ambitions with the same freedom as they had been accustomed to in their former homelands.

As before, German Jews suffered from all the restrictions imposed upon them. There were however some, who as Court Jews, enjoyed a greater freedom and also acquired much wealth. These Jews were able to donate elaborate Torah curtains and ritual objects in precious metals to their synagogues, and these ornaments beautified the interiors of the ancient structures.

Despite occasional uprisings, the Jews in Eastern Europe during the sixteenth, seventeenth, and eighteenth centuries had lived in comparative security and ease. This fact combined with their ardent religious fervor resulted in the building of a great number of synagogues.

Generally speaking, the persecutions in Europe gradually became less frequent and less bloody than in the fanatical Middle Ages, and a more peaceful life was conducive to the furtherance of art.

All the works of art of this period followed the predominating styles of the Modern Era until the end of the eighteenth century: the harmonious Renaissance, the pompous baroque, the delicate rococo, and the severe classicism. The adoption of these styles cannot have been merely superficial. The spirit emanating from them left its mark on those who lived and prayed under their influence.

But the spirit of the times penetrated still deeper into Jewish artistic life. The Second Commandment, so strictly observed in the Middle Ages, with the exception of the illuminated manuscripts, no longer played such an important part, at least in Western Europe. All the same, figures carved in the round were still particularly subject to condemnation; they were too vivid a reminder of the ancient idols against which the Jews had fought so long and bitterly. Nevertheless, the Jews of Siena possessed a fountain crowned by a stone statue of Moses, referring to his miraculous deed in causing water to gush forth out of the rock. The sculptor of this statue, which still exists in Siena, although no longer on the same site, was the non-Jew Antonio Federigh, a well-known Sienese artist of the fifteenth century.[46] As late as the eighteenth century, some Polish Jews, who happened to be in Siena as emissaries, were shocked when they saw the statue, but were told that it had stood there for many centuries and no rabbi had ever voiced an objection to it.

In the synagogues of the Modern Era, the Jews generally confined themselves to floral and animal decorations, but a

133. THE TEN COMMANDMENTS
By Aaron de Chaves. London, Bevis Marks Synagogue.

few attempts were made to break through these reserves. Bevis Marks, the S'fardic synagogue in London, possesses a wooden tablet painted in 1675 by the Dutch-Jewish artist Aaron de Chaves,[47] showing the Ten Commandments flanked by the figures of Moses and Aaron (Fig. 133). One of the synagogues in Cracow, called "Hohe-Schul," erected in the late sixteenth century, has ten oil paintings with Biblical scenes. Such scenes are also found on a ceiling in the synagogue of Rohoncz (Rechnitz) in Austria. The Town Hall of Monheim in Germany, formerly a synagogue, has a ceiling with a few Biblical scenes in stucco dating from the time of its erection in 1715.

A similar tendency can be noticed in the applied arts. German Chanuko candelabra of the eighteenth century often have a statue on the top of the middle arm depicting Judas Maccabeus or Judith (Fig. 33). In Italy, the makers of

small Chanuko lamps were not afraid to depict mythological figures in the style of the Renaissance, such as tritons
who blow horns of shell, and a nude nymph in the center (Fig. 134). It goes without saying that these last mentioned pagan figures had no meaning for the Jews, but neither had they for the Christians. They both looked at them
from an aesthetic point of view, the only difference being
that the Christians probably knew more about the origin of
these figures than did the Jews.

In yet another way the Jews in a few countries adopted
the spirit of the Modern Era. They included portraiture
among the permissible subjects. We have already noticed to
what a degree the modern cult of the worth of the individual had increased the scope of this branch of art. An interesting passage dealing with this question can be found in a
book about Hebrew rites by the famous Italian rabbi Leone
da Modena (1571–1648). He emphasizes the Second Commandment and adds: "But in Italy, there are many who
have freed themselves of this restriction, and have paintings
and portraits in their homes, although they avoid sculpture,
both in relief and in the round" (*Riti Ebraici* Part I, Chapter 2, section 3). From this we learn that the practice of
portrait painting was widely spread among Jews, and only
busts and portrait reliefs were wanting.

As to the latter, an exception must be made for the art of
medallion portraiture, a favorite at the time of the Italian
Renaissance. A medal portraying the beautiful Grazia
Mendes, niece of the more famous Grazia Mendesia, has
come down to us. It is the work of a non-Jew, Pastorino,
noted medallist of the sixteenth century. A second Italian
medal of the sixteenth century shows on one side a man by
the name of Elia de Lattes and on the reverse, his mother.
Finally, a plaque exists, made in honor of Benjamin ben

134. ITALIAN CHANUKO LAMP
New York, Jewish Museum

Eliahu Beer, an Italian-Jewish physician, who lived about
1500. We show an illustration of this plaque (Fig. 135) because we assume that it was made by a Jew. It is not only the
elaborate Jewish inscription which points to this conclusion, but also the manner in which this inscription is applied. It fills up all the available space around the head. An
Italian artist would have carried out the design with greater
tranquillity. The head itself with its laurel wreath leans in
style towards the medals of the early Renaissance, but seems,
nevertheless, to be the likeness of the Jewish physician. This
opinion is upheld by the fact that the name Benjamin, divided into two parts, is inscribed on each side of the head.

There seems to have been no further use for medals in
the next centuries; at least we know of the existence of only
one medal before the time of the Emancipation. It was made
in 1735 for Eleazar ben Samuel Schmelka when he was
elected rabbi of the Ashk'nazic congregation in Amsterdam.

135. Medal of Benjamin ben
Eliahu Beer
Paris, Bibliothèque Nationale

The artist was also a Jew, who signed his Hebrew initials on the reverse.[48] It is interesting to note that the medal was fashioned in honor of an Ashk'nazic rabbi, because they had always regarded the art of portraiture with suspicion. Shortly before this another Dutch Ashk'nazic rabbi, Zebi Ashkenazi, had been portrayed at the request of an admirer when on a visit to London in 1714–15, but this had been done without the rabbi's knowledge. The artist observed his subject from another room, for the rabbi would never have agreed to sit for his portrait.[49]

The S'fardic Jews' reaction to portraiture was very different, at least in the Christian countries. It is very probable that they were already acquainted with this art in Spain and Portugal where their conversion to Christianity had made them fully aware of the surrounding customs. This tendency was increased in Holland where portrait painting had reached its peak. There they did not hesitate either to act as models for artists who were greatly attracted by their foreign, oriental appearance or to have their portraits painted for their own pleasure.

Later on, when the S'fardic Jews were allowed to settle in England again, they continued the art of portraiture. The following illustration (Fig. 136) is a mezzotint of David Nieto (1654–1728), chief rabbi of the S'fardic congregation in London. The canvas, now lost, was painted during his lifetime; the engraving was only made after his death. This happened frequently, and gives us an insight into the degree of veneration accorded to the rabbis. The rabbi was for the Jew what the prince was to the non-Jewish world. This is why the rabbi was the model for most of the earlier portraits.

The painter of the above-mentioned portrait was a Jew, his name—David Estevens—indicates his S'fardic origin. He had settled in Denmark but occasionally visited other countries. Judging from the intelligent, lifelike face of the rabbi and the skill with which the whole picture is composed, we can assume that Estevens was a very able artist. The mezzotint, however, was done by a Christian.

This happy collaboration of Jew and non-Jew leads us to ask what were the relations between Jews and Christians in art during this period. This question arose already in the Middle Ages. For more than a thousand years the Jews had taken part in manifold artistic activities which, during the Middle Ages, had gradually diminished owing to the numerous restrictions imposed upon them. The expulsion of the Jews from Spain, which took place at the beginning of the Modern Era, intensified their loss. They had reached the highest plane of craftsmanship there but their work was suddenly disrupted by the expulsion. A few artists

136. RABBI DAVID NIETO
Portrait by David Estevens.
Mezzotint by I. McArdell.

fled to other countries, but we are inclined to believe that
the majority remained as Christians in the Iberian peninsula and did not even leave it later as the Marranos did.
Their connections with Christian employers had always
been friendly, mainly because they were so much in demand. This friendship may have become intensified after
their conversion. The fact, that no architects, and at least in
the first generation, no illuminators, and no goldsmiths
were to be found in the new S'fardic communities, is further
proof that they never left Spain. As far as we know all the
synagogues erected by the S'fardim in Italy, Holland, England and North Germany were built by Christians.

In Germany, the Jews had already lost many of their artistic abilities in the Middle Ages, and they did not regain
them under the more favorable conditions of the Modern
Era. We come across excellent silverware such as rimonim,
breastplates, Torah pointers, Chanuko candelabra, even silver book covers in the seventeenth and eighteenth centuries,
but they are all made by Christian goldsmiths, as we can see
by their trade marks.

In Holland the Jews usually commissioned Christian artists to paint their portraits.[50] Rembrandt towers above the
rest in this field. The contact achieved between this great
artist and the Jews in Amsterdam was of great significance
for both. Rembrandt found the models for the scenes of his
beloved Old Testament among the Jews, who were so much
more expressive than the placid Dutch. The Jews on the
other hand discovered a portrait painter who was not only
a great artist, but who showed deep insight into the Jewish
character; who understood their wisdom and their melan-
cholic resignation. A number of masterpieces resulted from
this combination. Most of them are paintings, but there are
some prints as well, as for instance the etchings of the fa-

mous physician Ephraim Bueno and the rabbi and pub-
lisher Menasseh ben Israel. Menasseh could even boast that
Rembrandt illustrated one of his books.[51]

Just as we find Christian artists universally in demand by
the Jews, we occasionally come across Jewish artists who executed works of art for Christians. This happened particularly in Italy. In this country Jewish art had not attained to
the same splendor as it did in Spain during the Middle Ages,
but on the other hand, it never suffered an eclipse since
there was no expulsion from Italy as a whole.

In the seventeenth century a Jew by the name of Josua
Ostiglia lived in Florence. He painted landscapes in the
manner of Salvator Rosa, and often sold them to Italian
noblemen and even to other painters. Here is a Jew who
was not only accepted by Christians, but who also added
landscape painting to the more accustomed field of portraiture.

Usually a Jew only had access to Christian circles after his
conversion. Thus a Jewish armorer, Salomone da Sesso
(about 1465–1518) was baptized, acquired the name of Er-
cole de Fideli, and entered the service of the Duke of Fer-
rara. His swords, the scabbards of which he engraved or
etched with nude figures from mythological scenes, rank
among the best of this period. One of them, made for the
bloodthirsty Cesare Borgia, and today in private hands, has
been named "Queen of Swords." The Musée des Invalides
in Paris, the South Kensington Museum in London, and the
Zeughaus in Berlin own further examples of his skilled
craftsmanship.

In Venice in the second half of the seventeenth century,
there lived a bronze caster—Guiseppe Levi di Verona. The
name denotes his Jewish origin, but the artist himself was
probably no longer a Jew. In the Venetian church S. Giorgio

Maggiore, there is a statue of a Christian saint, John the
Baptist, designed by Angelo de Rossi, cast by Guiseppe Levi.
Guiseppe Levi, it appears, was not a creative artist, but he
was very much in demand for the reproduction of the works
of contemporary artists as well as the masterpieces of earlier
centuries.

A contemporary of Guiseppe Levi was the Venetian
Pietro Liberi (1614–1687), the son of a Jew who painted
altar pictures and church frescos. His art is an echo of the
classic art of Titian, Veronese, Tintoretto and Correggio.
The work of Francesco Ruschi, who lived in Venice at the
same time and was the son of a converted Jewish physician,
is more progressive. He strove for dramatic light effects,
derived from Caravaggio, and a decorative use of space in
the manner of Pietro da Cortona. He became one of the
forerunners of the style of decoration which distinguishes
Venetian painting at the turn of the eighteenth century.
Guiseppe Fiocco, in his book, *Venetian Painting of the Sei-
cento and Settecento,* written as late as 1929, praises Ruschi
in the following words: "He breathed new life into all the
younger generation."

In England, in the seventeenth century, Samuel Cooper
gained renown. He was an excellent painter of portrait miniatures. He has been taken for a Jew because his lesser
known brother Alexander, also a miniature painter, is recorded in 1647 in a list of persons living at that time in
Stockholm as "Abraham Alexander Cooper, the Jew, portrait painter." It is quite possible, however, that Alexander
became a Jew in his early years and added Abraham to his
name, in which case we have no reason to assume that Samuel was a Jew.

The well-known English painter John Zoffany (1722/23–
1810) was the son of a Jew called Zaufely, who was a cabinet

137. CAPTAIN JAMES COOK, SIR JOHN BANKS, AND JOHN ZOFFANY
DISCUSSING COOK'S SECOND EXPEDITION
By John Zoffany. England, private possession.

maker from Prague and became the court architect of the
Prince of Thurn and Taxis in Regensburg. John Zoffany
reached England about the year 1761 after an adventurous
youth and acquired a great reputation as a painter of famous
actors and actresses. His fresh, natural style, probably influenced by Hogarth, contrasts favorably with the somewhat
affected manner of the majority of English portrait painters
of that time. A self-portrait (Fig. 137) shows the artist leaning against the pedestal of a statue, listening to the words of
the renowned Captain James Cook, who sets forth his plans
for one of his expeditions of discovery. Zoffany was to go
along in the capacity of designer, but in the end he did not
go with the others. The picture breathes all the freshness
and amiability of his style without being sentimental.

Besides this occasional participation of Jewish or Jewish born artists in the Christian world, there were two kinds of crafts in which the Jews excelled and were therefore in great demand.

One of these crafts was the art of embroidery, and there are several examples to show how popular were the Jewish craftsmen. Salomo Isaac was embroiderer at the court of Prussia about 1700. A Christian writer in the early eighteenth century wrote of the Episcopal court in Fulda, "a Bohemian Jew has been living here for twelve years as artistic gold embroiderer for missal robes and other clerical vestments." [52] In Bamberg, Germany, in 1738, an elaborately embroidered cover was executed by Gerson Mayer for the tomb of Emperor Heinrich and his wife Kunigunde in the cathedral of Bamberg. In Mainz we come across a Jew who was elevated to the rank of court embroiderer in 1725 but only after he had been converted. We know none other than his Christian names: Johann Sebastian Stein. All this shows that the old textile art, going back as far as Biblical times, still flourished in the Modern Era.

The second handiwork, which was very much in demand by the Christians, was the art of stone cutting and metal engraving for cameos, seals, coins and medals. This craft can also be traced to its oriental origin and shows once again the persistence with which some Jewish arts continued through the ages.

To mention a few examples: in the eighteenth century a Jew, Samuel Judin (1730 to after 1800), was a coin minter and medallist at the Russian court. He made the silver ruble for Peter III and also a number of medals in memory of important events of the time. Aaron Jacobson from Hamburg in 1750 became the royal engraver at the Danish court. Abraham Aaron (about 1744–1824) was engaged at the court of the tolerant Duke of Mecklenburg as a seal engraver. When this artist moved to Stockholm because of the small salary which he received in Germany, the government of Schwerin submitted a petition to the duke in which was written: "Thus much can be said, that Your Highness has lost an artist without an equal in Lower Saxony, for orders used to come to him from Berlin, Hanover, Hamburg and Lübeck. Since his departure to Sweden, there is no one in Mecklenburg with the skill to cut a graceful coat-of-arms in stone, let alone engrave a clean die for a coin." As a result of this petition, the artist was brought back to Mecklenburg. A number of his medals have been preserved. They are works in classical style, and their execution shows good taste and precise finish. Some Jews practiced this craft with equal success at the courts of France, Belgium, Italy, and Austria.

We have a particularly full account of two such seal engravers at the Prussian court, because most of their work has been preserved. They were father and son: Jacob Abraham (1723–1800) and Abraham Abramson (1754–1811). The elder was commissioned by Frederick the Great to perpetuate his successes on the battle-field by medals. It is interesting to note that an inscription on one of the medals contains the words "Novus incipit ordo"—"a new order is beginning," which reminds us of the "new order" of a modern would-be conqueror, one who, however, would not have allowed such a task to be executed by a Jew. Jacob Abraham even designed a new Prussian eagle for the "thaler" pieces which the king issued. His work was inspired by the picturesque style of the late baroque period.

His son, on the contrary, adopted the clear-cut classical lines of the later eighteenth century. Besides executing his official duties, the latter, together with his father, issued a series of medals in honor of the great philosophers and poets

138. MEDAL OF DANIEL
ITZIG
By Abraham Abramson

of Germany at that time: Kant, Lessing, Schiller and so forth. With great pride he has included Moses Mendelssohn in his series. One of his medals (Fig. 138) portrays with particular charm the well-known Jewish court banker and leader of the Jews in Prussia, Daniel Itzig. The obverse shows the sharp profile of the seventy-year-old banker, softened by the cap and folds of his cape. The bust is placed in the circle with a fine assurance and framed by a few, clear-cut letters. The figure on the reverse is an allusion to his chief virtue, Charity, and depicts a graceful woman protecting a nude boy with her gown and at the same time offering him fruit out of a basket. The medal shows the noble style of the period. It is easy to understand that Abramson was considered one of the best medallists of his time.

From the above we see that there was some relationship between Jews and Christians in the field of art. Let us turn to specifically Jewish themes and see how they were treated in this Modern Era.

The synagogues continued to be the center of all Jewish activity. Their ground plan usually conformed to the old tradition of a plain rectangular, longitudinal form. Only one change can be observed. Whereas the entrance in mediaeval times was placed unobtrusively at the side of the synagogue, it is now found in the west wall, giving to this side the appearance of a facade. As an example we show the S'fardic synagogue in The Hague, Holland, erected in 1726

(Fig. 139). Here we not only see the portal, but also further elaboration of the facade by a gable resting on two tall pilasters.[53]

By placing the entrance in the west wall, the eye of the person entering is immediately drawn to the Torah shrine which faces him. We have followed the growth of the shrine from its modest beginnings in Antiquity to its increased importance in the late Middle Ages, and this trend continued during the following centuries. Once again we refer to the Torah shrine from the *Scuola Italiana* in Padua, which we have mentioned before (Fig. 9). The metal doors of the

139. S'FARDIC SYNAGOGUE
In The Hague, Holland

shrine are elaborately ornamented, but the main attraction lies in the flanking columns, supporting a lively and richly designed entablature and gable in the baroque style.

Without a doubt such Torah shrines were influenced by contemporary church altars. The latter also had developed into towering structures, framing immense paintings which in the synagogues were replaced by the doors of the shrine.

The bimo did not always follow this elaborate pattern. In the Berlin synagogue it is purposely kept very low so as

140. THE PORTUGUESE SYNAGOGUE OF AMSTERDAM, HOLLAND
Engraving by B. Picart

not to interfere with the view of the ornate Torah shrine.
Now and again, however, the Jews were inclined to lend
the same splendor to the bimo as to the Torah shrine. In
the synagogue of Padua to which we have just referred, a
particularly large and elaborate bimo faces the Torah
shrine (Fig. 12). To give it the necessary height, a steep
flight of steps on either side, curved according to the baroque style, leads to the platform, and a lofty structure
above it forms a canopy.

Most synagogues are comprised of nothing more than a
single hall, but a few divide the interior into aisles. We have
come across such partitions already in the Middle Ages. At
that time, as we have seen in the synagogues of Worms,

141. Scuola Spagnola at Venice

Prague and Cracow (Figs. 108, 111, 112), the hall was divided into two aisles or, as in the synagogue of Toledo (Fig. 105) into five aisles. The partition into three aisles had been avoided intentionally for fear of resembling the churches too closely. Apparently, in the Modern Era, these interpretations were not given much consideration and the Jews constructed their synagogues like churches if they so desired.

The most imposing example of a synagogue with three aisles is found in the S'fardic house of worship in Amsterdam, which was constructed in 1675 by the Dutch architect Elias Bowmann, the Elder (Fig. 140). Here the middle nave is twice as broad as the aisles, and high columns support the barrel vaultings. The broad and imposing Torah shrine, characteristic of S'fardic synagogues, adds to the grandeur of the interior.

In this synagogue still another feature can be observed
which, besides its practical purpose, contributed to its embellishment: it is the women's galleries, barely seen in our
engraving because the high columns hide them from view.
We have already found them in the synagogues of Antiquity. From there they were taken over by the S'fardic Jews
in Spain although there they didn't protrude but receded
behind the walls. The exiled S'fardim had brought that
custom with them. The *Scuola Spagnola* in Venice, erected
in 1584, and more richly decorated in 1635, is a fine example
of such a gallery (Fig. 141). The rectangular interior en-
closes an oval-shaped balcony giving an impression of elegance, which is heightened by the arched windows, the
elaborate Torah shrine, beautiful chandeliers, and the ornamented ceiling. Even more worldly is the eighteenth century
interior of the synagogue of Leghorn with its two balconies
which suggest a theater rather than a synagogue.

The Ashk'nazic Jews with few exceptions clung to their
old habit of placing the women in rooms outside the main
hall, into which they could look through arched openings
in the wall. These adjoining rooms were sometimes constructed with two stories, as in the synagogue in Fürth,
Germany and in the Pinkas Synagogue in Prague, both
erected in the early seventeenth century. The latter was
the work of a Jew—Judah Goldschmied de Herz (d. 1625).

The synagogue in Frankfort-on-the-Main, built in 1711
and pulled down in the nineteenth century, even has a
three-storied room for the women. Our illustration taken
from an old print (Fig. 142) clearly shows the arched openings in the wall. Strange to say, this synagogue was built in
Gothic style, instead of in the baroque style which was
prevalent at the time of its construction in the beginning
of the eighteenth century. The Gothic style was also used

by the well-known architect Sonnin, when he built the Ashk'nazic synagogue in Altona, Germany, in 1682.[54] Such a return to styles of the past occur only occasionally. In general, the synagogues adhere to contemporary styles.

In Eastern Europe the synagogue construction embarked on a course of its own. We have already mentioned that the Jews of Poland, in spite of occasional persecutions, found a certain economic security there. A particularly active religious life went hand in hand with this. We need only state

142. SYNAGOGUE AT
FRANKFORT-ON-THE-MAIN
Demolished in 1854

the names of a few outstanding rabbis, such as Moses Isserles in Cracow; Solomon Luria in Lublin; Elijah ben Solomon in Vilna, to show that Talmudic research attained a new peak in this part of Europe. The erection of many new

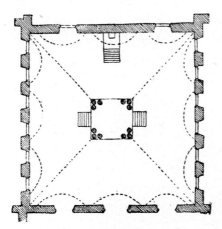

143. MAHARSHAL SYNAGOGUE
Lublin, Poland. Ground plan.

synagogues resulted from this religious activity, first in large cities such as Vilna, Cracow, Lemberg, Lublin, Brest-Litowsk, and Przemysl and later on in the smaller towns and villages.

The architects of these synagogues were probably at first non-Jews. Some were Italians, who played an important part in Polish architecture since the Renaissance and therefore were occasionally employed by Jews as well.

The Italian Renaissance in its churches greatly favored the central structure with its walls equally distant from the center, its resulting regularity and the possibility of crowning such constructions with magnificent domes.

The Jews, delighted in this style because it made it possible for them to express freely their religious feelings. In the preceding chapter we have mentioned that the Ashk'-nazic Jews placed the bimo in the middle of their synagogues; thus giving a visual center to the reading of the Torah. The importance of this was further stressed by the central structure plan. This can be clearly seen in our illustration (Fig. 143) depicting the ground plan of the Maharshal synagogue in Lublin, erected in 1567. It is a square, and this simple form of central structure is the one most frequently used among the Jews. The bimo is in the center. Three columns at each corner support a kind of arched canopy over the bimo which carries the vaulting of the whole synagogue (Fig. 144). In this way the interior from the floor to the ceiling forms *one* piece, centering in the bimo itself, thus giving it tremendous weight. The whole spiritual direction of the synagogue is to be found in this type of construction and we must add that to a certain degree, the solution is an original one, because churches never made the same use of the center structure, preferring to leave the center free by placing the altar on the east wall.

The exterior of these Polish stone synagogues is generally very unassuming. In the synagogue of Zolkiev, which we have chosen as an example (Fig. 145), the edifice is char-

144. MAHARSHAL SYNAGOGUE
Lublin, Poland. Interior.

acterized by large windows and by buttresses which carry the weight of the interior vaultings. Furthermore this synagogue possesses a superstructure which adds to its appearance, but also served a practical purpose. Ever since the uprising of the Cossacks and their Tartar allies—an uprising not only directed against the Jews, but mainly against the Poles—the necessity had arisen for protection from similar invasions, and the Jews were obliged to assist in the defense of the country. Consequently the walls of these superstructures were erected as forts, from which the Jews themselves

145. Fortress-Synagogue at Zolkiev

could help to defend the city. These are called "fortress-synagogues" corresponding to the "fortress-churches" which came into existence simultaneously.

Small communities, which were unable to afford the luxury of stone synagogues, had to content themselves with buildings of wood, which were easily erected on account of the abundant forests in the East European countries. Such wooden synagogues needed no fortifications. In the event of an approaching hostile force, they could be destroyed by fire, so as not to afford a foothold for the enemy.

The synagogues constructed of wood have one point in common with the stone synagogues: they are also central structures and the bimo is also placed in the middle or, as in the synagogue of Gwozdziecz erected about 1650 (Fig. 146), not far from the middle. The ceilings were likewise

vaulted, but as wood is so much lighter than stone, it was
not necessary to support them with columns. Consequently
the bimo had no part in the architectural construction. But
vaultings of wood invited elaboration. Thus in the above-
mentioned synagogue, the square walls become octagonal as

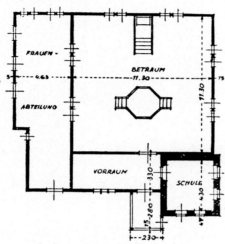

146. SYNAGOGUE AT GWOZDZIECZ
Ground plan

they curve upwards, and the illustration (Fig. 147) shows
clearly how the corners are bridged. These eight penden-
tives do not close at the top, but form another square which
in its turn supports new curved vaultings surmounted by a
dome (Fig. 148). This is all very intricate but it adds to the
aesthetic pleasure of the building. The decorative effect was
heightened by the paintings of tendrils, animals, and Hebrew verses which covered all the available space on the
walls as well as on the ceilings.

The bimo and Torah shrine were included in this elaborate ornamentation. The synagogue in Gwozdziecz possesses
a particularly fine example of such a bimo (Fig. 149). An

147. GWOZDZIECZ SYNAGOGUE
Part of the vaulting

148. Gwozdziecz Synagogue
Center vaulting showing dome

octagonal balustrade frames the platform and supports finely shaped columns, upon which a vaulted cover of pierced woodwork rests. The lantern crowning the canopy seems to float rather than to be carried by the lightly swung fillets.

The Torah shrine in the stone synagogue in Selwa may serve as an example of Polish Torah shrines of the pompous baroque period (Fig. 150). The entrance to the stairway suggests a portal. The Ark itself is artistically enlarged by a superstructure and by wings at the sides, which consist of a labyrinth of animals and tendrils in pierced work. The playful tendency already observed in Jewish art found an outlet in these intricacies.

We have already mentioned that the synagogues of the Modern Era generally adhered to their simple rectangular outline. In this respect the Polish wooden synagogues form an exception. Elaborate exteriors go hand in hand with the rich interiors. We refer once again to the ground plan of the synagogue of Gwozdziecz (Fig. 146). It can be distinctly seen that various other rooms adjoin the square main hall; a long, narrow one for the women, a small anteroom and a larger schoolroom. Western synagogues have similar rooms, but they are only loosely connected with the main hall and play no part in the architectural beauty of the exterior as a whole. In Poland, on the other hand, they are woven into the plan of construction. A sloping roof gives them an upward-striving impression which is accentuated by an intermediate roof, terminating in a third one. The whole edifice thus has an exotic appearance which is very attractive (Fig. 151).

In another Polish synagogue in Wolpia (Fig. 152) the low anteroom has a separate roof. The rooms to the left and right of it are constructed in the manner of turrets, decorated with balustrades, all three forming a kind of upbeat to the actual synagogue, the scaled roof of which corresponds to theirs.

These synagogues of wood, original as they seem to be on first observation, are not entirely free from outside influence. We see the steplike roofs on the wooden churches of

149. BIMO OF GWOZDZIECZ
SYNAGOGUE

these East European countries as well,[55] and the balconies are to be found in Polish manor houses. This appropriation of the native styles in the construction of these synagogues does not lessen their artistic value, which is measured by the originality with which all these ideas are combined. The finished work grows out of the imagination of the builder.

The importance of these synagogues is increased by the fact that they were mostly built by Jews. They differ in this from the synagogues of Western Europe which, as we have seen, were usually constructed by non-Jews. The names of some Jewish architects have come down to us. Simcha ben Salomo Weiss at about the end of the seventeenth century built the beautiful synagogue in Nasielsk of which we have nothing more today than a drawing. The synagogue in Wolpia, which we have just shown, resembles it so much, that we can without a doubt, ascribe it to the same architect. Hillel Benjamin of Lasko in Poland built the synagogue of Lutomiersk in the second half of the eighteenth century. By this time, the elaborate baroque style of the older synagogues had given way to a simpler type, corresponding to the newly developed classicism.

In order to erect synagogues of wood it was not necessary to be conversant with all the details and intricacies of architecture. There could be no fear of these edifices collapsing. The builders were probably carpenters possessed of special architectural skill, and a certain aesthetic imagination.

The carvers of the bimos and Torah shrines were also Jews. We know that a wood-carver by the name of Beer ben Israel who lived in the early eighteenth century made the magnificent Ark of the Law in the synagogue of Uzlany, and there must surely have been others.

The artists who painted the interior of the synagogues so elaborately and lavishly were Jews as well. Occasionally they signed their murals and the names found are always those of Jews.

One of these Polish painters, Eliezer Sussmann, wandered as far as Germany early in the eighteenth century and decorated the synagogues of Bechhofen, Horb, Hall-Unterlimburg, Kirchheim, small towns in Franken in southern

150. Torah Shrine in the Synagogue of Selwa

151. Exterior of Gwozdziecz Synagogue

Germany. The exterior of these synagogues is extremely plain—the one in Bechhofen is rightly called the "barn synagogue." Consequently, one is all the more astonished to find in the interior a barrel vault richly painted and walls decorated with Hebrew letters, vases, tendrils, city views, and so forth. In their love of bright colors and the urge to fill up every available corner and space, also in their charm, all these Jewish paintings remind one of peasant art. Before the Nazi rule, German museums were very eager to acquire such interior decorations, which by now have most likely disappeared.

To these architects, wood-carvers, wall painters, we must add the Polish coppersmiths, who fashioned a great number of ritual objects of equal artistry. They made the many-branched hanging lamps in the synagogues as the one in Figure 112. They made the star-shaped Sabbath lamps (Fig. 21) and the Sabbath candelabrum (Fig. 22) which is known by the name of "Lamp of Cracow," the old Polish

152. SYNAGOGUE AT WOLPIA, NEAR BYALISTOCK

capital. They also made the small metal Chanuko lamps of which we have given an example (Fig. 32). These objects were sometimes presented to a synagogue, the gift of the pious artist, as was that of the poor brassmaker Baruch, who lived in Pohrebyszcze in the early eighteenth century. He gathered scrap brass for many years and was at length able to present the synagogue with an eight-armed Chanuko candelabrum of great richness.[56]

The small and charming silver Chanuko lamps, a few of which are to be found in Jewish museums in America, are likewise of Polish origin. Patiently and lovingly the fine silver wires are spun into delicate filigree work. Our example (Fig. 153), probably early eighteenth century, owes its particular charm to the little doors flanked by columns surmounted by griffins, and to the crown, on the top of which a crowing cock is perched. A rooster as the messenger of the approaching dawn is an appropriate motif for a lamp.

We have thus come to the subject of ritual accessories,

and it may be useful to say a few more words about their development and the artists who made them in the Modern Era in Eastern and Western Europe.

As the bimo and Torah shrine increased in splendor, so did the Torah curtains. The embroiderer of the curtain in Figure 10 was a German Jew, Jacob Koppel Gans, living in Bavaria in the eighteenth century. Another example of his art escaped the plundering and incendiarism of the Nazis and is now in the Jewish Museum of New York.[57]

Elkone Naumburg, also of Bavaria and the same century, was still more famous. The Augsburg synagogue contained two of his works and in Hildesheim there was a third example. All three pieces showed the same motifs: the spiral columns and the top-piece embroidered with the utensils of the Tent of Meeting. In all probability the lost curtain in the Hambro synagogue in London was also a product of his art. The Ashk'nazic Jews of Amsterdam also ordered one of his curtains but refused it because it was too elaborate. Such display was acceptable to the splendor-loving Bavarian but offensive to the sober Calvinistic Dutch.

In 1736 an Italian Jewess, Magdalena Bassan, embroidered the fanciful Torah curtain which hung formerly in Padua, and is today in the Jewish Museum in New York.[58] We can assume that all these textile works were carried out by Jews, as well as the colorfully embroidered prayer-shawls of the same period, which were illustrated before (Fig. 17). Since Jewish embroiderers were employed by non-Jews, why should it not be taken for granted that they were also able to work for their fellow Jews? The name "Goldsticker" (gold embroiderer) is not an uncommon family name among Ashk'nazic Jews, and indicates that the embroiderers were particularly fond of using gold and silver threads for their needlework to heighten its splendor.

153. SILVER CHANUKO LAMP
Poland, 18th century. Cincinnati, Hebrew Union College.

Needless to say, the beautiful Torah mantles of this period were also made by Jews. The illustration, Fig. 5, shows a specimen, the work of an English embroiderer of the early eighteenth century. Such richness of ornamentation was only achieved during the baroque period.

The fancifully designed silver rimonim on this Torah Scroll are also a product of the baroque period. How much richer they are compared to the simple stopper-like caps of the Middle Ages of which there is unfortunately no original but only a painting in an illuminated manuscript (Fig. 114). The English rimonim are the work of a Jewish goldsmith, Abraham Lopez de Oliveira by name.

The demand for these metal ornamentations had increased since the beginning of the Modern Era. In the Middle Ages the only metal decorations on the Torah were the rimonim. The Torah shields and pointers were added in the following centuries. The Torah shield in Amsterdam, the oldest preserved example, dates from 1607, and is fashioned in Renaissance style. It is still comparatively simple with its

Fellmann Photo Service

154. TORAH SHIELD
Germany, about 1700.
New York, Jewish Museum.

clearly outlined pattern in which every detail is easily discernible (Fig. 7). The fullness of the design in the baroque shield made around 1700 by a German silversmith (Fig. 154) obliterates the clarity and gives it a heavy, restless appearance.

The Chanuko lamp of the Middle Ages, presumably lit only in the home, was modest in size and ornamentation (Fig. 118). Although this triangular form was still retained in the Modern Era, it was, nevertheless, executed far more elaborately. In our example of a Renaissance lamp (Fig.

134) we can still clearly see the single figures and decorative motifs, whereas in the baroque lamp (Fig. 153) the intricate design sacrifices all details in favor of the whole.

Besides all these lamps of the "bench-type" the vertical Chanuko candelabrum makes its appearance from the time

155. CHANUKO CANDLESTICK
Italy, 15th century. Padua, Synagogue.

of the Renaissance on, as well for the home as for the synagogue. The earliest known example (Fig. 155) probably dating from the fifteenth century, was not found in Italy by mere chance. We know that there is a seven-branched candelabrum on the arch of Titus in Rome (Fig. 64). The rediscovery of Antiquity through the Renaissance may have furthered the closer study of this arch and the Italian Jews may thereby have been attracted anew to the beauty of the candelabrum. On the other hand, as the Talmud forbade the direct imitation of the seven-branched candelabrum, a way out was found by transforming it into an eight- or even nine-branched Chanuko lamp as in the illustration. The artist has skilfully contrived to vary the shape of the lamp by graduating the height of the sockets.

The baroque period strove to outdo the well-balanced harmony of these simple, clear lines. As can be seen by the illustration (Fig. 33), a baroque lamp, made in Germany about 1710 stands in great contrast to the Renaissance style. The simplicity has given place to a grouping of a great many figures, beginning with enameled scenes on the base, continuing with the rampant lion and terminating in a small statue of Judith, which stands above the horizontal line of the oil containers.

In the Middle Ages, engraved pewter plates were used for the Seder service. They were still in use in later centuries but with far richer decorations (Fig. 39). In the Modern Era a second type was introduced in Italy: Seder plates of majolica. S'fardic Jews brought this craft from Spain. This is proved by the fact that many of these plates were signed with the name of Azulai, a family of S'fardic origin. These plates were made in Padua, Mantua, Faenza, Urbino, and Pesaro, the earliest in the sixteenth century, the latest in the eighteenth or even nineteenth century, and were subject to very little change. The center of the plate is inscribed with blessings and the rim is filled with floral motifs, figures and Biblical scenes in bright colors. In this example (Fig. 156), the standing figures of Moses, Aaron, David, and Solomon can be recognized. The Biblical scenes depict Joseph revealing himself to his brothers, and opposite under the inscription, the Israelites partaking of the first Passover bread in Egypt, "with your loins girded, your shoes on your feet, and

156. ITALIAN SEDER PLATE
1614, Fayence. New York, Jewish Museum.

your staff in your hand," as we read in Exodus (12:11).

In Italy, too, for the first time in the Modern Era, we come across the quaint bridal rings surmounted by small houses. The ring which we have already shown (Fig. 57) was probably made by a Jewish-Venetian goldsmith of the sixteenth century. Venice was full of goldsmiths at that time, and the Jews, who suffered no restrictions in this respect, were no doubt able to fill their own needs.

We have seen that the rich funereal art of late Antiquity became lost during the Middle Ages. Nothing had remained

157. TOMBSTONE OF DAVID DA ROCHA
(DIED 1708)
*S'fardic Cemetery in Ouderkerk
near Amsterdam*

but the plain tombstone which only acquired a slightly more elaborate appearance in the later Middle Ages (Fig. 119). The Modern Era changed this habit for the Christians, who wanted to alleviate the fear of death by beautifying the graves. The Jews followed them in this. Here and there in Italy, the Jews erected large tombs against walls, the inscription flanked by columns supporting a semicircular arch.[59] In the S'fardic cemeteries in Amsterdam, Hamburg, and Altona, from the middle of the seventeenth century on, the flat tombstones were decorated with ornaments, symbols and even Biblical scenes. The Dutch cemetery in Ouderkerk near Amsterdam has an abundance of such stones. The graveyard attracted non-Jews as well. Jacob Ruisdael, the well-known Dutch landscape painter, made it the subject of several of his works.

The Biblical scenes on these tombstones allude to the names of the deceased person. The Jewish composer, David da Rocha (d. 1708), was honored by a figure of his great

158. Tombstone of Samuel Teixeira
(died 1717)
*S'fardic Cemetery in Ouderkerk
near Amsterdam*

musical ancestor King David
playing the harp (Fig. 157).
The pathos with which the
king is striking the chords of
his instrument gives this relief
a particular attraction. On the
tombstone of Rachel Teixeira
who died in childbirth, the Biblical scene of Rachel on her
death-bed mourned by her family has been carved. The memory of her husband Samuel,
who died in 1717, is perpetuated by a scene depicting the
infant Samuel, who was called
at night by the Lord in the
Temple of Shiloh (Fig. 158).
The representation of God by
a human figure done as late as
1717, when the Marranos had
long since returned to Judaism, is certainly strange. Obvi-
ously this stone was made by a Christian, to whom the representation of God was a natural thing. It is nonetheless
astonishing that the Jews accepted it. This indicates once
again a most liberal interpretation of the Second Commandment in contrast to the severity exercised in the Middle
Ages.

In Ashk'nazic cemeteries the upright tombstones were

richly decorated as well. In the cemetery of Prague, a number of them are still visible. The reproduction of figures of human beings was strictly avoided here as well as in other Ashk'nazic cemeteries, but the ornamental decoration became all the more important. The illustrations of the cemetery of Tarnopol (Fig. 63) can be examined once more in order to see the elaborate motifs and designs carved above the inscriptions. A single tombstone from the cemetery in Czernowitz (Cernauti) in Roumania, erected in 1791, demonstrates this in

159. TOMBSTONE OF ISRAEL BEN ZWI
(DIED 1791)

Czernowitz (Cernauti), Jewish Cemetery

greater detail (Fig. 159). The inscription itself is bordered by two columns and the upper half of the stone is filled with boldly swung tendrils. A bunch of stone grapes hangs from the tendrils over the inscription and alludes to the name of the deceased, Israel ben Zwi. We are reminded of the golden grapes in the Temple of Herod which symbolize the people of Israel. In this way, the motifs of the Ashk'nazic tombstones also allude to names, but only in symbolical forms.

We attributed the tombstone of Samuel Teixeira to a Christian sculptor and may assume that others were also executed by Christian artists. On the other hand, the Ashk'-nazic stones were no doubt made by Jews. A few names have come down to us, but most of the artists preferred to remain anonymous. They were mostly simple stone masons, some of whom were also grave diggers,[60] but they had a decided feeling for the vigor and beauty of ornamental motifs.

In conclusion we must ask what became of the graphic arts, which had flourished so highly in the Middle Ages in the form of illuminated manuscripts? In Europe printed books took the place of handwritten manuscripts in the latter half of the fifteenth century and these were no longer decorated by hand, but with woodcuts or engravings, which could be reproduced innumerable times.

Did this involve the disappearance of the Jewish scribe and consequently of the Jewish illuminator who was one and the same person? The scribe retained his profession to a certain extent. He was still required to write out the Torah Scrolls, which were not allowed to be printed and he wrote the Hebrew words in the parchments of the m'zuzo and the phylacteries as well.

Attempts were made to print the Esther story, read at the feast of Purim, but the rabbis did not approve of this, and only consented to the printing of the ornamentation which framed it. In general however, it was still the scribe who wrote and illuminated every scroll. He was able to frame the columns with an abstract design when the owner adhered strongly to the restrictions imposed by tradition, but added human figures when it was commissioned by a less Orthodox client. It is no coincidence that we have no decorated Esther scrolls of the Middle Ages, and that they only came into use from the sixteenth century on.[61] The illuminators had to find new fields to work in as they were no longer required to write books by hand owing to the invention of printing.

The scribe also retained the custom of writing marriage contracts. Though there were some decorated k'subos in the Middle Ages, they only came into general use in the

Modern Era. From now on we find woodcut or engraved
frames, similar to the Esther scrolls; the scribe only had to
write the individual text. But in general, the scribe preferred to ornament every contract himself, and most likely
the bridal couple attached greater value to a hand-painted
k'subo with its personal touch. The most beautiful examples
appeared in Italy (Fig. 59). The artist avoided figures of
human beings and was satisfied with intricate lines, and
floral motifs interwoven with Hebrew letters. Other k'subo
writers did not hesitate to make use of human figures in
their designs alluding to the name of the bridegroom. The
love for portrait painting, shared by the Italian and S'fardic
Jews, led them sometimes to add portraits of the bridal
couple, at least until Rabbi Abraham Hiyya de Boton, who
lived in Saloniki, forbade this towards the end of the sixteenth century.

To all these activities of the scribe, it may be added that
printed Hebrew books did not entirely supersede the hand-
written ones. The art of printing did not come into general
use in the Orient until the nineteenth century and the
Persian Jews, for instance, continued in the old art of writing and illuminating their books.[62] In Europe they often
clung to the handwritten and hand-painted Haggadahs,
probably because their coloring made them more attractive
for a family volume used by children. In Ashk'nazic countries during the eighteenth century, we come across scribes
in Germany, Poland, and Moravia, who roamed from place
to place writing and ornamenting Haggadahs. One of the
best was Moses Juda, called Loeb, from Trebitsch in Moravia, who lived in the early eighteenth century. The Mohel
book containing the ritual of the circumcision (Fig. 53) is
an example of his skill. These Mohel books also were preferably executed by hand. The grace and delicacy of this page

is found again in the Seder scene taken from a Haggadah, written and painted by the same artist (Fig. 160). It was made in 1723 for Lazarus van Geldern, the great-grand-

160. SEDER MEAL
From the Haggadah van Geldern.
Written in 1723 by Moses Juda Loeb.

father of Heinrich Heine. The head of the family, clothed in the traditional white garment, is seated at the table, opposite to his wife in a black skirt and red jacket. Between them we see two guests, according to the custom of inviting strangers to participate on this festive occasion.

The door is open in expectation of the arrival of Elijah, the forerunner of the Messiah. It seems as if spring is likewise invited, judging by the flowers in the window and the branches with leaves seen through the door.[63]

This illustration gives us an enlightening insight into the house of a wealthy Jew of this time. It is only natural that the owner of such a cultivated home should use equally beautiful Haggadahs.

All we have said about the art of illuminating in the Modern Era must not lead us to believe that the Jews looked upon the new art of printing with indifference or animosity. Their love of books was far too great to prevent them from welcoming an innovation which would enable people of lesser means to possess a Bible, a Talmud or other books. Therefore, it was only a matter of a few decades before they enthusiastically took over the new art of printing, and their activity in this field would have been still greater if, during the course of time, various restrictions had not been imposed on them.

Jewish love of beauty was just as much in evidence in the printing of books as it was in the art of manuscript illuminating, although the means of expression differed. The ornamented initial letters or words were still used, but were of more modest dimensions, and lacked the gold and the bright colors which contributed so much to their embellishment. In a page of a volume printed in Lisbon in the year 1489 (Fig. 161), the first letter only fills a small corner whereas the initial word of the Darmstadt Haggadah (Fig. 128), written about half a century earlier, took up more than half a page.

The ornamented borders, such as those framing the page from the Darmstadt Haggadah, were still used, but they did not flow so casually or loosely around the writing. Because

162. FROM RASHI'S PENTATEUCH COMMENTARY
Printed in Italy in 1487

161. PAGE FROM THE SEFER ABUDRAHIM
Printed in Portugal in 1489

they were cut into solid material from which they were then printed, they were somewhat stiffer and more compact in style. In our example, the material used seems to have been metal instead of wood which was usually employed, and this enabled the artist to carry out the smallest details. This delicacy imparted a special charm to the page. The finely drawn tendrils with leaves like snowflakes, interwoven with animals, may have been influenced by Islamic manuscripts; they, nevertheless, are adapted to the art of printing, which the Mohammedans still rejected for centuries.

Since the art of printing is dependent upon the contrast of black and white, the artist has intensified the effect by applying white motifs on a black background, whereas the text is printed in black letters on a white surface.

In Italy the same contrasting method was used (Fig. 162), but the design is more full of life and sometimes has a pagan touch. Notice for instance in this example the small nude figures playing among the tendrils.

A third example (Fig. 163) is taken from an Ashk'nazic book printed in Prague, a city which can be credited with the first Ashk'nazic printing-press. On this page of a Haggadah, dating from 1526, the initial word is in heavy black letters, which gives a strong and hard impression conforming to the German taste there prevailing. The border is equally massive with its large figures cramped into the available space. At the top we have Adam and Eve and below them Judith with a sword and the head of Holofernes, and Samson with the gates of Gaza. The design on the lower part of the border depicts the coat-of-arms of Bohemia, upheld by two wild men. Finally, a small drawing of the Messiah, entering Jerusalem on an ass, is squeezed into the left corner of the text.

Who were the designers of all these printed books? The

border of the Italian page (Fig. 162) is also to be found in a non-Jewish book, the *Fables of Aesop,* which appeared in Naples two years earlier. It is obvious that the Jewish

163. PAGE FROM A HAGGADAH
Printed in Prague in 1526

printer borrowed the woodcut and the artist had only to add the initial word. Such loans now became frequent—a procedure very different from that used in the days when individual artists had both to write and illuminate their book by hand, employing original ideas.

No doubt Jewish artists contributed sometimes to the

beautifying of Hebrew books. In Naples in 1492, there lived a Jewish "maker of woodcuts," Moses ben Isaac by name, who worked for his brother-in-law, the printer Azriel Gunzenhausen.[64] In Venice the painter Moise di Castelazzo (d. 1525) made illustrations for a Pentateuch from which his sons made woodcuts. The ornamentation of the Prague Haggadah repeatedly shows the Hebrew letter ש which in the example (Fig. 163) is placed to the left of the coat-of-arms between the arms of one of the wild men. This denotes

164. ABRAHAM AND THE THREE STRANGERS
*From the Amsterdam Haggadah engraved
by Abraham ben Jacob*

a Jewish designer or maker of woodcuts rather than a printer, because it was customary for an artist to sign his work in this modest way.

These are the only definite indications we have of Jewish artists in the field of printed books during the fifteenth and sixteenth centuries. We have seen that the Jewish scribes remained in their professions and were able to continue with the art of illumination. As a result there was most probably a lack of Jewish artists interested in the newer art of book decoration which required special training. This scarcity may have been the reason why the artistic embellishment of printed books gradually decreased in quantity and quality.

Holland formed an exception in the seventeenth and eighteenth centuries due to the favorable conditions there. Yet, it is worthy of note that here as well, non-Jews were employed as artists as for instance, a German clergyman, who

165. Title-page from the Pentateuch
with Commentary by I. Abarbanel
Engraved by Aaron Santcroos

was converted to Judaism and took the name of Abraham ben Jacob. His best-known work, a Haggadah, appeared in 1695 in Amsterdam, and soon acquired great popularity, not only in Holland, but all over the world. The numerous engravings are not of his own invention, but can be traced to Bible illustrations by the Christian artist Mathaeus Merian the Elder. But what did that matter to the reader? Here he found the familiar stories, illustrated simply but with

166. ESTHER SCROLL
Engraved by Salomo d'Italia. Hans Lamm, New York.

great vivacity. For instance, the three men appearing before
Abraham (Fig. 164) are white-clad angels with beautiful
wings. Abraham listens intently to the announcement of the
birth of a son and Sarah stands doubtingly in the doorway.
In the background we see a broad river covered with boats
as in Dutch landscape paintings.

In the eighteenth century the illustrations printed by
Jews in Holland sometimes acquired a rococo-like grace and
lightness, as in the Pentateuch with commentaries by Isaac
Abarbanel, which appeared in 1768 in Amsterdam. The
title (Fig. 165) is framed by a large columned portal and
small scenes depicting Abraham and Samuel in prayer, an

allusion to the publishers or financiers, Samuel and Abraham Halevi. How ably these two little scenes in light shades contrast with the dark and heavy drawing in the center, depicting the porch of the Temple. The artist was a Jew by the strange name of Aaron Santcroos, apparently adopted when he lived as a Marrano in the Iberian Peninsula.

In Holland, Hebrew books are sometimes illustrated with the engraved portraits of their authors. The reader was not always content with reading matter alone. He wanted to know more about the man who had written the book, and the portrait of the author satisfied this desire. Esther scrolls and marriage contracts, written in Holland, were also preferably decorated with engravings in contrast to the colorful hand-painted ones which were so greatly esteemed in Italy.

An Italian Jew, who had emigrated to Holland in the early seventeenth century, Salomo d'Italia, devoted himself to the above-mentioned tasks. His portrait prints are inferior works. One would not dare to place his engraving of Rabbi Menasseh ben Israel next to the etching made by Rembrandt. But his frame for marriage contracts, made in 1648, is a pleasing work, as well as his engravings for two Esther scrolls. Figure 166 shows an illustration of a part of the larger one, depicting the figures of the Esther story on

167. PARCHMENT BINDING
*From a written Haggadah,
Germany, 1756. Cincinnati,
Hebrew Union College.*

168. Silver Binding of a Printed Machzor
Venice, 1742. New York, Jewish Museum.

pedestals between huge portals. The details may not always
be naturalistically accurate, but the artist had a keen understanding, acquired from his native country, for pompous
architectural effects.

In the Modern Era as in the Middle Ages, the Jews loved
to furnish their books with beautiful bindings. But there
was a difference between the cover of the written and the
printed book. In the former we often come across parchment bindings, ornamented with hand-painted motifs in
vivid colors. The charm with which this was carried out can
be seen in the example (Fig. 167) taken from a German Haggadah of the year 1756. There is no doubt that the writer
and illuminator was at the same time the binder, as in the
Middle Ages.

For printed books, especially for prayer books, a new type
of cover made of silver came into fashion. Christians also
made use of them occasionally, but Jews were particularly
attracted by the decorativeness and had many books bound

in that fashion. The example (Fig. 168) once belonged to the Italian family Formiggini, and was the cover of a machzor published in Venice in 1742. The family coat-of-arms fills out the center of both covers and is surrounded by crowns, fruit and rococo motifs. Such a binding was probably made by a Jew, as we have already stated that in Venice the craft of the goldsmith was very familiar to Jews. German bookbindings in silver were, however, made by non-Jews as this craft had slipped out of the hands of German Jews.

We emphasized the relation between Jews and non-Jews during this period, because such friendly intercourse largely contributed to lessen the breach between them. This was the means of creating an atmosphere of reconciliation leading to the Emancipation.

XI.

The Emancipation to the Present

THE late eighteenth and early nineteenth centuries brought the Jews complete emancipation. They were freed from the ghettos and from most of the restrictions imposed upon them in their various professions, and they became citizens with full rights everywhere.

This means that in the field of art Jews were allowed to become architects, sculptors, painters, and craftsmen as they pleased, and that they could dispose of their work in whichever way they liked. The provision made for their artistic education, which had previously been very poor, was from now on no different to that granted to everyone else. Since the guilds were abolished, any Jew could become apprenticed to any Christian master. They could also become students at any art schools or academies, institutions which were now considered necessary for an education in the fine arts. Able to travel freely, the Jews found inspiration and incentive in foreign countries. Art exhibitions accepted their contributions and placed them thus in direct competition with their Christian fellow artists. The critics could condemn or praise them; art dealers sold their works; and collectors and galleries were interested in their achievements, regardless of their religious faith.

Parallel to this newly acquired political freedom, Jewish artists rejoiced in the spiritual liberation pervading Judaism at this time. The synagogues, it is true, remained faithful to their old principles forbidding the painting of Biblical scenes, and only permitting the artist the use of symbols and ornaments, though we must exclude some Reform communities in America from this statement. On the other hand, the Jewish home welcomed pictorial art of any kind and Jewish artists had no hesitation at all in freeing themselves of the early restrictions. Whether this spiritual freedom resulted from assimilation with Christian surroundings, or whether it sprang from an inner freedom or was merely a desire to throw off some of the old religious shackles does not concern us here. It suffices to say that both the Liberal and the Orthodox Jews were affected by the new trend.

The immediate result of this external and internal liberation was a gradual increase in the number of artists, in Western Europe, which first accepted the new ideas, and later in Eastern Europe, where the Emancipation was slower to take a hold and to overcome religious tradition.

In the United States where mass immigration took place during and after the nineteenth century, the first generations were too much concerned with making a bare living to have either the time or the desire for artistic activities, and Jewish artists were an exception. But the children and grandchildren of these immigrants had a leaning towards these professions and the twentieth century produced many more artists than the percentage of the total Jewish population warranted.

Towards the end of the nineteenth century, when the Zionist movement began to develop Palestine as a national home, it was considered a point of honor that the plastic arts should also have a place there. The sculptor Boris Schatz (1865–1933) must be credited with having planted this seed in Palestinian soil. He called the school of arts and crafts, which he founded in 1906 in Jerusalem, the "Bezalel School," after the oldest Jewish artist mentioned in the

Bible. In this way he symbolized the idea of the continuity of art in the life of the Jewish people.

The increase in the number of Jewish artists at this time was accompanied by a change in the quality of their work. The artist up to the time of the Emancipation was generally an artisan if not an amateur; his art was mainly folk-art. Now that the Jewish artist had every opportunity of developing his gifts freely and of entering into competition with others, he was able to imbue his work with his own personality, something which non-Jews had done for centuries. This growing individualism added so much to his stature as an artist that in many countries his name stood out among the best of his compatriots. The painter Ernst Josephson is hailed as one of the finest representatives of Impressionism and Isaak Grünewald as one of the leaders of Post-Impressionism in Sweden. In Russia, the work of the sculptor Mark Antokolski, the paintings of Isaac Levithan, the stage art of Leon Bakst, are considered to be the finest achievements in their respective professions. In England Jacob Epstein is the leader of modern sculpture in spite of the controversy which continually rages over his work. In America it is the painter Max Weber and the sculptor William Zorach, who aspire to these leading positions. Some Jewish artists even have a world-wide reputation: the Dutchman Josef Israels, the Frenchman Camille Pissarro, the German Max Liebermann, and the Italian Amedeo Modigliani.

The proximity of Jews and Christians inclined many Jews toward conversion. They wished to tear down the last barriers which in some countries were still erected against them, and to enjoy equal rights with their fellow citizens. These converted artists are not without significance for the development of the plastic arts. A daughter of Moses Mendelssohn married a banker Veit, but became a Christian after divorcing him, and educated her two sons, Johann and Philipp Veit, in the Catholic faith. These two highly artistic youths went to Rome in the beginning of the nineteenth century and joined the "Nazarenes," a group of artists who took the Christian Middle Ages for their ideal and

169. Moses Hidden by His Mother
By Philipp Veit

patterned their lives accordingly. Philipp (1793–1877) rose high in this circle. He painted altar pictures which are worthy of note and portraits which are still finer. His self-portrait, painted about 1815 in Rome, and unfortunately destroyed by fire, was considered an excellent work on account of its vigor and revealing characterization.

After his return to Germany, Philipp Veit became the director of the famous Staedel Institute in Frankfort-on-the-

Main, and later on of the museum in Mayence. His painting from the Old Testament, depicting the infant Moses hidden by his mother on the banks of the Nile, while his sister watches to see what will become of the child, may stand as an example of his style (Fig. 169). The subject is seen through Christian eyes. The mother resembles a madonna of Raphael, holding her child in her arms, and this maternal sentiment, corresponding to a similar tenderness in the soft flowing lines of the painting, is typical of the above-mentioned group. In spite of so complete an assimilation this artist deserves his place here, just as the still more renowned composer, Felix Mendelssohn-Bartholdy should be mentioned in a history of Jewish music. He was also a baptized grandson of Moses Mendelssohn and there can be little doubt that both inherited their talent from their grandfather whose religious and abstract philosophy became, in the hands of his heirs, tangible works of art.

In mentioning a few other converted artists from the beginning of this period, we must first refer to Eduard Bendemann (1811–1889), the son of a Berlin banker Bendix, who became professor of the Dresden Academy of Art and later director of a similar institute in Düsseldorf. It is astonishing how rapidly these baptized Jews rose to leading positions in German art circles. Bendemann, before his conversion, painted By the Waters of Babylon, considered a success in the time (Fig. 170). The particular attraction of this and similar pictures was to be found in the wave of sentimentalism which swept through this period. The man and the women are noble, well-clad figures, their sorrow being expressed in a resigned melancholy. The composition in its symmetry and balance exhales a similar noble calmness.

Julius Muhr (1819–1865) trod the same paths. After his conversion he was appointed director of the Schack Gallery

170. BY THE WATERS OF BABYLON
By Eduard Bendemann. Cologne, Germany, Wallraf-Richartz Museum.

in Munich, but his premature death prevented him from
acting in this capacity. His sentimental style makes his pictures seem antiquated today, but several small sketches in
oil show his astonishing talent.

In architecture we come across a grandson of Daniel Itzig,
whose medal we discussed in detail in the previous chapter.
He changed his name to Hitzig (1811–1881) and is known
as the builder of the Stock Exchange and the State Bank in
Berlin. In England the architect Joshua Basevi (1799–
1845) accepted Christianity and changed his first name to
George. He is known as the designer of the Conservative
Club in London and the Fitzwilliam Museum in Cambridge. These two last-named artists were well known in
their time, but are not of much importance today because
architecture of the nineteenth century plays little part in the
expression of the period. It is only interesting from a symp-

tomatic point of view that Jews became architects once more and thus regained an art which, at least in Central and Western Europe, they had lost for centuries.

A few words about artists born of mixed marriages must also be added. In Germany particularly, they were numerous and some of them played an important part in the art of that country. Gottfried Schadow, classicism's best-known sculptor, married a Jewess, who bore him two sons. Rudolph Schadow (1786–1822) became a sculptor as well, but his premature death cut short a promising career. His brother Wilhelm (1789–1862) became a director of the Art Academy of Düsseldorf and to him falls the merit of transforming the idealistic linear style of the Classicists and Nazarenes into a more colorful realism.

Hans von Marées (1837–1887), the son of a Jewish mother, painted the finest murals in German art of the nineteenth century. They are still to be seen in the Zoological Institute in Naples, Italy. Adolf Hildebrand (1847–1921), whose mother was also Jewish, was not only the finest sculptor in Munich, but also an important influence in the history of this art in his time. He demonstrated to the German people that sculpture has its own laws and that they are different from those of painting. Thus he brought back this art to a new florescence after years of decay.

The immense importance attained to by Jews and half-Jews since the Emancipation is so different from the earlier and inferior position of Jewish artists, that it would seem as if there were no connection between these epochs. It is, therefore, necessary to draw attention to the fact that there are certain threads linking them to one another. As we know, the Jews were considered to be good coin minters and medallists. In the nineteenth and twentieth centuries these crafts still have their prominent exponents. In Belgium the brothers Jacob (1815–1899), Leopold (1823–1891), and Charles Wiener (1832–1887); in Holland Solomon Cohen Elion (1815–1880) and his son Jacques (1842–1893); in Russia Avenir Griliches (1822–1905) and his son Abraham (b. 1852), and in America Victor David Brenner (1871–1924)—all left their mark as medallists and coin minters. In Hungary the founder of a modern style in medal designing,

171. MEDAL OF GUSTAV MAHLER
By Benno Elkan. Cincinnati, Dr. Hans Lion.

Fülöp Ö. Beck (b. 1873) by name, was a Jew by origin, and a number of other Jewish medallists followed his lead.

An example of this delicate form of art can be found in the work of Benno Elkan (b. 1877), a German-born sculptor whose best work is shown in his numerous medals. The one here pictured (Fig. 171) is dedicated to the memory of the famous composer Gustav Mahler. On the obverse his profile is characteristically outlined, while the reverse shows a youth devoured by flames. The inscription in Latin alludes to Mahler's premature death caused by the intensity with which his art burned in him.

Another field in which Jews attained great excellence after the Emancipation was that of the graphic arts. The beginning of the period of Emancipation is particularly marked by the emergence of a number of Jewish engravers, who sometimes did original work and sometimes reproduced the paintings of others. It would be too difficult to discuss them all.[65] Jewish artists became so numerous that we must, in this general survey, confine ourselves from now on to a judicious selection.

Even later, when the Jews were quite at ease as painters, they always retained an especial interest in the graphic arts, and the greatest of them, such as Israels, Pissarro and Liebermann, gave much of their time to etching and lithography.

Some Jewish artists devoted so much energy to the graphic arts that their paintings receded into comparative unimportance. Hermann Struck (1876–1943), for instance, could not free himself from a certain dryness in his paintings, whereas his prints are very natural and lifelike. He expresses a real depth of feeling in the etching of the old Jew studying the Talmud (Fig. 172). The seeming absorption in his book is not only given by thoughtful expression of the subject, but by the artist's skilful handling of light and shade. Hermann Struck was so familiar with all the secrets of graphic art, that a number of other artists, such as Max Liebermann, Lovis Corinth and Lesser Ury went to him for advice. In 1909, he published his book *Die Kunst der Radierung* (The Art of Etching) which won a high degree of acceptance and became a standard reference on that subject.[66]

His English contemporary, William Rothenstein (1872–1944), one of the best-known artists of that country, also devoted most of his energies to the graphic arts, chiefly drawings. Such specialists are also to be found amongst non-Jews, but the number and the excellence of their work leads to the conclusion that the Jews had a particular aptitude in this field. This is due to their old custom of writing, engraving and handling tools for their medals and coins, as well as

172. OLD JEW STUDYING THE TALMUD
Etching by Hermann Struck

to the fact that working in black and white offers an abstraction from the kaleidoscopic side of life—an avenue of expression well suited to their temperament.

It is worthy of note that amongst the prints by Jewish artists of this period there are to be found many heads of unknown as well as of known personalities. This art of portraiture also goes back to the Jewish past. Let us recall the medals, the portraits of authors in their books, the likenesses of rabbis. The Ashk'nazic Jews, however, had refused to accept this new field, and it was not until the Emancipation that they acquired an interest in this branch of art. Probably Moses Mendelssohn's example exercised a great influence in this respect. He was continually being painted, drawn, engraved.

At first, only well-to-do and famous Jews consented to
have their portraits painted, but a little later the middle-class
followed their example. The former were not particular as to
the religion of their portraitists, but the middle-class decid-
edly favored the Jewish artists who were to be found in all
cities where greater Jewish communities were established.
Our example (Fig. 173) is the work of Wilhelm Henschel

173. PORTRAITS OF CANTOR ISAAC WOHLFARTH AND HIS WIFE
By Wilhelm Henschel

(1785–1865) who lived in Breslau, Germany, with his brothers, who were also painters. The man who is evidently an
Orthodox Jew is portrayed with his cap on, and his wife
with the "sheitel," a wig which Jewish women put on after
cutting off their hair on the day of marriage. The artist has
shown particular skill in the drawing of the bonnet which
covers her head.

One of these portrait painters, Eduard Magnus (1799–
1872), baptized as a child, became a favorite in elite Berlin
society. His portrait of the famous singer, Jenny Lind, in the
Berlin National Gallery, is still very well known and owes

its popularity to its charm and grace, qualities in which the painter excelled in his portraits of women, as well as to his fine taste in colors.

Portrait miniatures were very popular at this period, and in this field Jews were particularly successful. This also is probably due to the fact that for many centuries they were accustomed to this detailed and delicate way of painting,

174. (*Left*) MINIATURE OF MISS ADOLPHINE VON BARNES. *By Lippman Fraenckel.*
175. (*Right*) MINIATURE OF COUNTESS BAUDISSIN. *By J. D. A. Fiorino.*

which they used for the illumination of books. Already in the eighteenth century a few artists had acquired fame by their miniature portraits, for instance, Juda Pinhas (1727–1793), court painter to the Prince of Bayreuth, his son Solomon (1759–1837), court painter in Kassel, and Johann Michael Siegfried Lowe, originally Moses Samuel Löwe (1756–1831), who made a good miniature of the philosopher Kant. The finest miniaturist of the next generation is Lippman Fraenckel (1772–1857), who emigrated from Mecklenburg, Germany to Copenhagen, Denmark, and became "the most able painter of miniatures in Denmark," according to the judgment of Ernst Lemberger, an expert on miniatures in Scandinavia.[67] Jeremias David Alexander Fiorino (1797–1847), who lived in Kassel and Dresden, is his equal in this field. We show an example of the work of each of them, the portrait of Fräulein von Barnes by Fraenckel (Fig. 174) and the one of Countess Baudissin by Fiorino (Fig. 175). The Jewish traits in the portrait of the latter clearly show her Jewish descent.

After the advent of photography, this pleasing branch of art went out of fashion, but we still find occasional examples of it. It is significant that in England it was a Jew, Alfred Praga (b. 1867), who was at the head of a group, the Society of Miniaturists, whose aim it was to revive this vanishing technique.

After the eventual decline of miniature painting, the Jews found other opportunities of making use of their skill in portraiture. Hermann Struck, whom we mentioned in connection with the graphic arts, devoted a great deal of his talent to etching well-known personalities, as did Emil Orlik (1870–1932), equally well known in this field. The most famous Jewish painter in the second half of the nineteenth century in Germany, Max Liebermann (1847–1935), was at that time one of the best portrait artists. How imposing is the likeness of the great surgeon Sauerbruch, which he painted at the age of 85 years (Fig. 176). How strongly the personality of the surgeon is expressed by his searching eyes, and his manner of sitting and folding his arms; how strikingly the colors of the white coat and the grey background are contrasted. It was the sitter and not the painter who first showed fatigue during the many sittings and asked how much longer it would take. Liebermann answered: "My dear professor, when you make a mistake in treating a patient, it is covered over by a grass mound, but when I make a mistake it continues to hang on the walls for centuries." This remark not only shows his quick repartee, but also his deep sense of responsibility towards his art.

Liebermann was surrounded by a number of good Jewish portrait painters who have succeeded in reaching other countries after their flight from Nazi Germany and Austria: Eugen Spiro (b. 1874), Joseph Oppenheimer (b. 1876), Max Oppenheimer called Mopp (b. 1876), Josef Bato (b. 1888),

176. PORTRAIT OF THE SURGEON SAUER-
BRUCH
By Max Liebermann

Victor Tischler (b. 1890), Georg Ehrlich (b. 1897), the latter also a good sculptor.[68]

In Russia the name of Leonid Pasternak (1862–1945) must be remembered as the friend and portrayer of Tolstoi as well as of the great political personalities, including the leaders of the Bolshevist revolution. William Rothenstein, whom we have mentioned before as an excellent exponent of the graphic arts, through his drawings, became the chron-

icler of the intelligentsia of France and England in the nineteenth and twentieth centuries. At the moment it is the
sculptor Jacob Epstein who has taken his place.

Jewish artists, not necessarily always of the first rank, also
penetrated into high mundane and ecclesiastical circles all
over the world. Vilma Parlaghi (1863–1921) and Philipp
Laszlo (1869–1937), both of Hungarian origin, became popular portrait painters in royal, political and ecclesiastical
circles in European countries.

There were naturally excellent non-Jewish portrait painters as well, but, as with the graphic arts, the great number of
good Jewish portraitists proves that in this branch of art the
latter felt particularly at home. The reason for this may be
that the hard fate of the Jews through the ages compelled
them to become keen observers of human nature. Always
obliged to be on their guard against possible enemies, the
Jews acquired the unconscious habit of rapidly summing up
the character of every individual with whom they came into
contact.

In the previous pages we touched upon modern Jewish
sculptors, but we must return to this subject and enlarge a
little on the part that sculpture played in the life of the Jews
at this period. We have tried to show that the Era of Emancipation is in many ways linked with the past, but the art of
sculpture brings the Jews into a field which they had up till
now purposely neglected. Let us refer once again to the
words of Rabbi Leone da Modena (about 1600) who, when
speaking about portraits in Italian-Jewish homes, said:
"they avoid sculpture both in relief and in the round." This
was the general attitude of the Jews until the Emancipation
and was probably even shared by Moses Mendelssohn, the
father of Emancipation, of whom no bust was made during
his lifetime, although he sat for many portraits. This point

of view was only very gradually eliminated and as late as 1864 the progressive German rabbi Abraham Geiger found it necessary to put in a good word for this art: "To acquire works of sculpture, particularly for the home, is not only allowed, but highly recommended as a means of education.

177. IVAN THE TERRIBLE
By Mark Antokolski

We are very pleased when the art of sculpture is practiced by a Jew; we certainly do not accuse him of encouraging idolatry. . . . It would be sheer folly to fight the advancement of art with a rusty law." [69]

The first Jewish representatives of this new branch of art were very mediocre and it was not until the second half of the nineteenth century that Jewish sculptors rose to a position of any importance. Mark Antokolski in Russia (1843–1902) had begun as a simple wood-carver, a craft with which

the Eastern Jews were familiar from their Torah shrines
and bimos. True to the spirit of the Emancipation, he carved
a head of Jesus, thereby attracting the notice of a wealthy
woman, who provided him with the means for study at the
Art Academy of Leningrad. His statue of Ivan the Terrible
(Fig. 177), made in 1871, created such a sensation that the
Czar bought this work and Antokolski's fame was assured.
The main reason for his great success lay in the fact that he
turned away from the conventional style reigning in Russian sculpture at this time, and boldly tackled reality, even
to the extent of depicting an insane monarch. This realism
made his name, but it is also the cause of a waning enthusiasm about his work today. His treatment of the garment
and the cushion is too picturesque, and too much attention
has been devoted to detail to give the impression which is
expected of a good work of sculpture; namely, massiveness
and simplicity in keeping with the material used.

This is even more true of a contemporary of Antokolski,
the American born Moses Ezekiel (1844–1917). He, too, was
a sculptor of repute in his time and his sumptuous studio
amidst the ruins of the Thermae of Diocletian in Rome was
a meeting-place for famous painters, musicians and writers.
An abundance of works issued from his creative mind: portraits, statues, monuments. His best-known work is the monument erected in 1871 in honor of Religious Liberty in
Philadelphia, commissioned by the Independent Order of
B'nai B'rith.

The number of Jewish sculptors has greatly increased
since these beginnings and today many of them rank among
the finest representatives of that branch of art.

Another field, new to the Jews, was that of landscape
painting. With the exception of Josua Ostiglia, Jews had
taken no part in the evolution of this type of art, which be-

178. PARISIAN BOULEVARD
By Camille Pissarro

gan in Europe in the Renaissance. Thus lacking precedent, Jews were at first reluctant to take up the subject of landscape painting. As late as 1870, such a keen observer as Bismarck declared that they lacked a feeling for nature and that as far as he knew, there never had been Jewish landscape painters.[70] But even as he expressed this opinion, a Jewish artist, Camille Pissarro (1831–1903), whose landscapes are today considered among the best of the times, had made his appearance in France. He was a S'fardic Jew, as the name denotes, born in the Antilles. When he came to Paris, he soon found himself under the influence of Corot, whose delicate, silvery landscapes impressed him deeply. Later he came into close touch with the Impressionist Claude Monet, who introduced Pissarro to the problems of plein air, of movement, and visible strokes of the brush which only at a distance merge into a complete whole. But he never quite lost the lyrical atmosphere of his early years as well as the preference for grey tones which he inherited from Corot. These techniques mastered, he painted landscapes of the utmost simplicity, for instance, a cottage half-hidden by bushes. The longer one contemplates them, the more one is affected by their unassuming calm beauty. In later years, when Pissarro was forced by his ailing eyes to place his easel indoors, he painted the crowded streets and squares of Paris as seen from his window (Fig. 178). In spite of this, he remained a landscape painter, insofar as light, air, and trees were the main subjects of his city scenes.

In Germany, Lesser Ury (1861–1938) followed in Pissarro's footsteps. His early landscapes, however, are of far brighter hues, born of fantasy more than of reality. In his later paintings of streets and squares, he varies Pissarro's style by preferring night scenes and streets in the rain in contrast to the sunny pictures of his predecessor. When towards the end of his life, he traveled again, he very significantly chose wet, foggy London in preference to sunny Paris.

Russia counts Isaac Levithan (1860–1900) amongst the foremost of her landscape painters. He was the first to feel the melancholy atmosphere of the Russian plains, her barren fields, her quiet woods and her poverty-stricken villages. In our illustration (Fig. 179), the loneliness of the landscape is accentuated by the high, smooth, grey sky, and the desolate fields.

The Austrian Eugen Jettel (1845–1900) and the Italian Clemente Pugliese-Levi (b. 1855) gained fame by the gentle, lyrical atmosphere which pervades their landscapes.

In Palestine, among the young artists gathered there, several endeavored to reproduce the air and coloring peculiar

179. Autumn
By Isaac Levithan

to this country, and the Roumanian Reuben Rubin (b. 1893), the Pole Elias Newman (b. 1903), and the Austrian Anna Ticho were particularly successful in this attempt. All this goes to show how premature Bismarck's judgment had been. As soon as the Jews were freed from the narrow confines of the ghetto they were just as susceptible to the beauties of nature as any other people.

In discussing Pissarro as one of the champions of the French Impressionists, we have touched upon a new characteristic of the Jewish artist after the Emancipation. He places himself in the front rank of all progressive movements and battles fearlessly to assure their success. This is very different from the Jewish artists' attitude before the Emancipation. Then he simply adapted to his own use the forms created by others, whereas now he is amongst those who take active part in the development of all new conceptions.

Philipp Veit was one of the founders of the group of young artists—the Nazarenes—who tried to demolish the "heathen" classicism. Antokolski struggled against the academic and conventional trend of Russian sculpture in favor of naturalism, although sculpture was not then the best means of expressing this revolutionary tendency. Painting was a more suitable field and on this account the most gifted Jewish artists turned their talents in this direction. By so doing they were instrumental in achieving the success of naturalism in art.

To the Dutch painter Josef Israels (1824–1911) falls the credit of leading his compatriots away from painting historical subjects with their grandiose gestures and bright colors, and bringing them back to truth-loving reproductions of their own surroundings. Israels himself in his youth had trodden the old paths, but during a stay in Zandvoort, at that time a simple fishing village, he became acquainted with the hard life of these fisherfolk. Possibly the deep sympathy he felt for these poor people rose out of his Jewish sensitiveness towards the poor and suffering. He was able to express their sorrows most realistically, as for instance, in his canvas, Alone in the World, which depicts a woman in silent despair at the death-bed of her husband. His pictures often have a sentimental touch which made them very popular, but he was not less successful when he painted uneventful scenes of every-day life as The Sewing School at Katwijk, now hanging in the Taft Museum, Cincinnati (Fig. 180). His picture shows diligent Dutch girls sewing, under the direction of an old lady who sits at a table in the window. The coloring is held to dull grey, brown, blue, and white, thus drawing all our attention to the sunlight which, shining in from the window, falls on the girls and their white needlework and caps.

Israels learned much from Rembrandt and was greatly impressed by his masterly handling of simple scenes and the magic of his light effects. These skills and techniques he adopted and used in his own paintings of scenes of contemporary life and thus contributed largely to a belated flourishing of Dutch art. The people of Holland take great pride in the room of the Ryksmuseum in Amsterdam devoted completely to his works.

The great German naturalistic artist of that period was Max Liebermann about whose portrait painting we had much to say. He too was attracted by simple folk and his first important painting depicted old women plucking geese (Berlin National Gallery). Bright colors attracted him no more than they did Israels. He cared more about the delicate nuances of light and shades. Following in the footsteps of his beloved friend Israels, he continually visited Holland and also painted Dutch folk, as in his pictures of the Old Folks' Home and the Orphans' Asylum in Amsterdam.

Yet another artist, a non-Jew, exercised a great influence over Liebermann. This was the Frenchman, Jean Francois Millet, who in contrast to the simple art of Israels, dramatized various aspects of the daily life of the peasant. In the picture Woman with Goats (Fig. 181), this influence is very noticeable, particularly in the way in which Liebermann has given a touch of heroism to the scene by placing the woman alone and towering above the horizon. Liebermann, however, has greater simplicity than Millet. The woman is seen from the back struggling with a recalcitrant goat and toiling up a barren hill. The whole atmosphere is one of solitude and melancholy.

Towards the end of the nineteenth century, Liebermann became acquainted with French Impressionism and from that time on it was his ambition to develop this technique

180. The Sewing School at Katwijk
By Josef Israels. Cincinnati, Taft Museum.

to the utmost by painting, with quick strokes of the brush, scenes bathed in light, and full of movement. In this style, he portrayed youths bathing, tennis and polo players, and a street in the Jewish quarter in Amsterdam on a market day. Due to the high quality of his work as well as to his dominating personality, Liebermann played a great part in introducing impressionistic art to Germany. He made inaugural speeches at exhibitions and published propagandistic books and essays. Both his artistic work and his great gift of organization gave an immense impetus to German art.

On a smaller scale Ernst Josephson (1851–1906) did for Sweden what Liebermann did for Germany. He stood at the head of a Swedish group of artists in Paris in the eighties, called "The Opponents," who fought against the antiquated

181. WOMAN WITH GOATS
By Max Liebermann. Munich, Germany, Museum.

art of the academies. His best works date from this time. One
such is the portrait of Mrs. Rubensohn (Fig. 182). This intelligent and expressive face is painted with a few accurate
strokes of the brush and framed by the bright colors of the
hat, the dress, and the plants. Besides this realistic tendency,
he showed a trend towards the fantastic, and delighted in
painting the fairy-tale characters of his native legends, for
instance the "nöck," a water-spirit, who sits by moonlight on
a rock by the side of a rushing cascade (museums in Stockholm and Göteborg). When this brilliant, young artist became insane in 1888, the visionary element took complete
hold of him. Had he continued his work in a normal, neutral
state, he would probably have become a keen partisan of
the new movement of Expressionism which followed. At all
events the drawings he made after his mental breakdown

were a source of great inspiration to the younger generation.

This one example, of an artist who was able to express his art in various fields and techniques, should be a sufficient warning that Jewish artists were not limited to the expres-

182. PORTRAIT OF JEANNETTE RUBENSOHN
By Ernst Josephson. Göteborg, Sweden, Museum.

sion of realism. They were not only able to reproduce the impressions gathered from the outer world, but could also express their own emotions. Therefore, when art turned away from too close an imitation of nature at the end of the nineteenth century, the Jewish artists were fully prepared for the change.

During the period of transition from one trend to the other, some branches of art came into the foreground whose very essence is quite remote from realism.

To begin with, there is the art of caricature, whose object it is to distort nature for satirical purposes. When, in 1896, the periodical *Simplicissimus* was founded in Germany, Thomas Theodor Heine (b. 1867), a Jew, was the leading cartoonist in political satire as well as in artistic merit. It was he who recognized the vain and empty boastfulness of Wilhelm II and lashed at the symptoms of decay visible in German domestic life. He made use of hard lines and aggressive colors to emphasize his points, and his cartoons were the talk of the day amongst those who even then, before the First World War, predicted the fall of the glittering, but inwardly hollow Imperial German Empire.

In England, Max Beerbohm (b. 1872) became famous through his cartoons which ridiculed individual personalities rather than institutions. The expressive caricature of Oscar Wilde, which shows up his stout dandified figure in a few elegantly swung strokes of the pen (Fig. 183), characterizes this talented cynic.

Frederick Burr Opper (b. 1857) was the leading artist of the magazine *Puck* in America, and later the cartoonist of the *New York Evening Journal*. A contemporary, William Gropper (b. 1897), who is also known as a painter, is counted among the best cartoonists. His interests lie chiefly in the fight against social injustice. We also find a good cartoonist Arjeh Navon (b. 1909) working in the contemporary paper *Dawar* which appears in Palestine.

Poster painting stands in close relationship to the art of caricature, because it must also simplify and conventionalize the forms of nature in order to catch the eye of the passer-by. When this art began to flourish in France in the

183. CARTOON OF OSCAR WILDE
By Max Beerbohm

closing decades of the nineteenth century, we know of only one Jew, Jules Alexandre Gruen (b. 1868), who took part in this movement. But the moment that it appeared in Germany, about 1900, an astonishing number of Jewish artists took up this art form: Thomas Theodor Heine, mentioned before as a cartoonist, Edmund Edel, Julius Klinger, Lucian Bernhard, R. Leonard, Walter Trier, Louis Oppenheim and Lindenstaedt. In Hungary, the most renowned placard painter was the Jew, Michael Biro, and in America, Henry (Hy) Mayer (b. 1868) gained an enviable reputation as a cartoonist and designer of impressive posters.

Without denying the excellence of the work of non-Jews, the great number of Jews who made names for themselves in this field indicates that this type of artistic activity suited them particularly well. They seem to have a special gift of expressing their ideas in the concise but striking manner, which is essential to this art. A typical example is the advertisement for the German shoe factory of Stiller (Fig. 184) in which Lucian Bernhard places nothing but the word "Stiller" and replaces the word "shoes" by drawing one shoe. The asymmetric composition of the whole adds to its strength.

Finally we come to the theater. It is a well-known fact that the Jews played a great part in the growth of the modern theater and in its closely related branches of pantomime, ballet, and film. They were playwrights, actors, producers, and stage managers. It is less well known that Jews contributed to a great extent to the art of stage-setting and costumes. All this occurred at a time when the stage turned away from naturalism and attempted to lure the onlooker away from every-day life into the realm of imagination.

The Russian, Leon Bakst (1868–1924), furnished the world-famous court ballet of his country with the colorful and vivid costumes and stage settings which have enthralled

184. POSTER
By Lucian Bernhard

audiences in Europe and America. In spite of the lack of color, our illustration (Fig. 185) gives a slight idea of the beauty of this art. The fluttering veil, the flowered dress, and waving ribbons merge into a fascinating combination, characterizing the vain Narcissus, who falls in love with his own image, mirrored in the water.

When the Russian Ballet made its first appearance in Berlin in 1909, it was again a Jew, Ernst Oppler (1867–1929), who seized the fleeting movements of the dancers, such as

Pavlowa and Nijinski, in a cycle of etchings. Quite recently
the well-known name of the painter Marc Chagall (b. 1887),
a pupil of Leon Bakst, has been added to the designers of
costumes and scenery of the ballet which has gained a firm
foothold in the United States.

On the subject of literary plays, we must mention a Russian, Nahum Altmann (b. 1889), who created the settings for

185. PROGRAM FOR THE RUSSIAN BALLET
By Leon Bakst

the famous play by Anski mirroring the life and imagination
of the Polish Jews: the Dibbuk. He also undertook the decorations for the first great triumphal celebrations after the
Russian Revolution.

In Vienna, the renowned architect and designer of stage scenery, Oscar Strnad (1879–1935) shared the honor of producing the most outstanding modern operatic and theatrical productions with Gustav Mahler and Max Reinhardt. For his Berlin theaters, Reinhardt (whose name was originally Goldmann) acquired the services of a Roumanian Jew, Ernst Stern (b. 1876), a master in the art of figurines.

The Jews' love and interest for the stage was extended to the actual building of theaters. When the construction of an opera house was planned in 1886 for Chicago, the firm Adler and Sullivan was commissioned to carry it out because the architect Dankmar Adler, the son of a rabbi, was considered the greatest expert in this field. We will have more to say about Adler later on.

After the First World War, Oscar Kauffmann (b. 1873) became the most popular theater architect in Berlin, because his interiors with their wood paneling, their beautifully curved balconies and charming decorations infected the audience immediately upon entering the theater with a spirit of gayety and expectation. After Hitler had set fire to the Reichstag, he transferred his puppet parliament to the Kroll Opera House, a building which had been reconstructed by Oscar Kauffmann.

While the cartoonists, poster painters, and stage decorators were setting out on their new ventures, a few individual artists had been searching for new ways which were to lead still farther away from nature and which were calculated to revolutionize the whole aspect of art: Cézanne, Gauguin, Seurat, van Gogh, Munch, Hodler and others. Among these isolated forerunners there were no Jews. They only made their appearance after the individual trends of these artists had combined to form a definite movement, but then they developed an astonishing activity.

In Munich, Germany, when the anti-naturalistic group "Der Blaue Reiter" (The Blue Rider) was founded in 1912, one of the leaders of the movement was Franz Marc, a descendant of Jewish ancestors bearing the name of Markus.[71] In the same year, a young painter from Prague, Eugen von

186. PRAYING JEWS
Drawing by Ludwig Meidner

Kahler (1889–1911), appeared in Munich. In spite of his aristocratic name, he was a Jew and very conscious of it. His paintings, particularly his still-lifes, express a visionary rather than a realistic conception. Let us hope that his paintings, which after his early death were faithfully taken care of by his family in Prague, did not fall into Nazi hands.

At the very same time an artistic scandal arose in Berlin when a number of young artists were refused permission to exhibit at the "Sezession" on account of the distorted manner in which they painted. The Roumanian Jew Arthur Segal (1873–1944) was one of the main agitators in this struggle, which ended in the formation of a new group of young artists, the "Neue Sezession." Segal remained a revolutionary all his life and in his last year fought for a new form of realism with the same enthusiasm with which he fought against it in his youth.

In 1911, three young artists who had come to Berlin united to form a group and two of these were Jews: Ludwig Meidner (b. 1884) and Jacob Steinhardt (b. 1887). They called themselves "Die Pathetiker" and this title expresses their aims. In place of the gay and lyrical Impressionistic movement, they wanted to substitute an art full of pathos and emotion as if they already sensed the tension which culminated in the First World War.

Ludwig Meidner occasionally attempted to express this note of pathos by realistic means, as for instance, in his drawing of two Jews praying (Fig. 186). But in comparing this work with the etching of Hermann Struck (Fig. 172), we see clearly how far Meidner is from actual realism. The Talmud Reader by Struck seems to have been sketched in an improvised manner, and the same casual effect is obtained by his handling of light and shade, making the reader one with the background. Meidner's heads, on the other hand, stand out plastically from an empty background expressing vigor and strength. Light and shade are used with dramatic effect and there is something threatening in the expression of their religious fervor.

A similar movement sprung up in Paris, but it showed less pathos. Some artists carried the departure from natural-

ism as far as cubism, so called because all objects were reduced to geometric and stereometric forms. The painter
Louis Marcoussis (b. 1883), a Pole who changed his name
from Markus, was one of the participants of this movement.
Jean Metzinger (b. 1883 in Nantes) was another, who to-

187. WOMAN WITH A BANG—ADRIENNE
*By Amedeo Modigliani. Chester Dale Collec-
tion, loan, The Art Institute of Chicago.*

gether with a non-Jew, A. Gleizes, formulated the new
ideas, publishing in 1910 what became a standard work *Du
Cubisme*.

Jacques Lipschitz (b. 1891), a Lithuanian by birth, carried out these principles in sculpture. The present writer
must frankly confess that this abstract sculpture means little

to him, but justice compels him to mention that the artist is highly esteemed by the art critics. "One of the most powerful, varied, and original of living sculptors" are the words of praise printed in the catalogue of the comprehensive exhibition "Art in Our Time" which took place in New York in 1939.

Most of the Jewish artists, however, who streamed to Paris, temporarily or in order to settle there, were no adherents of cubism. They contented themselves with acquiring a mastery over natural forms, and the changes they made served to express their own personalities. Life in this city was inexpensive, the atmosphere was gay and full of the love of art of every kind, and if an artist succeeded in making a name for himself in Paris, he was assured of success all over the world. All this tended to induce Jews to remain in this city, and an astonishing number acquired great reputation.

Among the pupils of the French artist Henri Matisse, we find a German Jew, Rudolph Levi (b. 1875), a painter of landscapes and still-life. He learned to replace the scintillating strokes of the brush with unbroken contours and colors, and to substitute for the veiled composition of the Impressionists a clearly conceived balance.

Another German-Jewish painter, Martin Bloch (b. 1883), likewise received his inspiration in the French capital. His streets and squares no longer merge into light and air, or rain and fog as in the works of Pissarro and Lesser Ury, but stand out with hard, sharp lines and untoned colors.

A third artist who must be included in this movement was Anita Rée (1885–1933). Born in Germany, she studied in France, but found her real sphere of action in southern Italy, where she painted the cubelike houses climbing up the rocks and hills and the dark-skinned, dreamy Italian fisherfolk. The Nazi domination of Germany which over-

took her while she was in that country made her so despond-
ent that she committed suicide and thus ended a very promising career.[72]

The Italian-Jewish painter, Amedeo Modigliani (1884–
1920), took with him to Paris the memory of Botticelli's
slender figures. His own paintings are imbued with the
spirit of the Italian master yet he did not lose his personality.
His young men and women clothed or in the nude, and
drawn with slim, elongated limbs, seem very fragile (Fig.
187). His contours are as fine as hair, his colors—silver-grey,
black, rose and mahogany-red—give a jewel-like impression. During his lifetime this poor, sick artist was unknown
except to the circle of a few ardent admirers who were also
attracted by his noble personality. He took pride in ac-
knowledging his Jewish birth. After his death, his fame rose
rapidly, and today his pictures are sought after by museums
and collectors who pay fabulous prices for them.

One of his friends was the Lithuanian Jew, Chaim Sou-
tine (1884–1943), who, in contrast to Modigliani's fragility,
was robust and vital. Whether he paints a church, game, or
slaughtered oxen, he sweeps across the canvas with bold,
broad strokes, but a delicate feeling for color is hidden behind this stormy temperament. American museums were
quick to recognize his talent and secured some of his works.

The Polish Jew, Moise Kisling (b. 1891), was also one of
Modigliani's friends. His peasants, beggars, and gypsies are
also more colorful, hardier and heavier than the frail characters of the Italian painter.

Georg Merkel, born in Poland in 1881, who spent the
best part of his life in Paris and Vienna, must also be included in this group. The example (Fig. 188) depicts his
fondness for idyllic scenes with simple, naive characters.
Here the contrasts between the shy, timid, young girl and

188. PAIR OF LOVERS
By Georg Merkel

the strong, decided man with his protective attitude is emphasized by the lines and colors. All of this makes a quite casual impression but it is really the outcome of the most careful calculation and study. "Lawfulness" is, in his opinion, the nucleus of art.

The Bulgarian Jules Pascin (1883–1934) who spent most of his life in Paris has depicted teen-age girls of doubtful reputation. The ease and sureness of his stroke and the delicacy of his colors make of his drawings and canvases great works of art.

Although the number of talented Jewish painters of this generation who found their way to Paris is too great for us to consider them all, we would not like to close this survey without at least mentioning the names of some other highly gifted Jewish painters of this same generation: the Poles, Eugen Zak (about 1884–1926) and Leopold Gottlieb (1883–1934), and the Czech, Georg Kars (b. 1880).

Among the sculptors living in Paris at this period, we must still mention the Russian, Chana Orloff (b. 1888) and the Bulgarian, Moise Kogan (b. 1879). Chana Orloff models her busts with an almost caricature-like exaggeration of the characteristic features of the model, and thus gives her works a masculine vigor. Kogan, on the other hand, is attracted by the softer lines of the female body, which he carves in the round as well as in reliefs of extreme delicacy. His work is apparently influenced by Greek art, but of the archaic period more than of the classical, which gives a certain severity to the grace of his figures.

Jacob Epstein (b. 1880) is similarly of East European origin and a sculptor, but he was born in New York, studied in Paris, and except on visits, never returned to America. He settled in London, England, and was looked upon in that conservative country, somewhat as a savage in a drawing

room. When, in 1907, he decorated the facade of the British
Medical Association Building with marble reliefs of nude
figures, a bitter newspaper feud was unleashed, although
these early works already showed his great talent. The up-
roar was renewed on the erection of a relief in memory of
the naturalist W. H. Hudson in Hyde Park, depicting a
nude female surrounded by birds. His statue of Christ, reminiscent of an African idol with its block-like body caused
a new wave of hostility, more intense than the others owing
to the affront given to traditional, religious feeling. As late
as 1939, a new scandal was created when Epstein exhibited
his figure of Adam, which resembles an ape staggering across
the earth more than a human being, although the head
thrown back is meant to indicate that he has already received the breath and the spirit of God.

Nevertheless, Epstein is remote from any blasphemy. He
is so strongly impressed by the Bible, the New as well as the
Old Testament, that he can only express his feelings in his
own unconventional manner. It would be more correct to
reproach him for attaching greater importance to his own
conception of the subject than to the possibilities of sculpture.

These objections vanish when we turn to his busts of outstanding men, temperamental women, and apple-cheeked
children. He was particularly successful with the latter,
whom he reproduced with great vivacity. Our example (Fig.
189) shows us one of his male busts in bronze. In his book
Let There Be Sculpture Epstein describes the impression
which the model for this bust made on him. "The Leeds
painter, Kramer, was a model who seemed to be on fire. Energy seemed to leap into his hair as he sat and sometimes he
would be shaken by a queer trembling like ague." This is
how the artist saw him, and thus he created him—with his

furrowed face, his tense expression and his flaming hair.

Isaak Grünewald is one of the best-known painters of Sweden. Born in Stockholm (1889), but of East European descent, he studied in Paris as did in earlier days his compatriot Josephson. As the latter brought Impressionism to

189. BRONZE BUST OF JOSEF KRAMER
By Jacob Epstein.
Cincinnati, Hebrew Union College.

Sweden, so Grünewald fought for the new Expressionistic ideas. His painting of the Negro cook (Fig. 190) shows the direction in which his art lies. He remains true to nature, but his accentuated outlines, simplified colors, and an increased plastic value of the body which he forces into a small space give great vigor to the painting.

In Russia, the sculptors, Antoine Pevsner (b. 1886) and

his brother Nahum, called Nahum Gabo (b. 1890), founded in 1920, after the Bolshevist Revolution, a movement called "Constructivism." "We call ourselves Constructivists," they say in their program, "because our pictures are no longer painted, our sculptures no longer modeled, but are built in

190. NEGRO COOK
By Isaak Grünewald.
Stockholm, Sweden, Museum.

space by means of space." By "building" they mean an abstract painting or sculpture, to which they add glass, metal and celluloid. The use of these different elements, however, is not intended for any practical purpose, but only to give aesthetic pleasure.

In the United States during the nineteenth century Jews did not participate to any degree in the development of art.

An exception must be made of the architect Dankmar Adler, whose name we have already mentioned and to whom we will return when dealing with modern architecture. It is all the more astonishing that the introduction of the post-Impressionistic movement in America in the twentieth century was due to a great extent to the exertions of a number of Jewish artists. When this trend first appeared in the United States in the second decade of the twentieth century, not only the organizer, the photographer Alfred Stieglitz, but half of the most prominent artists were Jews: Max Weber, Bernard Karfiol, Samuel Halpert, Abraham Walkowitz, and Maurice Sterne.

The paintings of the Russian-born Samuel Halpert (1884–1930) were at first very realistic, as he had begun his studies in France with Léon Bonnat and had then turned to Impressionism. But later he came under the influence of Cézanne, Matisse, and Dérain, and from then on his landscapes and still-life paintings assumed a more plastic form which filled his canvases with a decided and measured regularity.

Maurice Sterne (b. 1877), likewise a native of Russia, came to America as a child and in later years traveled extensively, spending three years in Bali. Like Gauguin, he attempted to break away from the sophisticated Impressionism of large cities, and sought his material in the simple lives of more primitive peoples. He was also attracted to children for similar reasons, and one of his best-known works is his portrait of a fair-haired, blue-eyed girl in a white frock, sitting on a plain wooden chair. The picture which we have chosen as an example (Fig. 191) also shows us a girl, this time in a pink dress with contrasting blue stockings, sitting on the grass in the foreground of the picture. She is holding a basket full of blackberries which match the black-

Courtesy, Detroit Institute of Art

191. BLACKBERRIES
By Maurice Sterne

ness of her eyes looking out innocently into the world. Here
again as in the later paintings of Samuel Halpert, one is
struck with the regularity and harmony of the composition
and the clear divisions of space into foreground, center and
background.

The poetic atmosphere emanating from Maurice Sterne's
picture is found in an even greater degree in the canvases
of Bernard Karfiol, born in Hungary in 1886. In one of his
paintings (Fig. 192) he portrays a boy sitting at a table in
front of an open window. The boy's dreamy attitude is emphasized by the vase with the long-stemmed flowers and the
calm waters of the bay which form the background. The
drawing is so meticulous as to detail and the composition so

satisfyingly symmetrical, that one is reminded of the works
of the painters of the Italian Renaissance.

The style of Abraham Walkowitz, born in 1880 in Sibe-
ria, is harder and more abstract, as can be seen in his oriental female heads, his still-life canvases of flowers, his heavily

Courtesy, Philips Memorial Gallery, Washington
192. Boy
By Bernard Karfiol

conceived nudes in rhythmical movement, and latterly in
his city scenes.

The strongest opponent to naturalism and the most
stormy temperament in this movement is the Russian-born
Max Weber (b. 1881). He occasionally breaks up natural
objects into geometric forms similar to the French Cubists.
Even when he seeks an approach to nature, as in flowers,
fruit or figures, he transforms them into clumsy, massive ob-

jects. In this manner, and with a decided oriental atmosphere, he paints women making music, adorning one another, or merely turning to each other with heavy gestures. There is more to be said about his purely Jewish scenes.

A contemporary of these artists, though he stands somewhat apart, is Leon Kroll (b. 1884). He made a careful study

Courtesy, Modern Art Museum, New York
193. CHILD WITH CAT
By William Zorach

of realism in Paris and is indebted to this school for the clarity of his forms. One of his works depicts a sleeping woman in a white robe, whose calmness is reflected in the tranquillity of the rocks, the meadow and the water. His well-balanced precision fitted him admirably for his work as a painter of murals.

Beside these American painters, we find a number of American sculptors of equal reputation. Jo Davidson (b.

1883) shows the oft-mentioned Jewish gift of portraiture in his busts, which tend toward realism.

Eli Nadelman, born in 1885 in Poland, demonstrates greater freedom towards nature in his mundane busts and even more so in his pleasing animal statues, for instance, in the two bronze deer in the museum in Detroit.

The most renowned is William Zorach (b. 1887) who was born, as so many of his fellow artists, in Russia. In his sculptures he strives towards a modern classicism. The Spirit of the Dance is far from the whirl of limbs and costumes that the subject would suggest. He models a beautiful nude female figure, with one knee bent, expressing an attitude of repose rather than of movement. When he employs more than one figure, his art lies in the gift of placing them close together so as not to destroy the impression of the solid block of stone or wood out of which they have been hewn. This is well demonstrated in the example (Fig. 193), in which the closeness of the figures is motivated by the love of the child for his cat. It is remarkable how, in spite of this compactness, the artist has been able to convey an impression of life and movement. Jacob Epstein has no doubt a greater scope of imagination and a more burning, passionate temperament, but Zorach better succeeds in remaining within the limits of the art of sculpture.[73]

Let us now devote a few words to modern Jewish architects. Out of the great number of capable artists, we can only mention a few, and we have chosen those who played a decisive part in creating a new style in architecture. As is well known, this branch of art had, during the greater part of the nineteenth century, no life of its own because it was too much concerned with the imitation of older styles. America may be credited with the fame of having given architecture its contemporary spirit. In this country there were no cathedrals, no castles and ancient mansions to serve as models. Moreover such a youthful country did not feel inclined to clothe itself in the historic garb of its antecedents. The birth of this modern spirit in architecture is closely connected with the works of Jenney, Sullivan, Richardson, and Wright. The full recognition of these aims is described by Sullivan in his book *The Autobiography of an Idea*. He clearly cites as his goal a "realistic architecture based on well-defined utilitarian needs—that all practical demands of utility should be paramount as basis of planning and design; that no architectural dictum, or tradition, or superstition, or habit should stand in the way." The realism which had invaded painting and sculpture was now transferred to architecture. This did not mean however, a reproduction of objects, but merely the consideration of the nature of the material at the disposal of the architect, the use of the new techniques of construction and the attention given to the demands of modern life.

None of the above-mentioned architects was a Jew, but the name of Dankmar Adler (1844–1900), already familiar to us as a builder of theaters, is closely connected with this new trend. He was born in a small German village and his father, a cantor, gave him the unusual name of Dankmar, a combination of "Dank" (German for gratitude) and "mar" (Hebrew for bitter, because his wife died in childbirth). The father came to America and settled in Detroit as a rabbi. In 1861 he moved to Chicago, a city which was growing with astonishing rapidity. Here Dankmar developed into a successful architect and in 1879, he made the acquaintance of Sullivan who was only twenty-four years old. Adler immediately recognized his capabilities and took him as a partner into his firm. This partnership lasted for fourteen years, during which time Adler and Sullivan executed

194. Auditorium in Chicago, Illinois
Dankmar Adler and Louis Sullivan, Architects

a great number of commissions: business houses, private
residences, theaters, hotels, exhibition halls, and synagogues.
An instance of the last named is the Anshe Ma'ariv synagogue in Chicago. There is no doubt that Sullivan was the
more creative of the two from the artistic point of view. He
is supposed to have designed a great part of the exterior of
the auditorium in Chicago (Fig. 194), this strange combination of hotel, opera and office building. According to the
ideas stated in his book, Sullivan does away with all superfluous ornamentation and strives for a clearly outlined structure in keeping with the material used. The beauty of the
building lies in the balance of the horizontal and vertical
lines, the tower being placed intentionally at the long side
to relieve the monotony of the length. Nevertheless, Sullivan still a novice in those days, would not have achieved all

this without the assistance of his partner, who was his superior in age, organization, business experience, and in technical knowledge. Adler was an expert in questions of acoustics and had already tested this capacity in the Central Music Hall in Chicago, a building no longer in existence. Sullivan himself praises this gift with the words: "I then discovered what Mr. Adler knew about acoustics. I did not know anything about them, and I did not believe that any one else did. . . . It was not a matter of mathematics, nor a matter of science. There is a feeling, perception, instinct—and that Mr. Adler had. He had a grasp of the subject of acoustics which he could not have obtained from study, for it was not in books. He must have gotten it by feeling." Whoever reads these words will realize what Sullivan owes to his partner and must concede to Adler a place of honor in the history of modern architecture.[74]

Albert Kahn (1869–1943) continued to develop this technical mastery. As Henry Ford's architect in Detroit, he revolutionized industrial architecture.

When news of this American movement reached Europe, one of the first to grasp its importance was an artist of Jewish descent, Alfred Messel (1853–1909). The department store of Wertheim in Berlin, whose construction was begun by him in 1896, was the first building in Europe to emphasize the idea of centralized management in an edifice expressed in a design of complete unity (Fig. 195). The observer of this illustration should first look at the receding part of the building which was the original construction. Pillars as slender as possible strive upwards in an unbroken line so as not to take away the light which was necessary for displaying so much merchandise. Here again we see the idea of realism in architecture motivated by modern demands and not only by aesthetic principles. At the same time Messel had a strong

195. WERTHEIM DEPARTMENT STORE IN BERLIN, GERMANY
By Alfred Messel, Architect

feeling for beauty and was able to express this still more in
the front part of the building, which he added in 1904. He
uses pillars once again, but interrupts the upright movement with a caplike roof. This contrast is increased by the
open arches of the ground floor and the more closely spaced
windows of the upper floor.

This building placed Messel among the best architects of
Germany and he was consequently entrusted with the construction of a building, which was to be the most representative one in the country—the Deutsches Museum in Berlin.
Unfortunately, Messel died before he had time to do more
than to draw the plans, and the unfinished edifice only gives
a faint idea of the grandeur of its conception.

The movement of Expressionism, which arose in the early
twentieth century, infiltrated the architecture of that period
as well. The small country of Holland was a pioneer in this
movement. It had remained unmolested during the First

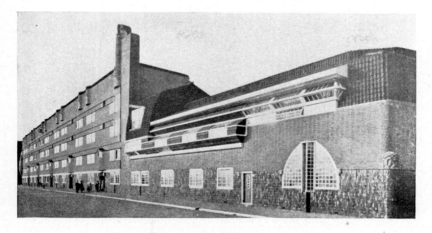

196. Apartment Buildings in Amsterdam, Holland
Michel de Klerk, Architect

World War, in fact, it had emerged from it considerably enriched and made use of its wealth by constructing new suburbs and erecting new buildings in such towns as Amsterdam, Rotterdam and so on. Among the group of outstanding architects, the Jew, Michel de Klerk (1884–1923) is in the front rank. His purpose is apparent in the apartment houses (Fig. 196) which he built in 1919. The old custom of building individual houses, however small, is replaced by a new conception, a row of buildings, each with its own entrance, but all joined together to form one uninterrupted edifice. From the aesthetic point of view, it forced the eye into motion by obliging it to follow the foreshortened lines. This dynamic feeling, characteristic of Expressionism is increased by the fact that the building is low at one end and rises abruptly by means of a chimney.

Dutch architecture exercised a great influence on Eric Mendelsohn (b. 1877), one of the best-known exponents of Expressionism in architecture. He went through the ex-

197. SCHOCKEN DEPARTMENT STORE IN CHEMNITZ, GERMANY
Eric Mendelsohn, Architect

citement of war, revolution and inflation in Germany and expresses these upheavals in his factories, motion picture theaters and department stores. Consequently, his works are imbued with greater pathos than those of de Klerk, who in comparison showed a certain lightness in all he undertook. This dramatic quality can be felt in Mendelsohn's department store of Schocken in Chemnitz, which he himself considered to be his maturest work (Fig. 197). The impression of motion, already created by the broad, white concrete "bands" is increased by the wide curve which the whole edifice describes. By night the same effect is obtained, but by opposite means, as the white "bands" recede into the darkness and the lighted windows take their place.

When, due to the Nazi government, Mendelsohn was forced to leave Germany, he lived in England a few years before coming to the United States. At a lecture delivered

198. Main Entrance, Hadassah University Medical Center
Mt. Scopus, Jerusalem. Eric Mendelsohn, Architect.

in London, he explained the aims of modern architecture in the following words: "The man of our day, out of the excitement of his rapid life, can find compensation only in an unrestrained horizontality. Only by the will to realize facts, will he be able to master his unrest; only by the highest degree of speed can he conquer his haste." [75] Nevertheless, in his later works, the artist has himself become somewhat quieter. The buildings he erected in Palestine during the years 1936–1941 are a proof of this: they are the Government Hospital in Haifa, the Hadassah University Medical Center (Fig. 198) and the Anglo-Palestine bank in Jerusalem, and the residences for Professor Chaim Weizmann and Salman Schocken.

It was due to the Zionist movement that Palestine developed great architectural activity since the turn of the century. Yet it was the Emancipation which gave the Jews

199. TECHNICAL SCHOOL OF HAIFA, PALESTINE
Alexander Baerwald, Architect

the opportunity of becoming well-trained architects, and
enabled them to undertake the construction of these edifices. The first important official building to be erected, the
Technical School of Haifa (Fig. 199), had not yet come
under the sway of modern ideas. The German architect,
Alexander Baerwald (1877–1930), began to build it in 1913
but owing to the First World War did not finish it until
1924. The high arch forming the portal and surmounted by
a dome, as well as by a roof with a crenelated border, gives
the building an oriental touch. In spite of this retrospective
tendency, the edifice has its merits, suggested by the clear
articulation of its parts and by the dearth of ornamentation,
which would have obscured its clarity.

After the First World War there was a definite striving
towards the latest trends of architecture. In 1920, Richard
Kauffmann (b. 1887), when he was commissioned to build
agricultural settlements, schools, sanitariums, and to plan
cities, was the first to introduce these principles in Palestine.
His school in Daganiah Aleph (Fig. 200) may serve as an

200. SCHOOL IN DAGANIAH ALEPH, PALESTINE
Richard Kauffmann, Architect

example. The impression of breadth is increased by the low flat roof. The windows follow the same lines and are no larger than necessary in order to give the proper amount of light and yet to keep out the heat of the oriental sun. The protruding roof is meant to give shade to the building, and thus the climatic conditions are taken into consideration without sacrificing the beauty of the architecture.

Side by side with Kauffmann there are a great number of talented younger architects who are working in Palestine and making that country one of the outposts of the newest ideas. Numerous sculptors, painters and craftsmen of applied art have settled there, partly voluntarily and partly forced there by the political disasters in Europe. We have mentioned a few of them. We have paid tribute to the memory of Boris Schatz, the founder of the Bezalel School of Arts and Crafts, and may add that his successor was the painter, Joseph Budko (1888–1940), a Pole, who went to Berlin in 1909, and became well known as a maker of prints. He left Germany on the advent of Hitlerism. Hermann Struck, of whom we have already made mention in connection with his ability in the graphic arts, had already settled in Palestine in 1920. In discussing the Jews' gift for landscape painting, we touched upon Reuben Rubin, Elias Newman, and Anna Ticho, and as a cartoonist, we mentioned Arjeh Navon.

The temptation to dwell at greater length on the budding art of Palestine must be resisted because we have restricted ourselves to artists who have already attained the summit of their ability. The same limitation is set in regard to the younger generation in Europe and America, gifted as some of them may be. The object of this book is to give a "history" of Jewish art, which implies a contemplation of past achievements rather than an appraisal of the ever-changing and ever-developing trends of the present.

Beside the artistic developments in Palestine, there is still another aspect of Jewish art which deserves comment. Over and above the interest shown in the growth of Palestine, what have Jewish artists done for Jews elsewhere during this period? We have seen how important their contribution has been to the art life of the countries in which they lived, but we have given no thought to the specifically Jewish themes, which formed the nucleus of Jewish art in all the previous centuries.

What about the synagogues of this period? Never at any time have so many been built as in the nineteenth and twentieth centuries. Never before were they so big, because the rapid development of the cities furthered large Jewish communities whose economic conditions enabled them to erect very large buildings. Freed from the narrow walls of the ghetto, Jews could settle where they would, and did not need to fear religious persecution when they expressed their religious devotion openly. Conditions were never more favorable; nevertheless, in reviewing all these synagogues, we must admit that in quality of architecture they do not come up to our expectations.

This disillusionment is not confined to Jewish structures, but applies also to Christian churches. The state of architecture in general was the cause. This branch of art was, as we stated once before, the one field which did not develop a style of its own because it depended entirely upon the styles of the past and therefore lacked inspiration. Consequently, we find synagogues with facades like Greek temples, with romanesque round arches and even with Gothic towers and pointed arches, as for instance, the synagogue in Budweis, Hungary, which could never be taken for a Jewish house of worship. This form however, was rarely chosen because churches of the nineteenth century were generally constructed in the Gothic style. On the other hand, an oriental touch was often added, usually derived from the art of Islam, a reminder of the era of florescence in Spain under Mohammedan rule.

This deviation from the surrounding architecture is very striking, coming as it does at a time when assimilation was at its height. But it may just be this assimilation which called forth the contrast. In previous eras the Jews had, without hesitation, adopted the styles prevalent in the countries in which they lived. The edifices were recognized as Jewish because they stood in the Jewish quarters of the cities. After the Emancipation, however, these buildings were freely erected wherever an available space was found and this resulted in the desire to define them clearly as Jewish houses of worship. These orientalized synagogues suffer from the same lack of originality as those of other styles.

When architecture freed itself from this historic retrospection towards the end of the nineteenth century and succeeded in finding its own expression, the best architects

201. SYNAGOGUE AT HAMBURG, GERMANY
Felix Ascher and Robert Friedmann, Architects

concentrated all their efforts on buildings close to the modern spirit, such as department stores, plants, railway stations, and theaters. Nevertheless, this modern trend was able to contribute something to the improvement of synagogues in doing away with superfluous ornamentation and in stressing the functional importance of these edifices. A good example of this new spirit is found in the Temple Beth Israel, Hartford, Connecticut, erected in 1936.[76] The interior with its vast dome which towers over the whole circular hall is particularly impressive, but no illustration can convey the sense of awe which seizes the visitor on entering the synagogue and looking upwards. We confine ourselves, therefore, to showing a synagogue erected in 1931 in Hamburg by the Jewish architects Felix Ascher and Robert Friedmann (Fig. 201). A few steps lead to a sort of forecourt formed by two side wings and a low porch. The bare wall rising behind this porch seems all the more massive in contrast to the open portals. The small, round window, decorated by a stone grill in the shape of the seven-branched candelabrum, adds to the solemnity of the structure. This proves that the functional architecture of our days is not only fitted for secular purposes, but is well able to convey religious feeling.

All the arguments regarding the synagogues of our period can likewise be applied to the ritual accessories. In the beginning of this period, under the rule of classicism, many beautiful pieces were fashioned (for instance Fig. 6, Fig. 40), but gradually these objects became mere imitations of different styles: Gothic as in the case of the domestic spice-boxes, and baroque or rococo as used for rimonim and Torah shields. In this field, a change has been wrought only in the last decades. We refer once more to the Seder plate in our Figure 41, which combines the container for the three pieces of unleavened bread, the six dishes for the symbolical food and the wine goblet, a creation of Ludwig Wolpert, who was obliged to leave Germany in 1933 and settled in Palestine. The materials used are metal and glass, and no ornament obscures the purpose of the different parts, yet the whole thing gives an impression of religious dignity. The finely curved goblet grows out of the center of the plate like a flower.

As to representational art dealing with Jewish subject matter, let us remember that in the last centuries before the Emancipation, it was only tolerated in books, with the exception of a few reliefs on tombstones and paintings in synagogues. Concerning the synagogues, the restrictions remained in general unaltered and the murals in the Wilshire Boulevard Temple of Los Angeles in California, depicting the history of Israel, form an isolated instance. Outside the synagogue, however, this Jewish subject matter appears frequently.

The Bible, glorified by Christian artists for many centuries, gradually became a favorite subject for Jewish painters and sculptors as well. When they at last turned to this field, Biblical art had long reached a climax and was already on the decline, and the Jews were drawn into this deterioration.

The Infant Moses Hidden by His Mother by Philipp Veit and By the Waters of Babylon by Bendemann, which we have already shown (Figs. 169–170), are pleasing works, but only echoes of earlier Christian Biblical art. Realism and Impressionism rarely turned to Biblical scenes. These movements grew out of the delight in contemporary life and there was little desire to depict religious subjects. Occasional attempts were made; Liebermann, for instance, produced a canvas called Samson and Delilah. The theme itself is characteristic—it has no religious significance—the seductiveness of women can be applied to all ages. Liebermann painted a fine picture but quite devoid of religious feeling.

Not before the turn of the nineteenth century, when Realism was on the wane, was there shown a renewed tendency towards Biblical scenes, and this time it was the Jews who caused the revival. The Zionist movement had made them conscious of their Judaism and the Bible stories became imbued with new life, because they were a part of that country in which the Jews were attempting to create a new home. In this spirit the sculptor, Henry Glycenstein (1870–1943), who spent his last years in America, created a statue of the Messiah, awaiting in semi-slumber the day of awakening. Ephraim Moses Lilien (1874–1925) began to illustrate the Holy Bible, but he devoted too much attention to the decorative details and the flowing lines, very popular in his time, to produce the effect of strength which the subject demands. Lesser Ury, whom we know from his Impres-

sionistic landscapes and city scenes, then often turned to
Biblical subjects. These huge canvases somewhat surpass
his technical abilities, yet they have a certain value because
he felt the greatness of the Bible narrative. An example of
this is shown in his Jeremiah (Fig. 202), painted in the year

202. JEREMIAH
By Lesser Ury. Last at Berlin,
Jewish Museum.

1897. The brooding prophet lies on the barren ground like
a stone. Above him, the vaulted heavens are studded with
gleaming stars, which increase the impression of dignity
and loneliness.

The Expressionistic movement found a new approach to
Biblical subjects. Its newly acquired freedom from the
bonds of nature led to the creation of paintings of imaginative content. When artists now depicted prophets—a favorite theme—they chose the moment of prophecy, a state
in which the characters were dominated more by divine

inspiration than by human reason. In this manner the figure of the prophet was depicted by the German Jew, Hugo Krayn (1885–1919). He is seen gazing ecstatically upwards, surrounded by an excited group of listeners (Fig. 203). The painting is strongly emotional in character, as is expressed in the foreshortening of the prophet's head, dramatically thrown back, and in the sharp contrasts of light and shade.

203. THE PROPHET
By Hugo Krayn

Jacob Steinhardt, whom we have already mentioned, conceived the prophet as an immense figure rising above the throng like a blue flame, the power of his prophecy being so great that even the houses collapsed.[77]

The same artist also gave new artistic life to the Haggadah; its miracles were newly conceived. We draw attention once more to the illustration of Moses leading the Jews through the Red Sea (Fig. 43). There is no attempt to make a natural phenomenon out of this miracle, and it is this supernatural effect which gives the woodcut its expressive power. Moses is not represented in the pose of a leader; on the contrary, he himself seems bewildered by the might of God, in whose behalf he is acting.

The second Jewish subject which comes to the fore in this period of Emancipation is aimed more at describing the

204. FRIDAY EVENING
By Moritz Oppenheim

present life of the Jews than depicting the past. Christian artists had rarely dealt with this subject. Why devote themselves to themes which they knew would not find popular favor? The Jews themselves often had occasion to illustrate their own life, namely, in Haggadahs, where they depicted their fellow Jews at the Seder meal or preparing the unleavened bread. But this was limited to books, whereas now they could reproduce these scenes in painting and sculpture.

The themes of these pictures were, at first, pleasing and friendly, corresponding to the comfort and peace in which the Jews lived at the height of the Emancipation. This led the portrait painter Moritz Oppenheim (1800–1882) to illustrate Jewish customs in a cycle of pictures which were issued in photographic form in 1866 and soon became very popular in Jewish homes. They were called "Bilder aus dem altjuedischen Familienleben" (Pictures of Old Jewish Family Life), and stressed the value of religion in the intimate family circle. This is clearly seen in the example (Fig. 204). It is a Friday evening and the Sabbath has just begun. The table is set and the housewife is blessing the Sabbath lights which she has just lit. Her husband consults his watch to see if it is time to leave for the synagogue and holds the hand of his little son, who with the prayer book under his arm, is eagerly awaiting the moment to set out. The same careful attention which is given to the detail of the contents is devoted to the form, showing the influence of Dutch genre paintings. This is particularly noticeable by the various light effects and the silk gown of the woman. In this delightful manner many other artists, for instance the Austrian Isidor Kaufmann (1853–1921), made names for themselves. It is impossible to mention them all.

Towards the end of the nineteenth century, a change took place in the atmosphere pervading these paintings. They gradually lost their amiable character and became more earnest, reflecting the increasing seriousness of the times. The few Jewish subjects painted by Josef Israels, whom we have alrady dealt with, clearly show this change. A Son of the Ancient People (Fig. 205), painted in 1889, depicts an old-clothes dealer seated amidst his scant merchandise. He could have made a cheerful scene of this, but he feels more strongly the melancholy side of the life of the poverty-

205. A SON OF THE ANCIENT PEOPLE
By Josef Israels. Amsterdam, City Museum.

206. WANDERERS
By Samuel Hirszenberg. Last at Berlin, Jewish Museum.

stricken Jews. Even his canvas of a Jewish marriage ceremony lacks a spirit of light-heartedness. He seems to stress
the seriousness of the moment by the heads of the bridal
couple bowed under the prayer-shawl.[78]

A still deeper melancholy pervades the works of a number
of East European painters and sculptors of the same decades.
The Jews of these countries never fully shared the benefits
of the Emancipation. Herded into a small space, the greater
number had nothing but poverty to look forward to and
from time to time they perceived the portents of renewed
hate and persecution. Their desire for wandering gradually
took hold of them again. This gave the Polish-Jewish artist
Samuel Hirszenberg (1865–1908) the material for a monumental canvas which he executed in 1904 (Fig. 206). A
group of men, women and children, old and young, are
moving across the snow-covered Russian steppe. One of
them carries a Torah Scroll, symbol of their unshakeable
faith in and attachment for their religion, which in spite of

207. INVOCATION
By Max Weber. New York, Mrs. Rose Gershwin.

their tragic fate, has bound them together through the ages.

As in previously described Biblical themes, so in scenes of contemporary Jewish life, Expressionism offered new possibilities. Max Weber, one of the first exponents of Expressionism in America, whom we have mentioned previously, in his picture Invocation (Fig. 207), painted three Jews gathered around a table, dreaming, arguing, and one of them lifting his hands and his eyes heavenwards. This is inten-

208. MY VILLAGE
By Marc Chagall

tionally drawn beyond the limits of naturalism, because the
feelings of the Jews are likewise far removed from nature.
These three figures have stepped beyond their material
existence and are mystically bound to God.

Still farther from nature are the paintings of Marc Chagall, who although he has spent the greater part of his life in
foreign countries, never forgot the tiny Russian village of
his birth. But he saw it more as a vision than a reality. In
our illustration (Fig. 208) he has painted the simple cottages
and barns of wood, but this poverty-stricken scene is lifted
from reality by bright colors, shimmering like a rainbow,
by a tree rising skywards, by fantastically shaped clouds,
while a Jew driving a goat before him seems to float in the

209. PASSOVER
By A. Raymond Katz

air. The boldness of Chagall's imagination, the beauty of his colors, have given these Jewish subjects world-wide renown.

Jacob Steinhardt, among other pictures with Jewish themes, painted a Jew dancing in exaltation with the Torah Scroll in his hands on Simchas Torah, the day of rejoicing over the Law. Similar themes of ecstatic religious enjoyment were frequently treated by other Jewish artists like Mané Katz (b. 1894) and Zygmunt Menkes (b. 1896), and they all show deep insight into Jewish religious life. King David executed a dance of joy when the Ark of Covenant was brought to Jerusalem and this primitive manner of expressing jubilation persisted through the ages, particularly in Eastern Europe, where the Jews have retained some of their more irrational traits.[79]

Our final example is the work of a young American artist,

A. Raymond Katz (b. 1895). During his childhood in Hungary, he became imbued with the essence of Orthodox Jewish life, and whenever he comes across Hebrew characters, the memory of these days strikes a chord of reminiscence. This led him to adopt the Hebrew letters as a starting point of his religious paintings in murals and in canvases. The Seder Meal (Fig. 209) is dominated by this idea and not only shows actual Hebrew letters, but the attitudes of the men and women remind one of them as well. The head of the family in a white garment is presiding at the table and the child, asking the four questions concerning the meaning of the ceremony, stands before him. The other participants are listening with deep emotion, the housewife waiting to place the dish on the table. The door remains open in order to welcome the prophet Elijah, and through the bare branches of the tree, one can see him approaching.

All of this shows us that Jewish artists after the Emancipation, contrary influences notwithstanding, retained and even intensified their Jewish interests.

It is impossible to prophesy the future of Jewish art. The very existence of the Jews, not to mention their culture and their art, depends upon conditions over which we have as yet no control. We can only express our ardent hope that both art and culture will survive the ordeal through which they have but recently passed, and will carry on in the spirit of the last 150 years. By this we mean that Jewish artists should keep in the closest contact with the artistic achievements of the rest of the world. But these influences should not permit them to forget their own unique characteristics. They should never hesitate to express their essential feelings; they should remain true to themselves. In this way alone, can they carry forward the tradition of Jewish art which has existed for three thousand years.

Bibliography

THIS bibliography, which lays no claim to completeness, is meant to give the reader the names of the books and essays which the writer of this work has consulted and to whose authors he gratefully acknowledges his indebtedness. These titles may also point the way to further study in one or another branch of Jewish art.

The articles from the Jewish encyclopedias as well as museum, library, and exhibition catalogues are omitted; so also, in the section of this bibliography entitled "Antiquity," are the accounts of the excavations in Palestine. These deal in a large measure with material predating the Israelite settlements in the Holy Land. Moreover the books here listed take account of the results of such excavations.

For the earlier Jewish artists, see the section "The Jewish Artist." Concerning the Jewish artists of the nineteenth and twentieth centuries, see the innumerable books and articles listed in the reference works on artists in general or in the Jewish encyclopedias. Because of the limited scope of this bibliography they are not included here.

I. GENERAL WORKS

KARL SCHWARZ, *Die Juden in der Kunst,* First Edition, Berlin, 1928. Second enlarged and revised Edition, Vienna and Jerusalem, 1936.

ERNST COHN-WIENER, *Die Juedische Kunst. Ihre Geschichte von den Anfaengen bis zur Gegenwart,* Berlin, 1929.

RAHEL WISCHNITZER-BERNSTEIN, *Symbole und Gestalten der juedischen Kunst,* Berlin-Schoeneberg, 1935.

FRANZ LANDSBERGER, *Einfuehrung in die juedische Kunst,* Berlin, 1935.

MARVIN LOWENTHAL, *A World Passed By,* New York and London, 1933.

JEAN-BAPTISTE FREY, La question des images chez les Juifs à la lumière des récentes découvertes, in the periodical *Biblia,* XV, Rome, 1934, pp. 265 ff.

II. THE JEWISH ARTIST

ALBERT WOLF, Etwas ueber juedische Kunst und aeltere juedische Kuenstler, *Mitteilungen der Gesellschaft fuer juedische Volkskunde,* IX, 1902, pp. 12 ff., XV, 1905, pp. 1 ff., XXIII, 1907, pp. 103 ff.

FRANZ LANDSBERGER, The Jewish Artist before the Period of Emancipation, *Hebrew Union College Annual,* XVI, 1941, pp. 321 ff.

CECIL ROTH, New Notes on Pre-Emancipation Jewish Artists, *Hebrew Union College Annual,* XVII, 1942–43, pp. 499 ff.

FRANZ LANDSBERGER, New Studies in Early Jewish Artists, *Hebrew Union College Annual,* XVIII, 1943–44, pp. 279 ff.

ALFRED RUBENS, Early Anglo-Jewish Artists, in *Transactions of the Jewish Historical Society of England,* XIV, London, 1940, pp. 91 ff.

III. ANTIQUITY

PAUL KARGE, *Raphaim. Die vorgeschichtliche Kultur Palaestinas und Phoeniziens,* Second Edition, Paderborn, 1925.

CARL WATZINGER, *Denkmaeler Palaestinas. Eine Einfuehrung in die Archaeologie des Heiligen Landes,* Leipzig, I, 1933, II, 1935.

ADOLF REIFENBERG, *Denkmaeler der juedischen Antike,* Berlin, 1937.

IMMANUEL BENZINGER, *Hebraeische Archaeologie,* Third Edition, Leipzig, 1927.

STANLEY A. COOK, *The Religion of Ancient Palestine in the Light of Archaeology,* London, 1930.

WILLIAM CREIGHTON GRAHAM and HERBERT GORDON MAY, *Culture and Conscience. An Archaeological Study of the New Religious Past in Ancient Palestine,* Chicago, 1936.

Kurt Galling, *Biblisches Reallexikon,* Tuebingen, 1937.

George Aaron Barton, *Archaeology and the Bible,* Seventh Edition, Philadelphia, 1937.

William Foxwell Albright, *The Archaeology of Palestine and the Bible,* New York, 1932.

———, *Archaeology and the Religion of Israel,* Baltimore, 1943.

Frederick Kenyon, *The Bible and Archaeology,* New York and London, 1940.

Nelson Glueck, *The Other Side of the Jordan,* New Haven, Conn., 1940.

Millar Burrows, *What Mean These Stones?* New Haven, Conn., 1941.

Adolf Reifenberg, *Palaestinensische Kleinkunst,* Berlin, 1927.

Samuel Krauss, *Talmudische Archaeologie,* 3 vols., Leipzig, 1910–12.

A. TENT OF MEETING

Martin Dibelius, *Die Lade Jahves,* Tuebingen, 1906.

Hugo Gressmann, *Die Lade Jahves,* Berlin, Stuttgart, Leipzig, 1920.

Harry Torczyner, Die Bundeslade und die Anfaenge der Religion Israels, in *Festschrift zum 50jaehrigen Bestehen der Hochschule fuer die Wissenschaft des Judentums,* Berlin, 1922, pp. 219 ff.

Herbert Gordon May, The Ark—A Miniature Temple, in *The American Journal of Semitic Languages,* LII, 1936, pp. 215 ff.

Julian Morgenstern, *The Ark, the Ephod and the "Tent of Meeting,"* Cincinnati, 1945.

B. TEMPLES

Kurt Moehlenbrink, *Der Tempel Salomos. Eine Untersuchung seiner Stellung in der Sakralarchitektur des Alten Orients,* Stuttgart, 1932.

Julian Morgenstern, The Book of the Covenant, *Hebrew Union College Annual,* V, 1928, pp. 1 ff.

F. J. Hollis, The Sun-Cult and the Temple at Jerusalem, in his book *Myth and Ritual,* Oxford, 1933, pp. 96 ff.

GEORGE ERNEST WRIGHT, Solomon's Temple Resurrected, in *The Biblical Archaeologist*, IV, 1941, pp. 17 ff.

R. B. Y. SCOTT, The Pillars Jachin and Boaz, in *Journal of Biblical Literature*, LVIII, 1939, pp. 143 ff.

W. F. ALBRIGHT, Two Cressets from Marisa and the Pillars of Jachin and Boaz, in *Bulletin of the American Schools of Oriental Research*, No. 85, 1942, pp. 18 ff.

H. G. MAY, The Two Pillars before the Temple of Solomon, in *Bulletin of the American Schools of Oriental Research*, No. 88, 1942, pp. 19 ff.

ADOLF FURTWAENGLER, Ueber ein auf Cypern gefundenes Bronzegeraet, Ein Beitrag zur Erklaerung der Kultgeraete des salomonischen Tempels, in *Sitzungsberichte der bayerischen Akademie der Wissenschaften*, Bd. II, Heft 3, Munich, 1900.

RUDOLF KITTEL, Die Kesselwagen des salomonischen Tempels, in *Studien zur hebraeischen Archaeologie und Religionsgeschichte*, Leipzig, 1908, pp. 188 ff.

S. A. HIRSCH, The Temple of Onias, in *Jews College Jubilee Volume*, London, 1906, pp. 39 ff.

F. I. HOLLIS, *The Archaeology of Herod's Temple*, London, 1934.

C. SYNAGOGUES

LOUIS FINKELSTEIN, The Origin of the Synagogue, in *Proceedings of the American Academy for Jewish Research*, 1928–30, pp. 49 ff.

SOLOMON ZEITLIN, The Origin of the Synagogue, *Proceedings, loc. cit.*, 1930–31, pp. 69 ff.

HIRSCH LOEB GORDON, The Basilica and the Stoa in Early Rabbinic Literature, in *Art Bulletin*, XIII, 1931, pp. 361 ff.

SAMUEL KRAUSS, *Synagogale Altertuemer*, Berlin and Vienna, 1932.

HEINRICH KOHL and CARL WATZINGER, *Antike Synagogen in Galilea*, Leipzig, 1916.

ELEAZAR LIPA SUKENIK, *Ancient Synagogues in Palestine and Greece*, London, 1934.

———, *The Ancient Synagogue of Beth Alpha*, Jerusalem and London, 1932.

———, *The Ancient Synagogue of el-Ḥammeh,* Jerusalem, 1935.

CARL H. KRAELING, *Gerasa, City of the Decapolis,* New Haven, Conn., 1938.

H. G. MAY, Synagogues in Palestine, in *The Biblical Archaeologist,* VII, 1944, pp. 1 ff.

MIKHAIL ROSTOVZEFF, *Dura Europos and Its Art,* Oxford, 1938.

MESNIL DU BUISSON, *Les peintures de la synagogue de Doura-Europus,* Rome, 1939. With an introduction by Gabriel Millet.

RAHEL WISCHNITZER-BERNSTEIN, The Samuel Cycle of Dura Europos, in *Proceedings of the American Academy for Jewish Research,* XI, 1941, pp. 85 ff.

FRANKLIN M. BIEBEL, The Mosaics of Hamman Lif, in *Art Bulletin,* XVIII, 1936, pp. 541 ff.

MORITZ SOBERNHEIM, Eine hebraeisch-aramaeische Inschrift aus Aleppo, in *Festschrift Ed. Sachau,* Berlin, 1915, pp. 311 ff.

ERWIN R. GOODENOUGH, Symbolism in Hellenistic Jewish Art, in *Journal of Biblical Literature,* LVI, 1937, pp. 103 ff.

D. IVORIES

JOHN WINTER and GRACE M. CROWFOOT, *Early Ivories from Samaria,* London, 1938.

E. BURIAL ART

KURT GALLING, Ein Etagen-Pilastergrab im Norden von Jerusalem, in *Zeitschrift des Deutschen Palaestina-Vereins,* LIX, 1936, pp. 111 ff.

NIKOLAUS MUELLER, *Die Juedische Katakombe in Monteverde,* Leipzig, 1912.

WOLFGANG BEYER and HANS LIETZMANN, *Die juedische Katakombe der Villa Torlonia in Rom,* Berlin-Leipzig, 1930.

J. B. FREY, Il Delfino col Tridente nella Catacomba Giudaica di Via Nomentana, in *Rivista di Archeologia Christiana,* VIII, 1931, pp. 301 ff.

F. SEALS

DAVID DIRINGER, *Le iscricioni antico-ebraiche Palestinesi,* Firenze, 1934, pp. 159 ff.

WILLIAM FREDERIC BADÈ, The Seal of Jaazaniah, in *Zeitschrift fuer alttestamentliche Wissenschaft*, LI, 1933, pp. 150 ff.

ADOLF REIFENBERG, Some Ancient Hebrew Seals, in *Palestine Exploration Fund Quarterly*, London, 1939, pp. 195 ff.

G. COINS

MORDECAI NARKISS, *Coins of Palestine*, Part I, Jewish Coins, Jerusalem, 1936 (Hebrew).

A. REIFENBERG, *Ancient Jewish Coins*, Jerusalem, 1940.

————, A Hebrew Shekel of the 5th Century B.C., in *Palestine Exploration Fund Quarterly*, LVII, 1943, p. 100.

E. L. SUKENIK, The Oldest Coins of Judaea, in *Journal of the Palestine Oriental Society*, XIV, 1934, pp. 178 ff. and XV, 1935, pp. 341 ff.

PAUL BONESCHI, Three Coins of Judaea and Phoenicia, in *Journal of the American Oriental Society*, 62, 1942, pp. 262 ff.

PAUL ROMANOFF, *Jewish Symbols on Ancient Jewish Coins*, Philadelphia, 1944.

H. GILT GLASSES

ERICH TOEPLITZ, Jewish Ornamented and Gilded Glasses, in *Milgroim-Rimonim*, Nos. 5 and 6, 1923–24 (Yiddish and Hebrew).

J. B. FREY, *Corpus Inscriptionum Judaicarum*, I, Rome, 1936, pp. 376 ff.

I. LAMPS

KURT GALLING, Die Beleuchtungsgeraete im israelitisch-juedischen Kulturgebiet, in *Zeitschrift des Deutschen Palaestina-Vereins*, XLVI, 1923, pp. 1 ff.

ADOLF REIFENBERG, Juedische Lampen, in *Journal of the Palestine Oriental Society*, XVI, 1936, pp. 166 ff.

RAHEL WISCHNITZER-BERNSTEIN, L'Origine de la lampe de hanouka, in *Revue des Etudes Juives*, LXXXIX, 1930, pp. 135 ff.

J. GOLDSMITHS

HUGO GRESSMANN, Der Festbecher, in *Sellin-Festschrift*, Leipzig, 1927, pp. 55 ff.

K. JEWISH INFLUENCE ON EARLY CHRISTIAN ART

JOSEF STRZYGOWSKI, *Orient oder Rom,* Leipzig, 1901.

DAVID KAUFMANN, Sens et origine des symboles tumulaires de l'Ancient Testament dans l'art chrétien primitif, in *Revue des Etudes Juives,* XIV, 1887, pp. 33 ff.

CARL MARIA KAUFFMANN, *Handbuch der christlichen Archaeologie,* Third Edition, Paderborn, 1922.

LUDWIG BLAU, Early Christian Archaeology from the Jewish Point of View, in *Hebrew Union College Annual,* III, 1926, pp. 157 ff.

IV. MIDDLE AGES AND MODERN ERA

A. SYNAGOGUES

HEINRICH FRAUBERGER, *Ueber Bau und Ausschmueckung alter Synagogen,* Frankfort-on-the-Main, 1901.

WILLIAM I. TACHAU, The Architecture of the Synagogue, in *The American Jewish Year Book,* 1926, pp. 155 ff.

RICHARD KRAUTHEIMER, *Mittelalterliche Synagogen,* Berlin, 1927.

ALFRED GROTTE, *Deutsche, boehmische und polnische Synagogentypen vom 11. bis zum Anfang des 19. Jahrhunderts,* Berlin, 1915.

ZDENKA MUENZER, Die Altneu Synagoge in Prag, in *Jahrbuch der Gesellschaft fuer Geschichte der Juden in der Chechoslowakischen Republik,* IV, 1932, pp. 63 ff.

ELIE LAMBERT, Les Synagogues de Tolède, in *Revue des Etudes Juives,* Vol. 84, 1927, pp. 15 ff.

ERNST MUNKACSI, *Der Jude von Neapel. Die historischen und geschichtlichen Denkmaeler des sueditalienischen Judentums,* Zurich, 1940.

MOSES GASTER, *History of the Ancient Synagogue of the Spanish and Portuguese Jews,* London, 1901.

HELEN ROSENAU, The Synagogue and Protestant Church Architecture, in *Journal of the Warburg and Courtauld Institute,* IV, pp. 80 ff.

MEIER BALABAN, *Die Judenstadt von Lublin,* Berlin, 1919.

——— , Wehrhafte Synagogen der oestlichen Randgebiete der polnischen Republik, in the periodical *Menorah,* IV, Vienna, 1927, pp. 369 ff.

MATHIAS BERSOHN, Einiges ueber die alten Holzsynagogen in Polen, in *Mitteilungen der Gesellschaft fuer juedische Volkskunde,* VIII, 1901 and XIV, 1904.

ALOYS BREIER, MAX EISLER, MAX GRUNWALD, *Holzsynagogen in Polen,* Baden near Vienna, 1934.

WILLIAM CHARLES WHITE, *Chinese Jews. A Compilation of Matters Relating to the Jews of K'aifeng,* 3 vols., Toronto, 1942.

DAVID KAUFMANN, Zur Geschichte der Kunst in der Synagoge, in *Gesammelte Schriften,* ed. M. Brann, I, Frankfort-on-the-Main, 1908.

ERICH TOEPLITZ, *Die Malerei in den Synagogen (besonders in Franken),* Frankfort-on-the-Main, 1929.

B. RITUAL OBJECTS

HEINRICH FRAUBERGER, *Ueber alte Kultusgegenstaende in Synagoge und Haus,* Frankfort-on-the-Main, 1903.

FRIEDRICH SARRE, A Fourteenth Century Spanish Synagogue Carpet, in *Burlington Magazine,* LVI, 1930, pp. 89 f.

ISRAEL ABRAHAMS, A Note on the Bodleian Bowl, in *Transactions of the Jewish Historical Society of England,* V, 1908, pp. 184 ff.

ELISABETH MOSES, Juedische Kult—und Kunstdenkmaeler in den Rheinlanden, in the collection: *Aus der Geschichte der Juden im Rheinland,* Duesseldorf, 1932, pp. 99 ff.

HENRI GUTTMANN, *Hebraica. Documents d'art Juif,* Paris, n.d. (1930).

RUDOLF HALLO, *Juedische Volkskunst in Hessen,* Kassel, 1928.

———, *Judaica. Juedische Kunst aus Hessen und Nassau,* Marburg, 1932.

CECIL ROTH, The Jewish Museum in London, in *The Connoisseur,* September-October, 1935.

ERICH TOEPLITZ, *Die Menorah des Chanukkafestes,* Frankfort-on-the-Main, 1924.

HERMANN GUNDERSHEIMER and GUIDO SCHOENBERGER, *Frankfurter Chanukkaleuchter aus Silber und Zinn,* Frankfort-on-the-Main, 1937.

MORDEKAI NARKISS, *The Hanukkah Lamp,* Jerusalem, 1939 (Hebrew).

Franz Landsberger, Old-Time Torah Curtains, in *Hebrew Union College Annual,* XIX, 1945–46 (in press).

C. ILLUMINATED MANUSCRIPTS

Heinrich Frauberger, *Verzierte hebraeische Schrift und juedischer Buchschmuck,* Frankfort-on-the-Main, 1909.

Carlo Bernheimer, *Paleografia Ebraica,* Florence, 1924.

Ernst Munkacsi, *Illuminated Manuscripts in Italian Libraries,* Budapest, n.d. (Hungarian).

Theo Harburger, Juedische Buchmalerei im 18. Jahrhundert, in *Bayerische Israelitische Gemeindezeitung,* 1928, pp. 113 ff.

Erwin Panofsky, Giotto and Maimonides in Avignon, in *The Journal of the Walters Art Gallery,* IV, 1941, pp. 27 ff. and V, 1942, pp. 12 f.

Elisabeth Moses, Ueber eine Koelner Handschrift der Mischne-Tora des Maimonides, in *Zeitschrift fuer bildende Kunst,* Vol. LX, 1926–27, pp. 71 ff.

Bibles

David Guenzburg and W. V. Stassoff, *L'Ornement Hébreu,* Berlin, 1905.

Moses Gaster, *Hebrew Illuminated Bibles of the 9th and 10th Centuries,* London, 1901.

Rahel Wischnitzer-Bernstein, Une Bible enluminée par Joseph Ibn Hayyim, in *Revue des Etudes Juives,* Vol. 73, 1921, pp. 161 ff.

Zofja Ameisenowa, *The Hebrew 14th Century Bible in Kracow and Its Pictorial Ornamentation,* Cracow, 1929 (Polish).

———, Eine spanisch-juedische Bilderbibel um 1400, in *Monatsschrift fuer Geschichte und Wissenschaft des Judentums,* Vol. 81, 1937, pp. 193 ff.

Jacob Leveen, *The Hebrew Bible in Art.* The Schweich Lectures of the British Academy, Oxford and London, 1944.

Machzors

Moïse Schwab, Un Maḥzor illustré, in *Revue des Etudes Juives,* Vol. 48, 1904, pp. 230 ff.

Martin Plessner, Eine illustrierte deutsche Machsorhandschrift in Breslau, in *Menorah,* V, Vienna and Frankfort-on-the-Main, 1927, pp. 85 ff.

RAHEL WISCHNITZER-BERNSTEIN, Der Streiter des Herrn. Eine Miniatur des Leipziger Machsor, in *Festschrift Moses Gaster*, London, 1936, pp. 539 ff.

———, The Messianic Fox, in *The Review of Religion*, 1941, pp. 257 ff.

Haggadahs

HEINRICH MUELLER and JULIUS V. SCHLOSSER, *Die Haggadah von Serajewo*, Vienna, 1898. Important also the appended essay by D. Kaufman, Zur Geschichte der juedischen Handschriften Illustration.

DAVID KAUFMANN, Les cycles d'images du type Allemand dans l'illustration ancienne de la Haggada, in *Revue des Etudes Juives*, Vol. 38, 1899, pp. 74 ff.

MOÏSE SCHWAB, Une Haggada illustrée, in *Revue des Etudes Juives*, Vol. 45, 1902, pp. 112 ff.

RAHEL WISCHNITZER-BERNSTEIN, Illuminated Haggadahs, in *Jewish Quarterly Review*, New Series, XIII, 1922–23, pp. 193 ff.

BRUNO ITALIENER, ARON FREIMANN, AUGUST L. MAYER and ADOLF SCHMIDT, *Die Darmstaedter Pessach Haggadah*, Leipzig, 1927.

MICHAEL FOONER, Joel Simeon, Illuminator of Hebrew Manuscripts in the 15th Century, in *Jewish Quarterly Review*, New Series, XXVII, 1936–37, pp. 127 ff.

FRANZ LANDSBERGER, The Cincinnati Haggadah and Its Decorator, *Hebrew Union College Annual*, XV, 1940, pp. 529 ff.

Esther Scrolls

RAHEL WISCHNITZER-BERNSTEIN, Der Estherstoff in der juedischen Illustration, in *Monatsschrift fuer die Geschichte und Wissenschaft des Judentums*, New Series, Vol. 38, 1930, pp. 381 ff.

K'subos

MOSES GASTER, *The Ketubah. A Chapter from the History of the Jewish People*, Berlin-London, 1923.

D. WOODCUTS AND ENGRAVINGS

ISAIAH SONNE, "Druckwesen," in *Encyclopaedia Judaica*, VI, Berlin, 1930, pp. 39 ff.

ARON FREIMANN, *Thesaurus Typographiae Hebraicae Saeculi XV,* Berlin, 1923 ff.

———, Zur Geschichte der juedischen Buchillustration bis 1540, in *Zeitschrift fuer hebraeische Bibliographie,* XXI, 1918, pp. 25 ff.

SALOMON HUGO LIEBEN, Der hebraeische Buchdruck in Prag im 16. Jahrhundert, in the collection: *Die Juden in Prag,* Prague, 1927.

ALEXANDER MARX, "Illustrated Haggadahs" and "The Literature of Hebrew Incunabula," in his *Studies in Jewish History and Booklore,* New York, 1944, pp. 271 ff.

MOSES MARX, Gershom Soncino, in *Sepher Ha-Yovel. A Tribute to Professor Alexander Marx,* New York, 1943, pp. 1 ff.

RAHEL WISCHNITZER-BERNSTEIN, Von der Holbeinbibel zur Amsterdamer Haggadah, in *Monatsschrift fuer Geschichte und Wissenschaft des Judentums,* New Series, 39, 1931, pp. 269 ff.

LAZARUS GOLDSCHMIDT, *The Earliest Illustrated Haggadah Printed by Gershom Cohen at Prague,* London, 1940.

ABRAHAM YAARI, *Hebrew Printers' Marks,* Jerusalem, 1943 (Hebrew).

SIEGFRIED SILBERSTEIN, *Eine in Kupfer gestochene Estherrolle aus der Universitaetsbibliothek zu Rostock,* Rostock, 1939.

SALLI KIRSCHSTEIN, *Juedische Graphiker aus der Zeit von 1625–1825,* Berlin, 1918.

ALFRED RUBENS, *Anglo-Jewish Portraits,* London, 1935.

E. BOOKBINDINGS

MAX JOSEPH HUSUNG, Ueber den sogenannten juedischen Lederschnitt, in *Soncino-Blaetter,* I, Berlin, 1925, pp. 29 and 179 ff.

ABRAHAM YAARI, A Silver-Binding from the d'Italia Family, in *Kirjath Sepher,* XV, 1938, pp. 513 f. (Hebrew).

———, Arms of Two Italo-Jewish Families on a Silver-Binding, in *Kirjath Sepher,* XVIII, 1941, pp. 190 f. (Hebrew).

F. TOMBSTONES

DAVID HENRIQUES DE CASTRO, *Auswahl von Grabsteinen auf dem niederlaendisch-portugiesisch-israelitischen Begraebnisplatze in Ouderkerk* (near Amsterdam), Leyden, 1883.

MAX GRUNWALD, *Portugiesengraeber auf deutscher Erde,* Hamburg, 1912.

LUBOMÍR JERÁBEK, *Der alter Prager Judenfriedhof,* Prague, 1903.

BERNHARD WACHSTEIN and SANDOR WOLF, *Grabinschriften des alten Friedhofs in Eisenstadt,* Vienna, 1912.

ARTHUR LEVY, *Juedische Grabmalkunst in Ost-Europa,* Berlin, 1924.

MAX DIAMANT, *Juedische Volkskunst,* Vienna and Jerusalem, 1937.

ALFRED GROTTE, *Alte schlesische Judenfriedhoefe,* Breslau and Dyherrnfurth, 1927.

G. SEALS AND MEDALS

MARKUS BRANN, Ein mittelalterlicher Siegelring mit hebraeischen Inschriften, in the periodical *Aus Schlesien's Vorzeit,* Neue Folge, IV, 1906, pp. 63 ff.

A. KISCH, Trois Sceaux Juifs du Moyen Age, in *Revue des Etudes Juives,* IV, 1883, pp. 278 ff.

S. FERARÈS, La médaille dite de Fourvières et sa legende Hébraique, in *Revue Numismaticue,* 1910, pp. 196 ff.

ALBERT WOLF, Die Hamburger auf oder von Juden gepraegten Medaillen, in *Mitteilungen der Gesellschaft fuer juedische Volkskunde, XIII,* 1904, pp. 151 ff.

MORITZ STERN, *Aus dem Berliner Juedischen Museum,* Berlin, 1937.

TASSILO HOFFMANN, *Jakob Abraham und Abraham Abramson,* Berlin, 1927.

V. EMANCIPATION TO THE PRESENT

MARTIN BUBER, Editor of the collection *Juedische Kuenstler,* Berlin, 1903.

SOPHIE M. COLLMANN, *Jews in Art,* Cincinnati, 1909.

KARL SCHWARZ, Juedische Kunstbauten, in the periodical *Kunst und Kirche,* VII, 1930, pp. 89 ff.

——— , *Modern Jewish Art in Palestine,* Jerusalem, 1941 (Hebrew) .

ELIAS NEWMAN, *Art in Palestine,* New York, 1939.

JACOB RASHELL, *Jewish Artists. Essays on Jewish Painters and Sculptors,* New York, 1943 (Yiddish).

MAX OSBORN, Immigrant Jewish Artists, in *The Chicago Jewish Forum,* III, 1945, pp. 191 ff.

Notes

[1] Cf. Fritz Baer, *Studien zur Geschichte der Juden im Koenigreich Aragonien waehrend des 13. und 14. Jahrhunderts,* Berlin, 1913, p. 168.

[2] The queen's letter appointing Francesco Chacon, resident of Toledo, "Court painter for life, with the duty of safeguarding that no Jew or Moor paint the figure of our Lord and Redeemer, Jesus Christ, or of Holy Mary the Glorious" is printed by M. R. Zarco del Valle in *Documentos inéditos para la Historia de las Bellas Artes in España,* Madrid, 1870, pp. 115 ff.

[3] Roman scrolls, since the time of the Caesars, also have two rollers, but only in exceptional cases where a particularly ornamental effect was desired. See Dziatzko's article "Buch" in Pauly-Wissowa, *Real-Encyclopaedie der classischen Altertumswissenschaft,* col. 956.

[4] In the so-called letter of Aristeas, we read that the Egyptian king Ptolemy Philadelphus (287–246 B.C.E.) desired a Pentateuch in order to have it translated into the Greek. The Jews sent him a scroll written in gold letters. Another scroll, which a certain Alexander had ordered for himself also had gold lettering. Cf. Ludwig Blau, *Studien zum alt-hebraeischen Buchwesen,* Strasbourg, 1902, pp. 150 ff. David Kaufmann mentions some further attempts in the Middle Ages to decorate the Scroll of the Law in: Zur Geschichte der Juedischen Handschriften —Illustration, in Mueller-Schlosser, *Die Haggadah von Serajewo,* Vienna, 1898, p. 297.

[5] The gathered curtain behind the doors of the Torah shrine can be recognized on a Roman gilt glass. See Figure 86. The Synagogue of Dura Europos had a curtain in front of the Torah niche. Cf. Mesnil du Buisson, *Les peintures de la synagogue de Doura-Europus,* Rome, 1939, p. 10, note 1.

[6] So also Maimonides in the *Mishneh Torah,* Hilkot Tefillah, 11, 3: "They put a platform in the middle of the house so that he who reads from the Law or he who speaks words of exhortation to the people may stand upon it and all may hear him." Yet Joseph Caro in his Maimonides commentary on this passage explains: "In our times when through our sins the synagogues are small and all the people hear, it is more beautiful if the bimo is on the side than if it is in the middle."

[7] Illustration in my *Einfuehrung in die juedische Kunst,* Berlin, 1935, Fig. 35.

[8] Cf. William Rothenstein, *Men and Memories,* three volumes, London, 1931–1939, Vol. II, p. 35.

[9] Cf. Leopold Loew, *Graphische Requisiten und Erzeugnisse bei den Juden,* I, Leipzig, 1870–1871, p. 176.

[10] The illustration and its explanation are taken from the book by Rahel Wischnitzer-Bernstein, *Symbole und Gestalten der juedischen Kunst*, Berlin-Schoeneberg, 1935, Fig. 37 and p. 65.

[11] For instance in Dirck Bouts' picture in the Art Museum in Cincinnati, O.

[12] Two examples are reproduced in my *Einfuehrung in die juedische Kunst, loc. cit.*, Figs. 24 and 25.

[13] A separate essay on illustrated Esther scrolls describing their origin and distribution according to countries and times would be welcome.

[14] To fulfil the Law of Erub a member of the community hands a loaf of bread, or, on Passover, a piece of matso to a representative of the community. See the article "Erub" in the *Encyclopaedia Judaica*, VI, col. 738.

[15] A reproduction of the k'subo fragment which is in the Bodleiana, Oxford, in Moses Gaster, *The Ketubah*, Berlin-London, 1923, pl. 2. The fragment came from Fostat, Egypt.

[16] The fourteenth century Austrian k'subo in the Staatsbibliothek, Vienna (Cod. hebr. 218) is reproduced in M. Gaster, *loc. cit.*, pl. 7. Rahel Wischnitzer-Bernstein, *Symbole und Gestalten, loc. cit.*, Fig. 31, also reproduces the k'subo but mistakenly describes the crown on the head of the bride as the crown of the Torah.

[17] At least that is the interpretation given by Josephus to the lamps of the seven-branched candelabrum in his *Jewish Antiquities*, V, 5, 5.

[18] See First Maccabees, 4, 48.

[19] For the details of the division of the Biblical description among the several sources see *Handbuch zum Alten Testament*, ed. Otto Eissfeldt, in the Vol. *Exodus,* ed. by Georg Beer, Tuebingen, 1933.

[20] The ivory plate in Arslan Tash is reproduced in F. Thureau-Dangin, *Arslan Tash,* 1931, pl. 27, the similar fragment from Samaria in J. W. and G. M. Crowfoot, *Early Ivories from Samaria,* London, 1938, pl. VI, 2.

[21] See, for instance, W. F. Albright, What Were the Cherubim? *The Biblical Archaeologist,* I, 1938, pp. 1 ff.

[22] For the details on this orientation and its significance see Julian Morgenstern, The Book of the Covenant, *Hebrew Union College Annual,* V, 1928, pp. 45 ff.

[23] Nelson Glueck discovered one of these copper mines in Khirbet en-Nahâs. Cf. his book *The Other Side of the Jordan,* New Haven, 1940, pp. 50 ff.

[24] Illustrations of the stables in *Megiddo I, Seasons of 1925–1934, Strata I–V,* by R. S. Lamon and G. M. Shipton, Chicago, 1939, Figs. 43 and 53. They are long halls with their ceilings supported by two rows of pillars. In Megiddo were also found the remains of administration buildings of which the authors of the book have attempted interesting reconstructions.

[25] Adolphe Lods, *The Prophets and the Rise of Jerusalem,* New York, 1937, p. 308, writes concerning these goddesses: "The deities associated with Jahu are not Egyptian, but Palestinian; that is certainly true of Anat and probably true of Ašan."

[26] In Alexandria, Egypt, a synagogue inscription was found dating from the reign of Ptolemy III (246–221 B.C.E.). The first of the synagogues of which traces remain are ascribed to the second or third century of our era.

[27] Ground plan and reconstruction in Carl Watzinger, *Denkmaeler Palaestinas*, II, Leipzig, 1935, Figs. 17, 50 and 51.

[28] Cf. E. Babelon, *Catalogue des Monnaies Grecques de la Bibliothèque Nationale. Les Rois de Syrie*, Paris, 1890. An anchor occurs on a coin of Seleucus I, Nicator (305–281 B.C.E); a cornucopia in coins of Demetrius Soter (162–150 B.C.E).

[29] On the other hand the prohibition would surely not have been pronounced had there not been such attempts at imitation. We learn, for instance, that the synagogue in Sideh, Pamphylia had two seven-branched candelabra. Cf. Samuel Krauss, *Synagogale Altertuemer,* Berlin-Vienna, 1922, p. 236.

[30] The cherubim on the cover of the Ark of the Covenant are described as birds by Philo in his *Life of Moses,* III, 8.

[31] To Mrs. Rahel Wischnitzer-Bernstein goes the credit for the working out of this eschatological significance. See her article The Samuel Cycle in the Wall Decoration of the Synagogue at Dura Europos, *Proceedings of the American Academy for Jewish Research,* XI, 1941, pp. 85 ff. However I cannot agree with her identification of the here illustrated figure (Fig. 92) as that of Samuel. Samuel communicated to the people by word of mouth the rules concerning the kingdom about to be established, and wrote them down later on, not in order to read them but rather to lay them "before the Lord" (I Samuel 10:25).

[32] Cf. Humann, Cichorius, Judeich, Winter, *Altertuemer von Hierapolis,* 1898, pp. 46 and 174.

[33] See note 4.

[34] Cf. David Kaufmann, Zur Geschichte der Kunst in der Synagoge, 1897, in *Gesammelte Schriften,* ed. M. Brann, I, Frankfort-on-the-Main, 1908.

[35] Thus Obadiah of Bertinoro, who visited the city in 1486, reports in a letter. See *Jahrbuch fuer die Geschichte der Juden und des Judentums,* III, 1863, pp. 195 ff.

[36] The Hebrew inscription has been published frequently; most recently in the *Hebrew Union College Annual,* XVIII, 1944, p. 283. Other illustrations of the synagogue in Ernst Munkacsi, *Der Jude von Neapel,* Zurich, 1940.

[37] The sources for these and the following notes on Jewish artists of the Middle Ages in my article Jewish Artists Before the Period of Emancipation, *Hebrew Union College Annual,* XVI, 1941, pp. 340 ff.

[38] However—as Dr. Franz Rosenthal brought to my attention—Sumair is first mentioned as a Jew in an Arabic source of about 1200. Cf. *Hebrew Union College Annual,* XVIII, 1944, p. 290.

[39] Cf. Leopold Loew, *Graphische Requisiten und Erzeugnisse bei den Juden, loc. cit.,* pp. 55 f.

[40] Cf. Cecil Roth, New Notes on Pre-Emancipation Jewish Artists, *Hebrew Union College Annual,* XVII, 1942–43, p. 505.

[41] See Ch. R. Post, *History of Spanish Painting,* Cambridge, Mass., 1930 ff., III, pp. 168, 180, 186 ff., IV, 2, pp. 626 ff., and VIII, 2, pp. 658 ff., with illustrations. See also the article by José Mª Sanz Artibucilla, Guillem y Juan de Levi, Pintores de Retablos, in the Spanish periodical *Sefarad,* IV, 1944, pp. 73 ff.

[42] Cf. D. Guenzburg and V. Stassoff, *L'Ornement Hébreu*, Berlin, 1905.

[43] Cf. Theodor Birt, *Die Buchrolle in der Kunst*, Leipzig, 1907, p. 286.

[44] Cf. *Die Darmstaedter Pessach-Haggadah, herausgegeben und erlaeutert von Bruno Italiener*, Leipzig, 1927. Concerning the dating of text and pictures, see my article "The Cincinnati Haggadah and Its Decorator," *Hebrew Union College Annual*, XV, 1940, pp. 552 ff.

[45] There are some miniatures from this manuscript in Elisabeth Moses, Ueber eine Koelner Handschrift der Mischne-Tora des Maimonides, *Zeitschrift fuer bildende Kunst*, LX, 1926-27, pp. 71 ff.

[46] For the sculptor and his statue see Paul Schubring, *Die Plastik Sienas im Quattrocento*, Berlin, 1907.

[47] The tablet painted in 1675 comes from the Great S'fardic Synagogue in London which is no longer extant. For other works by the same artist see *Hebrew Union College Annual*, XVIII, 1944, p. 304, with two illustrations.

[48] It is the letters יבכלל that must be read as Joel ben Lipman Levi. Cf. *De Vrijdagavond*, I, 2, 1924-25, p. 314.

[49] The portrait in the Jewish Museum in London is perhaps by the painter David Estevens who lived in Denmark and occasionally came to London.

[50] The only Jewish artists who painted portraits are to be found in Amsterdam: Samuel da Silva and Jacobe da Carpi. Silva's portrait of the Rabbi Gomez de Mesquita (1688–1751) has only been preserved in a mezzotint by F. Faber. Cf. *Hebrew Union College Annual*, XVIII, 1944, p. 310, Fig. 10. None of the works of Jacobe da Carpi

(1685–1748), a Veronese immigrant, has been preserved.

[51] The title of the book is *Piedra Gloriosa; o De la estatua de Nebuchadnesar*, Amsterdam, 1654–55. See my book *Rembrandt, the Jews and the Bible*, Philadelphia, 1945.

[52] Cf. I. I. Schudt, *Juedische Merckwuerdigkeiten*, IV, Frankfort and Leipzig, 1718, p. 252.

[53] Other examples: the large Portuguese synagogue in Amsterdam, the synagogue in Leghorn, the synagogue in the Heidereuter Strasse in Berlin, Germany.

[54] A picture of the building to which in the nineteenth century a western balcony has been added in *Jahrbuch fuer die juedischen Gemeinden Schl's-wig Holsteins und der Hansastaedte*, 1934–35.

[55] Cf. Arthur P. Coleman, The Wooden Churches of Ruthenia, *Art and Archaeology*, XXXIV, 1933, pp. 137 ff.

[56] This and a second lamp made by him illustrated in the *Mitteilungen der Gesellschaft fuer juedische Volkskunde*, VIII, 1901, pp. 174 ff.

[57] Other curtains by Jacob Koppel Gans and by the still more renowned Elkone Naumburg are reproduced in my forthcoming article, Old-Time Torah Curtains, *Hebrew Union College Annual*, XIX, 1945–46.

[58] The Torah curtain itself is not signed but a Torah binder closely resembling it (Fig. 3) is signed. The beautiful curtain is pictured in the book of C. Adler and J. M. Casonowicz, *The Collection of Jewish Ceremonials in the United States National Museum*, Washington, 1908, pl. LXI.

[59] Cf. the sepulchre of Menachem F. di Abramo da Ventura (died 1555) in Bologna, Museo Civico. Illustrated in Heinrich Frauberger, *Ueber alte Kultusgegenstaende in Synagoge und Haus,* Frankfort-on-the-Main, 1903, Fig. 146.

[60] Cf. Max Diamant, *Juedische Volkskunst,* Vienna-Jerusalem, 1937, which deals with the gravestones of Cernauti (Czernowitz), Roumania, and their makers.

[61] The earliest dated illustrated Esther scroll is from the year 1567. Cf. Georg Swarzensky and Rosy Schilling, *Die illustrierten Handschriften und Einzelminiaturen des Mittelalters und der Renaissance in Frankfurter Besitz,* Frankfort-on-the-Main, 1929, p. 263. Certainly the scroll written in Italy, which was offered at auction by Gilhofer and Rauschburg in Vienna, is also from the sixteenth century. See the auction catalogue 253, no. 36, with illustration.

[62] Some Persian-Jewish illuminated manuscripts of the seventeenth century are in the possession of the Jewish Theological Seminary in New York. They came from the Elkan Adler collection and are described in the *Catalogue of Hebrew Manuscripts in the Collection of Elkan Adler,* Cambridge, 1921, no. 1440 (Yussuf and Zuleika by Janni) and no. 62 (Nizami's Khasraw and Schirin). Illustrations on plates 37 and 38. The *Catalogue of the Hebrew and Samaritan Manuscripts in the Sassoon Library,* I, London, 1932, p. 473 and Fig. 51 mention another Persian-Jewish illuminated manuscript.

[63] A very similar Haggadah by the same illuminator of the year 1717 is mentioned in the *Notizblatt der Gesellschaft zur Erforschung juedischer Kunstdenkmaeler,* no. 22, 1928, with an illustration. For further works of the artist see Theo Harburger, *Jue-dische Buchmalerei im 18. Jahrhundert, Bayerisch-Israelitische Gemeinde-Zeitung,* 1928, pp. 113 ff.

[64] This Moses ben Isaac gives his name in the Pentateuch commentary of Bahia ben Asher, printed in Naples, 1492. See Steinschneider's Catalogue of Hebrew Books in the Bodleian Library, Oxford, England, col. 777–78.

[65] Most prominent are Solomon Bennett (1761–1838), Michael Jacob Abramson (about 1775–1825) and Heinrich Bendix (1768–1828). Cf. Salli Kirschstein, *Juedische Graphiker 1625–1825,* Berlin, 1918, and my correcting notes in *Hebrew Union College Annual,* XVI, 1941, pp. 400 f.

[66] Emil Orlik (1870–1932), Hugo Steiner-Prag (b. 1880), Erich Wolfsfeld (b. 1884), Gustav Wolf (b. about 1885) were particularly versed in all the techniques of the graphic arts and thereby made a reputation as teachers in German art schools.

[67] Cf. Ernst Lemberger, *Meisterminiaturen aus fuenf Jahrhunderten,* Stuttgart, 1911, catalogue p. 34; further his book *Die Bildnisminiatur in Skandinavien,* Berlin, 1912, II, p. 172. Compare also the article by the same author on Jewish miniature painters in *Ost und West,* XIV, 1914, pp. 195 ff. and 289 ff., and in *Cicerone,* VII, 1915, pp. 117 ff. (M. L. Lowe) and VIII, 1916, pp. 127 ff. (Die 5 Pinhas).

[68] I regret that here I can only name these excellent artists and hope that I may be able, at some later date, to write a separate book on the place of the Jew in the artistic world of the nineteenth and twentieth centuries.

[69] Abraham Geiger's decision concerning the justification for sculpture in Jewish houses is to be found in his article: Das Mosesbild in einem Syna-

gogenfenster. Ein Gutachten, *Juedische Zeitschrift fuer Wissenschaft und Leben*, III, 1864–65, pp. 136 ff.

70 Cf. Moritz Busch, *Graf Bismarck und seine Leute,* II, 1878, XII, 19, 1870.

71 In the book of Alois I. Schardt, *Franz Marc,* which appeared during the Nazi regime, this fact was naturally suppressed, yet I received my information from reliable sources.

72 When the artist died, the director of the Kunsthalle in Hamburg, Gustav Pauli, gave a funeral oration in which he expressed his admiration.

73 A number of good German Jewish sculptors might well be added here, at least by name: Emil Pottner (b. 1872), Arnold Zadikow (b. 1884), Kurt Kroner (b. 1885), Tina Haim-Wentscher (b. about 1890), and Elisabeth Wolff (b. 1898).

74 The architect Frank Lloyd Wright, who in his earlier years served an apprenticeship with Adler and Sullivan, accords him even greater recognition. He quotes a saying of Adler's: "Form follows function," and adds to this the question: "Has it occurred to none, then, that Dankmar Adler, not Louis Sullivan, deserves the credit for that dogma? It was Adler's contribution to his young partner when he was teaching him practically all the young man knew about architecture below the belt. As an architect Louis Sullivan went to school not to the Beaux-Arts but to Dankmar Adler. Out of his association with Adler came Sullivan's whole sense of building as a functional experience in function." From the Saturday Review of Literature, De-

cember 14, 1935, in a review of Hugh Morrison's book on Sullivan. See F. L. Wright, *Selected Writings,* New York, 1941, pp. 200 f.

75 Cf. Arnold Whittick, *Eric Mendelsohn,* London, 1941, p. 71. Other highly esteemed architects of about the same age were: in Germany, Leo Nachtlicht (b. 1872), Max Landsberg (b. 1878), Fritz Landauer (b. 1883), Erwin Gutkind (b. 1886), Fritz Nathan (b. 1891), the brothers Hans and Oscar Gerson; and in Austria, Oscar Wlach (b. 1881), Josef Frank (b. 1885), Ernst L. Freud (b. 1892).

76 The synagogue was erected by the well-known synagogue architect Charles R. Greco, Boston, Mass. An illustrated description by Rabbi Abraham Feldman appeared in *The Jewish Layman,* XIX, 1944–45.

77 The painting was in the Jewish Museum in Berlin which was stolen by the Nazis in 1938.

78 The picture painted in 1903 is in the possession of the Rijksmuseum in Amsterdam, a second version in the museum at Tel-Aviv, Palestine. The beautiful picture, The Torah Scribe, painted in 1902, in the Community Museum in The Hague, also deserves mention.

79 Among other contemporary painters of Jewish themes should be mentioned Jankel Adler (b. 1895) and Arthur Szyk (b. 1894), both born in Lodz, Poland. In large paintings Adler gives the Polish Jew monumental stature. Szyk, on the contrary, strives for the detailed and the delicate in his hand-painted Esther scroll and Haggadah.

Index